Why New Hampshire?

With warm regards,

R. Sean O'Kane

The Center of New Hampshire

WHY
New Hampshire ?

The First-in-the-Nation
Primary State

Hugh Gregg
Former Governor

Bill Gardner
Secretary of State

RESOURCES–NH

ISBN: 0-9637615-5-2
Library of Congress Control Number: 2003094015

Designed and composed in Baskerville MT
at Hobblebush Books,
Brookline, NH (www.hobblebush.com)

Printed in the United States of America

Published by:

RESOURCES—NH

20 Gregg Road · Nashua, New Hampshire 03062

Books are available from Enfield Distribution Co.
Box 699, Enfield, NH 03748
Web: www.enfielddistribution.com
E-mail: info@enfieldbooks.com
Phone: 603-632-7377 · Fax: 603-632-5611

Contents

Preface · ix

Chapter 1
Handshakes, Shoe Leather and the National Spotlight · 1

Chapter 2
Beginnings · 18

Chapter 3
The Three Fathers · 39

Chapter 4
From White Steeples to High-Tech
The New Hampshire Political Culture · 49

Chapter 5
The Primary Isn't For Sale · 67

Chapter 6
On the Fringes · 74

Chapter 7
Third Parties and Independents · 95

Chapter 8
Leaving the Party Early
Buchanan and Smith in 2000 · 105

Chapter 9
The Hare and the Tortoise I
Ten Candidates Who Did Not Finish the 2000 Race · 118

Chapter 10
The Hare and the Tortoise II
Seven Who Made It to the Finish Line in 2000 · 149

Observations on the Primary – Some Good, Some Bad · 176

Chapter 11
The 2004 Primary
The Democrats Who Are Now in the Starting Gate · 184

Chapter 12
Are Retail Politics Being Threatened? · 213

Chapter 13
Back off! · 223

Chapter 14
New Hampshire Holds Its Own · 248

Chapter 15
Clouding the Crystal Ball
Perplexing the Pollsters · 262

Chapter 16
A New Generation Votes · 268

Chapter 17
It Gets Earlier and Earlier · 273

Chapter 18
Will New Hampshire Stay First-in-the-Nation? · 278

Appendix A
Chronology of Major Candidates
Participating from 1952 to 2000 · 285

Appendix B
2004 Presidential Primary Calendar · 299

Appendix C
Testimony of the Honorable Judd Gregg · 302

Appendix D
History of Legislation Governing
the New Hampshire Primary · 306

Appendix E
As Others See Us, 1979 · 309

Index · *317*

Dedication

This book is dedicated to The Library and Archives of New Hampshire's Political Tradition—more commonly known as The Political Library—because it is the only nonpartisan, nonprofit organization in the state committed exclusively to the election process, with a mission of protecting and preserving New Hampshire's tradition of holding the first-in-the-nation presidential primary.

Preface

THOSE OF US WHO LIVE IN New Hampshire take the presidential primary for granted, a sort of birthright which we don't pay much attention to until every third year of our existence. Being first hardly explains its consistent appeal to candidates and the media. More likely, it's our unlimited enthusiasm for politics, the fact that we prefer handshakes and voting booths to political polling, and because it remains the quickest, easiest, least expensive and most effective place to start the presidential contest.

The primary was born not in an attempt to be first, and not for any economic benefit to the state, but simply to give more of its citizens a chance to be heard. It would later become first-in-the-nation, as other states either moved to later dates in the calendar or reverted back to a caucus format. Today it has become an event of national significance, although its reason for being has not changed one bit. This is what the New Hampshire primary was meant to be: Let the people decide.

But there's a lot more to it than that. It's fun. It's an adventure. It's enlightening. It's informative. It's one of a kind. It has a history all of its own. Granted, it's special to Granite Staters. Yet the world participates with the TV sound bite and the Internet. Presidential candidates may not shake your hand or come into your living room, but you don't have to live here to enjoy such a sensory experience offered nowhere else. Just turn on your television and participate in it with us.

It's fun—you meet so many luminaries right up close, be they journalists or public figures. You observe their demeanor. Do you like their looks? How are their manners and behavior? Would you want them in your home? The so-called "fringe" or lesser-known candidates are sometimes a circus with strange and often eccentric ways of presenting themselves. Anything for publicity.

It's an adventure—occasionally it seems as though a distant culture has suddenly transferred itself to our Main Street. Wondrous to us are the variety of twangs and images created by the storytelling of our visiting "foreigners." Some are like nomads or vagabonds, here only as yarn-spinners about how much better things could be—as though we weren't happy here already.

It's enlightening—*New York Times* journalist Phil Rosenthal confided that it can also be an experience for those who might otherwise attend the World Series, The Final Four or the Super Bowl. For the past several primaries, Phil and two or three friends have come here at the height of the season, not as reporters, rather as political junkies, just to enjoy what's going on. "It's the run for the White House as a spectator sport, politics as performance art. All the passion and excitement of campaigning—the part that's filtered out by the world-weary, subjective news coverage—comes alive as we shiver in the cold or sweat in the back of an overheated Legion hall."

It's informative—whatever the issue, those who choose to run better have an answer and an answer as good or better than the competition. Staged debates bring out all sides. Better yet, there's also the face-to-face opportunity for the voter to single out the candidate of personal choice, and to applaud or condemn statements made. There's an unbounded fountain of knowledge on limitless subjects for a quick education on all matters relating to government. The participants give us all of this free of charge.

It has a history—for over three-quarters of a century we've constantly honed the process for adapting to changing times. Our conduct of the primary has been smooth, satisfying all concerned and serving the nation well. Never has there been scandal, corruption or questions of ballot count. Nor has any other state a better long-standing record of citizen turnout on primary day.

It gets back to the fact that we're a small state, otherwise frequently unnoticed, but every four years when national elections roll around this is the place to be. This is where it all starts and sometimes finishes. Adam Nagourney writing in the *New York Times* sums it up when he says New Hampshire, "is the last remaining spot in the nation where a regular citizen can shake hands and converse with someone who might very well be the next president of the United States."

If we were novelists, the story of New Hampshire's vital service to the nation could be parlayed into a best-seller. Until some writer does it, this book is designed to record the process by which it all happens, and to assist the novelist who writes the story.

This book is designed "to set the stage" for the 2004 New Hampshire Presidential Primary. It also contains valuable historical information and copies of artifacts that have never appeared in any other book.

Based solely on the experience of the 2000 primary, this book augers—from a bipartisan approach—what might happen in presidential primaries in 2004 and beyond.

—*Hugh Gregg and Bill Gardner*
August, 2003

Why New Hampshire?

Chapter 1

Handshakes, Shoe Leather and the National Spotlight

EVERY FOUR YEARS, FOR MORE than half a century, New Hampshire has captured national headlines with its first-in-the-nation presidential primary, and enlivened the process of electing our presidents. Being first hardly explains its consistent appeal. The state also has singular geographic, governmental and communal characteristics not found anywhere else, much of which accounts for its perpetual political attraction.

Subliminally, the state's primary is always in media focus, maybe not always consciously, but always there. It is the longest-running convention held anywhere in the United States. It doesn't start every four years with candidate filings and end with the primary. Rather it begins the day after the last primary election and continues for four years to the next primary.

For example, a few days after the Tuesday of the primary election in 1996, Lamar Alexander, who had been defeated, was identified by the plaid shirt he wore throughout the state, had plaid bumper stickers on the street overlaid with the figure "2000." He did run again in the 2000 campaign. In fact, he hosted a mammoth lobster bake on the New Hampshire seacoast for potential supporters, but he made the mistake of buying the lobsters in Maine.

Also, just a week after Clinton had been re-elected in November of the same year, Sam Berry, Jr., a Republican lawyer from Oregon, ran an ad in *Manchester Union Leader* announcing his presidential candidacy for the year 2000. He subsequently set up a website, came to the state, and was the first person to file in 2000; but he didn't campaign actively and he received only 61 votes.

New Hampshire offers a user-friendly primary process. It has an open-door policy. The state is alone in making its ballot available to anyone with a $1,000 filing fee who qualifies to hold the office of president by complying with the provisions of the United States Constitution. Not so elsewhere. Ballot access varies from state to state, some of which are extremely restrictive and exclusive to the point where the parties or the secretary of state make the final choice of the names to be listed.

The secretary of state's office, which accepts candidate filing papers, perpetually answers all inquiries, dispatches requested information, and hospitably receives applicants one-by-one. It's easy to be listed on the ballot. It can even be done by mail. Many are potential "fringe" candidates who never actually file. Yet the ballot contains more names than appear in other states. Fourteen-term Secretary William Gardner knows more thwarted presidential candidates than the 400 members of the legislature with whom he deals every day. Though defeated, they still call him to reminisce.

New Hampshire is a strong grassroots state where people take part in civic affairs with enthusiasm. Political leadership comes from the grass roots, complemented by a plethora of unpaid commissions supervising vital agencies.

Participatory government is a hallmark of the Granite State. Except for Vermont, New Hampshire is the sole state which elects its governor for only a two-year term. Thus there is no need for a recall provision, as in California, which has recently developed a circus atmosphere. Governors in New Hampshire are not trusted for the customary four years. They have to run again if they plan to stay longer in the Statehouse. Though, in fairness, no governor was ever deprived of a second successive term if he wanted it. This system is also a trap door for the Executive Council and lawmakers, who get the same treatment.

As previously noted, in honor of New Hampshire's 400 member legislature, it means every two years New Hampshire goes to the polls with the possibility of ending up with a whole new cast of characters running the show. Politics and elections are a way of life. More elections are held with greater frequency at state and local levels than in any other state. Citizens are constantly in an election mode. They are forever voting about something, whether it be at town meetings or on the municipal affairs of cities in the off-years. Easy ballot access is provided in presidential primaries and general elections by permitting voter registration on election day. Jimmy Carter spelled it out, "In New Hampshire the primaries are the state industry."

Though unrelated to its presidential primary, and perhaps it's only political trivia, New Hampshire has also elected more governors than any other state. Eighty to be exact. Again, that's pretty convincing evidence that it spends a lot of time behind the polling curtain.

Voting is made easy, particularly for those who call themselves Independents or who do not wish to be registered as a permanent member of a specific party. New voters of either party or Independents (undeclared voters) can register and vote on primary day by picking up the ballot of a qualifying national party. After voting, they have the same day alternative of remaining registered as a member of the party whose ballot they chose or they can again revert to an independent or undeclared status.

Fun along the Campaign Trail

Democratic Congressman Morris Udall of Arizona walked into Joe Swiezynski's busy barbershop on the Oval in Milford. In a friendly gesture of greeting to the assembled cluster of regulars both in and out of the chair, he announced, "I'm Congressman Morris Udall. I'm running for president."

"Yes, we know" replied Joe, the town's leading Republican, "we were laughing about it this morning."

Former New Jersey senator and New York Knicks basketball hero Bill Bradley greets voters at a campaign event in Hampton.

Nearly all the state's qualified voter population is registered. Traditionally, New Hampshire ranks among those states with the highest voter turnout in national elections. Studies have found that many of its citizens actually shake hands with a presidential candidate. Depending on the handhold, it often results in identifying candidates as conductors who will lead the country to political paradise or, in the alternative, as gluttonous freeloaders at the public trough.

In 1999, a telephone survey by Dartmouth College professors of government contacted 2,296 voters. They reported 19.76 percent of the voters said they had met one of the top four presidential candidates or attended one of their rallies. As stated in the report, "If nearly 20 percent of New Hampshire's one million voters report meeting a candidate, then roughly 200,000 people are met." Or, as the *Concord Monitor* editorialized, "Twenty percent! In some places, a figure like that could pass for voter turnout."

A 2001 study under the direction of Economics Professor Ross Gittell at the University of New Hampshire arrived at similar statistics on the "engagement" of the state's citizens in the primary process. The UNH report concluded, "More than in any other state, New Hampshire residents seek opportunities to meet with candidates." Because so many want to get in on the action there's an unlimited supply of experienced volunteers always available. An effective campaign can be run with a smaller paid staff than in larger states.

For years, the state boasted its slogan, "Always First, Always Right." Up to the 1992 primary, when Clinton was beaten by

---

Fun along the Campaign Trail

Pat Paulsen, the professional comedian and frequent primary participant was a Democrat. One year he filed as a Republican on the intuition, "I don't think all the comedians should be in the Democratic Party."

Massachusetts Senator Tsongas, the state had an unblemished ten-game record of picking the candidate who would eventually sit in the Oval Office. In that year the popular, vicarious native son (his home was just a few miles from the New Hampshire border) bested the relatively unknown southerner. Further, the neighborhood kid had campaigned hard and didn't stop to pick Flowers. Though the incident was excusable as an explainable aberration, nonetheless it somewhat tarnished New Hampshire's guru-ish reputation.

After Senator John McCain's "Straight Talk Express" bus toured the state in the 2000 primary, when he'd held 114 town meetings for an upset victory over Texas Governor George W. Bush, and when in the general election thereafter, Al Gore didn't even retain his apprenticeship office in the White House, the slogan was reduced to two words, "Always First." By nature, New Hampshire people aren't long-winded anyway, particularly when its blowing in the wrong direction.

Now there's the increasingly popular idea that the state should scrap the old slogan and adopt a new one, "The Do or Die State." But that is not necessary, as we can still claim, *no one has ever become president who did not win in New Hampshire.* Although Clinton lost to Tsongas in the 1992 primary and Bush lost to McCain in the 2000 primary, both Clinton and Bush carried the state in the general election thereafter.

As an aside to the "Always Right" end of the slogan, one wag asked: "If New Hampshire voters are such Magis, how come 273,599 of them in the general election of 2000 thought George W. Bush should be president, yet only 71,494 thought him worthy of being the Republican candidate at the time of the primary election?" It takes a few minutes of cogitation to get a good answer. Maybe it's only the New Hampshire voter's occasional quirkiness.

In 2000, a heartbreaker occurred in the town of Hudson, the only town in the state which previously held an unbroken record of voting for the eventual national winner of each major party

The following communities have correctly chosen the winners of all New Hampshire REPUBLICAN presidential preference primaries since 1952:

Claremont	Pembroke
East Kingston	Richmond
Lancaster	Rochester
Newmarket	Sanbornton
Newton	Washington

The following communities have correctly chosen the winners of all New Hampshire DEMOCRATIC presidential preference primaries since 1952:

Bennington	Laconia
Epping	Merrimack
Hudson	Rollinsford
Kingston	

in every primary since 1952. But in 2000 it picked McCain and Gore in the primary and then struck out a second time in the general election when Gore trimmed Bush by 36 votes out of a total of 9,110 votes cast by the two parties in that town. Hudson's flag should be forever flown at half staff!

After the 2000 primary, there were still a few towns that had an unbroken record of selecting at least the Democratic or the Republican winner, as shown in the chart above.

Because so relatively few national convention delegates can be gained here, presidential candidates do not put their names on our ballot solely to gain seats at the national conventions. The state picks only one percent of the delegates elected to the national conventions. Rather, campaigning in the Granite State is valuable as a quick means of achieving national recognition.

Sometimes, winning results here are not duplicated elsewhere. Though not much talked about, the state does maintain a Presidential Wannabees Retirement Home. Accommodations have been provided there for Estes Kefauver, Michael Dukakis, Patrick J. Buchanan, Paul E. Tsongas, Gary Hart, Edmund S. Muskie, Henry Cabot Lodge, Al Gore and John McCain.

There are those who continually raise the musty argument that New Hampshire citizens are not representative enough of the American electorate to speak for it. Others frequently have alleged that it doesn't have enough Asians, Hispanics, African-Americans, Eskimos or others to be a true cross-section of the general populace. Except for neighboring Vermont, where they used to say the cows outnumbered and had more sense than the voters, there probably remains a bigger residue of "Ay'up" Yankees in New Hampshire than elsewhere.

Though perhaps not necessarily with the same ethnic, economic or social groups, the diversity of the population is as mixed as any other state. So who is to determine which combination of minorities best represents the American profile? California, frequently thought of as today's melting pot, has more racial minority groups than white people. Is that a better test?

Most important of all is the service New Hampshire renders to the country and the national election process by winnowing out the weaker candidates. The ticket is shortened before other states see it. If it weren't for New Hampshire, with Senator Phil Gramm's fear of running for president and Elizabeth Dole's fear after running for president, either or both of them might have ended up playing golf on a presidential pension. While in the state, the competitors have the opportunity to test their issues, find out what works and what doesn't. It sets them up to avoid mistakes later on.

Dr. Emmett N. Buell, Jr. of Denison University believes that New Hampshire's reputation for momentum is even more significant than its service for winnowing. He writes, "unexpected winners often get an extraordinary bounce from this primary. Whether it propels them to final victory is another matter." It's these two ingredients working together which accounts for the state's unique contribution to the overall presidential nominating process.

Other well-known hopefuls, such as Senators Robert Taft and Howard Baker, have had their dreams of the Oval office dashed. Conversely many politicians with little name identification and/

or financial resources have been able to attract nationwide attention as viable presidential candidates by entering the quadrennial event. President Carter started as "Jimmy Who?" Even George Bush, the elder, was, as he said, "an asterisk" when he joined in 1978. New Hampshire voters conscientiously pick the survivors from the aspirants.

New Hampshire inhabits a small, homogeneous area where its citizens enjoy a unity of purpose and quality of life unequaled elsewhere. It honors the right of privacy and the privilege of "doing your own thing." It abhors big government and resists it to whatever extent it can.

The locale is readily accessible by ground or air. It is compact, easy to traverse, replete with diverse communities and their equally versatile inhabitants engaged in a wide range of employment. If the candidate had only a boat, he could dock in Portsmouth harbor. Otherwise it's quick access by Interstate from Boston or direct by air into Manchester's modern airport.

To save money candidates often choose to seek lodging in the homes of supporters, who are happy to host coffees and receptions for them as well. President Clinton rewarded such hosts with reunions at the White House. Often fringe candidates have settled in at churches and college dormitories. Thanks to an extensive tourist industry, venues host innumerable overnight accommodations. Once here the state is geographically small; relatively short tours take the candidates to its population centers from Concord or Manchester.

Of course once in a while some visitors find traveling around this small state to be a burden, as did Peter Kaye, an aide to President Gerald Ford, who found it, "a hell of a state to walk in, because if you go forty miles outside of a city, there's nothing but bears and trees."

Morry Taylor, a candidate in 1996, nicknamed the "Griz" because he loved bears, and his staff, campaigned in their own traveling hotel consisting of six brightly colored red, white and blue large mobile units. His portable house had all the comforts of a home and office, from a queen-sized bed to a shower, from a computer to a fax machine, not to mention five cellular telephone numbers. He shared these quarters with his wife, Michelle, and his dog, named after him, Griz. Who knows who came when she called Griz?

Uniquely New Hampshire, a favorite campaign stop is the local dump. In the smaller towns it is a social event for its residents to convene there on Saturdays to assess each other's trash and discuss other affairs of state. When the town of Newton got tired of politicians cluttering up the place with their literature, the selectmen ruled that campaigning among garbage bags was becoming a safety issue. They didn't say whether it was the paper, or the issues advocated, that was the danger. Nonetheless, they voted to ban the practice.

But a local disciple of the primary's significance filed a complaint in court that the restriction violated candidates' right of free speech. He also noted that the town center had burned down in the 1800s and the "transfer center" was the only central place where the candidates could press the flesh. The case was eventually settled out of court, with the town designating a privileged zone where the politicians could set up shop, a typical example of the grassroots support generated for politicians with the courage of stepping forward to represent them.

Campaigns in some states have become so expensive it even takes lots of money to get beaten. Even worse, in 1999, Senators Ashcroft and Bob Kerrey were good examples of spending money just to think about starting a campaign. But in New Hampshire it is relatively inexpensive. The skinflint natives, proud to be only one of two states without a sales or income tax, challenge any other state, be it smaller or bigger, to charge a candidate less money for his or her campaign.

For so few bucks, nowhere else could there be such a cash bargain for the unknown who wants to be the next president of the United States, and with the odds of winning astronomically better than Powerball's. Jimmy Carter would so testify! There's no need for extensive spending of money on radio and television. Steve Forbes demonstrated that in 1996, when it cost him something approaching four million of his own money to come in fourth.

But winning does require putting up with the residents. The candidate wears hard on shoe leather, handshakes and listening to a lot of stuff he couldn't care less about. Apparently, though, New Hampshire does make exceptions for five-star generals, because the only candidate who ever won here without following this time-tested procedure and became president was Eisenhower.

Eyeball-to-eyeball encounters with New Hampshirites is the standard operating procedure on which the voters' convictions are based. In years past, they have been described as a shy, humble, quiet, retiring people and as granite and loquacious as was their Great Stone Face in Franconia Notch. But it ain't so in today's political caldron. During primary season everybody has an opinion. Even more boring, it's freely expressed, when the listener may not give a damn. But all such good advice still doesn't tell how the loudmouths are actually going to vote. Minds are changed faster than new candidates enter the race.

Washington Post columnist David Broder said it well, "I am firmly of the belief that the term 'front runner' should never be applied to anyone until the voters of New Hampshire have per-

---

Fun along the Campaign Trail

President Reagan always carried a stack of 3″ x 5″ cards in his pocket which could fit any situation. When he got a question critical of the way Social Security payments were being paid, he reminded the malcontent, "Don't worry about it. I ran into a guy the other day who had complained that, because the agency thought he was dead, his Social Security checks had stopped coming. But, on second thought, the man wasn't too concerned, as they sent him a good check for his funeral."

GOP candidates in 2000 attend a state Republican Party candidate's night. Steve Duprey, chairman of the state party, at left, shares a lighter moment with the assembled guests, McCain, Bush, Keyes, Hatch, Forbes and Bauer.

formed their God-given right to sort out and shrink the presidential nomination field."

Maura Carroll, a Carter/Mondale staffer in 1980, told a reporter, "A lot of people say, 'I'll take your literature, but I can't say I'm voting for the president right now.' That's not a positive response, but it's not negative either. People here consider themselves politically sophisticated, independent thinkers. Not that they're all undecided, many just don't want to say."

Brian Lamb, president of C-Span, believes our primary is "always going to be important … Just because you're smart enough to figure out for yourselves if a candidate is pulling your chain."

The eyeball scenario can be tough. Lamar Alexander found that out when he was pontificating to customers at a convenience store on the national budget and bringing down the federal debt. The clerk, as reported by Rick Wenck, stopped him in mid-sentence and asked, "In that cooler is our milk. Can you tell me how much a gallon costs today within ten cents?" The candidate had no clue, so he got a follow-up question. "How about a loaf of bread, how much is that going for?" Again, don't know. Which allegedly resulted in the clerk saying if he didn't even know the price of a gallon of milk or loaf of bread he had no business talking about the budget, and she wouldn't vote for him.

The candidate is also measured by the weather. It's figured that any foreigner who can slosh around in the snowdrifts without catching pneumonia or distemper can withstand the rigors of a presidency. It's always a tough choice to decide whether to bundle up in a fur coat or wear the clothes he came in and look presidential. No matter how cold or windy, they have to brave it to tell their story. So many of them come during the campaign season that the air is constantly full of speeches and vice versa. Franklin D. Roosevelt was visiting on April 12, 1934 when the highest wind ever recorded in the world hit 232 miles per hour on New Hampshire's Mount Washington.

Perhaps the effects of weather were best described by Senator Eugene McCarthy when, campaigning in 1968, he noted, "I think more people die in New Hampshire than win. New Hampshire is like a suit of long underwear frozen stiff on a clothesline."

The Media love coming to New Hampshire. They're attracted from all over the world. The internationalists are taken with the state's scenic beauty and economic diversity. The national pundits like bunking in Manchester from where they can quickly and conveniently travel to most major events in any direction. Better still, they can return at night to file their stories while taking advantage of the state-controlled low liquor prices. The lounges at the Holiday Inn or the Wayfarer are the places to get autographs of your favorite columnist or TV anchor. John DiStaso of the *Manchester Union Leader* said CNN claimed to have 300 people here covering the 2000 primary.

Near election day, when there's a saturation of media, it is occasionally true, as William Safire wrote in the *New York Times,* that candidates, "are unable to climb over a cameraman to touch a voter." But their presence translates into free television, radio and print exposure. At the same time, as CNN's anchorman Bernard Shaw commented, "It's important for journalists to listen to real voters express their views."

David Paletz and Robert Eastman in their book *Media Power Politics* underscore the importance of the press with their view that, "Were it not for the media . . . the New Hampshire primary would be about as relevant to the presidential nomination as opening-day baseball scores are to a pennant race." James Perry of the *Wall Street Journal* echoes the same theme, describing the

---

Fun along the Campaign Trail

Once in a while a contestant contests too much, like Vice President Walter Mondale: "New Hampshire, the Mt. Everest of Democratic primaries."

Senator Robert B. Dole echoed the same theme: "Now I know why it's called the Granite State—it's so hard to crack."

primary as, "part reunion, part convention, part warm-up for what's to come." All agree the media set the pulse for the national attention attributed to the state's presidential primary.

Dr. Emmett Buell of Denison University, who quadrennially brings his students to the state for their field work, credits New Hampshire as being the mouse which gets "the lion's share of coverage." Still, as they say in dogsledding, if the candidate can't achieve a lead dog image, the scenery along the trail never changes.

David Nyhan, the former *Boston Globe* columnist, emphasizes the critical role the media play in building the candidate for what comes later. "But do well in New Hampshire and your mug is on the cover of *Time* and *Newsweek*, the cable networks go bananas making you a household name, and with the calendar scrunched toward the weeks just after New Hampshire, the single biggest bang you can get is to come out of the Granite State as the man who is hot-hot-hot!" Even more sophisticated readers find the primary an interesting study in publications like the *New Yorker*.

Photo-ops are also a major media allurement. There's a voracious appetite by the video recorders for backdrops of skiing, sledding and snowbanks, farms and their animals, church steeples, country stores and their country characters, ice fishing and bob-houses and in some years even maple sugaring, which one writer noted as "sap doesn't only come from trees in New Hampshire." Obviously he hadn't had enough syrup. Significantly, these photographs receive wide circulation. Favorable ones resonate directly to a candidate's benefit at no cost to him. Freelance TV production crews find the primary a great source for documentaries.

For example, in 1992, President Bush, running for re-election, made a "spontaneous" stop beside a field where there happened to be a farmer standing with his cow. Bush got out of his vehicle and shook hands with both the farmer and the cow. The whole scenario was aired on national television. The following morning it made the front page of the *New York Times* and a few days later appeared in full color in *Newsweek*. It was tremendous gratuitous publicity for the campaign.

New Hampshire offers a further advantage. If running for president seems like too much of an undertaking, it happens to be the only state where an aspiring candidate can file and run for vice president. Or better yet, he or she can run for both president and vice president simultaneously, except the candidate must come up with an additional $1,000 to file for both offices. In 1984, Gerald Willis tried it and got 50 votes for president and 14,870 for vice president. Four years later David E. Duke, the former National Imperial Wizard of the Ku Klux Klan, did the same thing. New Hampshire voters didn't respond quite as well to him as to Willis because while the Wizard also received 50 votes for president, he conned only 10,531 for vice president.

New Hampshire comes as close to a level playing field for any seeker of the presidency as could possibly be designed. The state is small, diversified and politically sophisticated. Its politics are retail. Its citizens are accustomed to meeting the candidates one-on-one and are not easily influenced by the national media. They tend to make independent judgments based on the character of the candidates to whom they have been personally exposed, and they keep these opinions to themselves.

Fun along the Campaign Trail

During his hectic New Hampshire campaign, Senator John McCain appeared before the state's Senate where members noted his exhaustion. One commented that McCain need not worry, as Senator Squires was a doctor. This prompted lawyer Senator Gordon to remark, "Don't worry, John, if the doctor doesn't give you the right treatment, we'll sue him." Whereupon the Senate Chaplain spoke up, "If the condition gets very serious, I'm here." The final offer of help came from Senator Eaton, an undertaker.

New Hampshire voters require candidates to share their views in person. Whatever comes over a nationally televised network program is merely an add-on that doesn't replace the handshake. The candidates' positions are not formulated by national polls or national news commentators, but rather by the personal familiarity with the voters of New Hampshire. The state's primary reflects positively on the openness of its electoral process.

Jean Davidson, writing in the *Los Angeles Times* put it a little differently, "Americans choose their elected leaders, in part, the same way they buy vegetables—by appearance." That leaves a little flexibility. How many times have you thought the melon was ripe?

That's why the pollsters are so frequently wrong in reading New Hampshire's political sentiment. And maybe that's also why every presidential candidate who has won in New Hampshire has always pledged to support the continuance of its first-place primary.

*

Chapter 2

Beginnings

EVEN THOUGH NEW HAMPSHIRE HAS maintained the tradition of holding the first-in-the nation presidential primary since 1920, it was not until 1952 that its importance in the national nominating process was recognized.

The increasing influence of electronic media, such as television and the Internet, has done more to bring attention to the Granite State's role in presidential elections than anything else. The media have developed a sustained and lofty image of how candidates present themselves and how campaigns are conducted. When the political historians write their books on 20th century presidential electioneering, or when the TV anchors give their versions, inevitable comparisons will be made with its beginning in New Hampshire.

Its first settlers administered public affairs within each of its own communities independently of any overall authority. It was not until 1641, when the area became part of the Province of Massachusetts, that a central government was formed, and in 1679, King Charles II permitted the establishment of a Royal Province of its own. In the early years of British rule all affairs of state were handled by appointees of the King of England. After the last of the royal governors had left New Hampshire, a "Revolutionary Assembly" met in Exeter in the summer of 1775.

The first overt act of aggression against the King occurred in December 1774. Paul Revere rode from Boston to warn the citizens of Portsmouth of the likelihood of a British blockade of the harbor, just like had happened to Boston. The citizens reacted quickly and attacked Fort William and Mary, taking the guns and ammunition that were later used at the Battle of Bunker Hill on June 17, 1775. Over half the soldiers who fought in that battle came from New Hampshire.

On January 5, 1776, New Hampshire's Fifth Provincial Congress was the first of any legislative body in the thirteen original colonies to assert its independence from Great Britain, six months before the nation's Declaration of Independence on July fourth. It stated, in part, "The sudden and abrupt departure of His Excellency John Wentworth, Esq., our late Governor . . . We conceive ourselves reduced to the necessity of establishing a form of government, to continue during the present and unhappy and unnatural contest with Great Britain. . . . We do resolve that this Congress assume the name, power, and authority of a House of Representatives, or Assembly, for the colony of New Hampshire."

A proclamation to the people outlining a proposed constitution emphasized that one of the purposes of the newly formed government was "to quell all appearances of party spirit, to cultivate and promote peace, union, and good order, and by all means in their power to discourage profaneness, immorality and injustice." It ended with the words, "God save the people." With those four words, never let it be said that our forefathers didn't have insight into the future and today's government!

> *Fun along the Campaign Trail*
>
> **Austin Burton, known as Chief Burning Wood was a frequent primary contender. One year he tried to beat the $1,000 filing fee. Instead, he sent the secretary of state a package of wampum—a four foot length of snake skin. Not such a dumb idea; it got him enough national publicity that he didn't have to file.**

When the Declaration of Independence came to a vote, the first to vote was New Hampshire's Josiah Bartlett, because the delegates decided to start with the northernmost colony.

On June 5, 1779, a New Hampshire Constitutional Convention presented the first free constitution of the people, by the people and for the people in world history and it was ratified by the people in 1783, after two additional revisions in 1781 and 1782. The state was also the ninth and deciding vote of the thirteen original colonies to ratify the federal Constitution on June 21, 1788, thereby making it the law of the United States. On December 15, 1788, New Hampshire residents cast their first popular votes for presidential and vice presidential electors. When our first president George Washington took the oath of office, he stood next to Senate President Pro Tem John Langdon, one of New Hampshire's two senators who held the bible that Washington rested one of his hands on as he stated the oath.

Though redrafted several times, the state's constitution has retained many of the vestiges of colonial days. New Hampshire is one of only two states with an Executive Council. The Council holds veto power over the governor in matters of government, including certain appointments, expenditures and contracts. It is also one of only two states which maintains a two-year term for its

---

Fun along the Campaign Trail

When Vice President Bush's motorcade was routed through a small town, the police department agreed with the Secret Service to be responsible for securing the town's one intersection. They were there, all four of them, dutifully on station, when the advance team of several state cruisers zoomed by. Figuring they'd seen the motorcade pass and duty completed, the locals left. Five minutes later, the motorcade sailed through the unsecured access roads, with concern and embarrassment to the Secret Service.

governor. The governor is uniquely identified in the constitution as the Supreme Executive Magistrate and most governors imagine they comport themselves as though they fit that role.

After the Parliament of England and the Congress of the United States, New Hampshire's four-hundred member House of Representatives is the third largest English-speaking deliberative body in the world. Since the state constitution was adopted in 1783, more than 23,000 individuals have served in the New Hampshire House. Today, every 3,089 citizens have a state representative. Compare this to California where it takes 423,395 citizens to have a representative in Sacramento. For California to have representation like New Hampshire, it would need 10,965 House members. For the U.S. House to have representation like New Hampshire, it would need 91,105 members.

From the nation's founding, the state's military and political leaders have received national acclaim. It was the Revolutionary War hero of Bunker Hill and the Battle of Bennington, General John Stark, who penned the phrase "Live Free or Die" which is now the state's official motto. In the 1830s, settlers on the state's northern boundary seceded from the state and established their own independent country known as the Indian Stream Republic. It was native son Daniel Webster who assisted in terminating the secession. And, while he was U.S. secretary of state, he helped write the treaty that set the boundary between Canada and the United States that became known as the Webster-Ashburton treaty. Statues of both Stark and Webster are exhibited in the rotunda of the Capitol in Washington.

Native Granite Staters take particular pride in Daniel Webster's famous quote: "Men put out signs representing their different trades. Jewelers hang out a monstrous watch, shoemakers a huge boot. Up in Franconia, God Almighty has hung out a sign that in New Hampshire He makes men." The reference was to the Great Stone Face, as referred to by Nathaniel Hawthorne, which quietly cogitated what went on up here every four years while blessing the presidential primary tradition. Now that he has left us, we pray it may last as long as he did.

In 1777, Captain John Paul Jones commanded the U.S.S. Ranger, built at the Portsmouth Navy Yard. As it sailed against the British it was the first navy ship to fly the Stars and Stripes.

The Republican Party as we know it today was founded by Congressman Amos Tuck in Exeter on October 12, 1853. Earlier that year, in March, General Franklin Pierce, a New Hampshire Democrat, took the oath of office as president of the United States and served from 1853 to 1857.

New Hampshire played a prominent role in organizing the first national party nominating convention of what is now the Democratic Party. Prior to the presidential election of 1832, presidential and vice-presidential party nominations were decided by what was known as the "Congressional caucus," sometimes derisively referred to as the "King Caucus." These meetings of members of the United States House and Senate were not without controversy and in some years were sparsely attended. If you were being represented in Congress by someone of a different party, you had no voice in the caucus nomination process of your party. The King Caucus was not popular, and by the 1820s it was ready to be replaced. Andrew Jackson's election in 1828 became the catalyst.

During Jackson's first term, a rift developed between the president and his vice president, John C. Calhoun. On several of the most important issues facing the administration, the two took different positions and gradually their relationship deteriorated. It got so bad that during the last year of Jackson's first term, when he nominated Martin Van Buren to be minister to England, his own vice president undermined the nomination and cast the deciding "no" vote as president of the Senate.

When Jackson decided he would run for a second term, he wanted Martin Van Buren to be his vice president. Understanding the uneasiness and friction between his administration and the House and Senate, his friends and political advisors discussed alternatives to the Congressional caucus. They knew Calhoun had

Fun along the Campaign Trail

In 1999 when Lamar Alexander withdrew from the presidential race, he left homeless a great quantity of his trademark red/black checkered shirts. Pat Buchanan's comment, "Let me tell you, you can get a lot of those Howdy Doody shirts for cheap today."

many friends among House and Senate members and decided that in order to prevent him from being Jackson's running mate and have someone more to the president's liking they needed to broaden the nomination process by ending the role of the Congressional caucus.

New Hampshire party leaders were receptive to this idea and took the lead in organizing the first national nominating convention. They decided it was time to end the Congressional caucus and let the nomination for vice president be decided by a national convention.

The Jacksonian Democrats controlled two-thirds of the membership of the New Hampshire General Court after the March 1831 election. They were led by 26 year-old Franklin Pierce, who was elected speaker of the House for that session. A party legislative caucus was called for the elected party members, including House, Senate, governor, councilors, secretary of state, treasurer, and clerks of each chamber. Pierce played a leading role in this debate and made the motion creating the committee, of which he became a member, that drafted the language calling on the other states to join New Hampshire at a national convention.

At that caucus, held on June 23 and 24, 1831, they voted their support for President Jackson to be their nominee for a second term and also voted that there be a national convention to be held on the third Monday of May 1832 at Baltimore for the purpose of choosing a party nominee for vice president. They voted to send a resolution to each of the other states calling for their participation in the proposed national convention and asking each state to send delegates equal to their number of electors. The call was successful, as 23 states sent delegates (only Missouri did not) and the national convention took place at the time and place New Hampshire had proposed. Martin Van Buren was selected by the delegates to be Jackson's' running mate. Thus, the national convention was established and continues to this day.

Because New Hampshire was credited with organizing this first national party nominating convention, New Hampshire Delegate Frederic Augustus Sumner was given the honor of calling the convention to order. He was a respected lawyer from Charlestown whose opening remarks to the delegates explained why New Hampshire had decided to call for the convention in the first place. His remarks were published in several newspapers.

Before 1878, when most states held their elections in the fall, New Hampshire cast ballots in March on the traditional town meeting day. New Hampshire was always the first state to have it's election, and all state office holders served one-year terms. With the ascendancy of the Republican Party during the late 1850s, and throughout the Civil War, the state played a significant role in the national competition between Republicans and Democrats. With its first-in-the-nation state elections every year in March, much attention was paid to New Hampshire by the rest of the country.

The state was looked to as a barometer of how each political party was doing in the eyes of the voters. New Hampshire campaigns for governor and the state legislature garnered national attention during this period and many national political figures came to New Hampshire to campaign for their fellow party candidates. This was particularly intense during the early years of the Civil War, when the Republicans were afraid that if the New Hampshire elections went Democratic, it would create momentum in other states to do the same, and thus hurt President Abraham Lincoln's chances of being re-elected in 1864. The concern was that General McLellan, a Democrat, would gain support, particularly because of the defeats of the Union army in the early years of the Civil War. The campaigns during those elections were very spirited party affairs and generated interest beyond the state's

NEW HAMPSHIRE PATRIOT AND STATE GAZETTE

CONCORD, MONDAY, JUNE 27, 1831.

Voice of the Granite State !
The Republican Members of the Legislature, to the number of more than ONE HUNDRED AND FIFTY, being nearly TWO THIRDS of that body, met in Convention on Friday evening last. This Convention UNANIMOUSLY passed resolutions approving of the nomination of ANDREW JACKSON to the Presidency, *and recommending a general Convention of Republicans friendly to the re-election of Gen. Jackson, to be holden at Baltimore in May, 1832, for the purpose of nominating a Vice President.*

These pages show clippings from the New Hampshire Patriot and State Gazette, *a newspaper published in the capital city in the 1800s. The paper ran several articles describing the process—led by New Hampshire—leading up to the first national nominating convention of the Democratic Party.*

Note: At the time, the Democrats referred to themselves as Republicans, a relic of the Jeffersonian era. There were also fewer state representatives than today.

THE PATRIOT.

REPUBLICAN CONVENTION.

At a meeting of the Democratic Members of the Legislature, at the Hall of the Eagle Coffee House, in Concord, on Thursday evening, June 23, 1831,

JAMES FARRINGTON, Esq. Chairman :

B. B. FRENCH, Esq. Secretary.

On motion of Mr. PIERCE of Hillsborough, a Committee of ten was appointed to report an Address and Resolutions for the consideration of this Convention ; which committee consisted of Messrs. CARTLAND and STARK of the Senate,—Messrs. PIERCE, HARVEY, of S. PRESCOTT, WALDRON, GOVE, of Grantham, WILLIAMS, DEARBORN, and SAWYER of Swanzey, of the House of Representatives.

On motion,

Resolved, That the Chairman of this Convention be directed to invite the Democratic members of the Council, the Secretary and Treasurer, and the Clerks of both Houses, to attend at the next meeting of this Convention, and to take part in the deliberations thereof.

The Convention then adjourned to Friday evening, June 24.

FRIDAY, June 24.

Met according to Adjournment.

Upon a call of the Convention, the following gentlemen appeared and answered to their names :

COUNSELLORS.

Messrs. Jacob Freese, Samuel C. Webster.
Stephen Peabody,

SENATORS.

Messrs Bradbury Bartlett, Nathaniel Knowlton,
Frederick G. Stark, Eleazer Jackson, jr.
Aaron Whittemore, Robert Burns,
Henry B. Rust, Samuel Cartland.
Benning M. Bean,

HOUSE OF REPRESENTATIVES.
ROCKINGHAM.

Messrs. Richard Greenough, Benning Leavitt,
Henry T. Eaton John Harvey jr

{ VOL. 3. NO. 106....NEW SERIES. }
{ VOL. XXIII...,WHOLE NO. 1162. }

Resolved, That this Convention, aware of the salutary effects which may attend the interchange of sentiments of the great republican party throughout the Union—believing that the great interests of the North and the South, the East and the West, can be better conciliated by holding communion with each other, and yielding points of minor local difference, than by a reiteration of epithets, calculated to widen the breach by fanning the flame of local prejudices,—do recommend to their republican brethren in other States, friendly to the reelection of ANDREW JACKSON, to elect Delegates equal to the number of Electors of President in each State, to attend a general Convention to be holden at Baltimore, in the State of Maryland, on the third Monday of May, 1832 ; which Convention shall have for its object the adoption of such measures as will best promote the reelection of Andrew Jackson, and the nomination of a candidate to be supported as Vice-President at the same election,

Resolved, That JOHN LANGDON ELWYN, JAMES FARRINGTON, ARLOND CARROLL, CHARLES F. GOVE, FREDERICK A. SUMNER, NATHAN G. BABBITT, SAMUEL C. WEBSTER, and JARED W. WILLIAMS, be delegates for the State of New-Hampshire, to attend a National Convention at Baltimore on the third Monday of May, 1832, provided a majority of the States shall accede to the recommendation contained in the foregoing resolution ; and that the gentlemen herein named shall have authority to choose a substitute or substitutes to supply any vacancy that may happen in their number.

27

THE PATRIOT.

From the Baltimore Republican.
GENERAL CONVENTION.

The convention met at the Athæpeum at 11 o'clock, yesterday morning, when Mr. SUMNER, of New-Hampshire, ad.'ressed the meeting as follows :

GENTLEMEN : The proposition for calling a general convention of delegates, to act on the nomination of a candidate for President, and to select a suitable candidate for the office of Vice President of the United States, originated in the State of New Hampshire, by the friends of democracy in that State ; and it appears that the proposition, although opposed by the enemies of the democratic party, has found favor in nearly and perhaps all the States in the Union ; so that we find collected at this time and place a greater and more general delegation from the people than was ever before assembled upon an occasion of this sort.

The object of the representatives of the people o f New Hampshire who called this Convention was, not to impose on the people, as candidates for either of

This final article on the national nominating convention appeared in the New Hampshire Patriot and State Gazette *on June 4, 1832. In recognition of New Hampshire's status as the organizing state, one of its delegates, Frederick Augustus Sumner, was given the honor of calling the convention to order and explaining why New Hampshire felt this was for the good of the country. Sumner was born in Claremont and practiced law in Charlestown. He served 15 years as a town clerk and 15 years as a selectman and later became a judge of probate.*

the two first offices in this government, any local favorite ; but to concentrate the opinions of all the States. They believed that the great body of the people, having but one common interest, can and will unite, in the support of important principles ; that the operation of the machinery of government confined within its legitimate sphere is the same, in the north, south, east, and west ; that although designing men, ever since the adoption of the constitution, have never ceased in their exertions to excite sectional feeling and sectional interest, and to array one portion of the country against another, the great and essential interests of all are the same. They believed that the coming together of representatives of the people from the extremity of the Union, would have a tendency to soothe, if not to unite, the jarring interests, which sometimes come in conflict, from the different sections of the country.

They considered the individuals, who might be selected as candidates for office, to be of much less consequence than the principle on which they are designated ; they thought it important to ascertain the fact, whether the people themselves, or those who should frustrate the voice of the people, should succeed in our elections.

They believed that the example of this convention would operate favorably in future elections ; that the people would be disposed, after seeing the good effects of this convention in conciliating, the different and distant sections of the country, to continue this mode of nomination.

The states heeded the call of New Hampshire to hold the national nominating convention on the third Monday of May of 1832.

borders, like our modern day presidential primary—without the modern inventions of radio and television and computer.

As historian James O. Lyford wrote in 1906, the "Eyes of the country were fixed on New Hampshire. The New Hampshire election was the first of the year, and, being a debatable state, the election was regarded as the keynote of subsequent elections of the year. The state was visited by correspondents of leading metropolitan newspapers, who gave to their readers thrilling accounts of the campaigns, forecasting the results. Men of national reputation on both sides, distinguished members of Congress, took part in the campaigns, speaking upon the stump."

The countrywide attention given to the statistical results of New Hampshire's voting before 1878 may be considered the genesis of the conventional "polling" so widely practiced today. These elections were a precursor of what was to follow with the birth of the first-in-the-nation presidential primary. In 1878, the state shifted its state elections from March to November in even-numbered years, rather than every year. Elections became more a matter of local interest and New Hampshire temporarily lost national attention.

For the remainder of the 19th century, the national political parties nominated candidates for president and vice president at nominating conventions. The convention sites were determined by the national parties, and those delegates attending were selected, for the most part, by party caucuses of state legislators. Those delegates would meet at a national convention and represent the voters of their respective political parties in selecting their party nominees. There was virtually no involvement by the rank and file voters of the various states in the delegate selection process until the beginning of the 20th century.

As researched by Mark A. Siegel, an authority on national delegate selection, Wisconsin in 1905, in line with its Progressive Movement, introduced the first political party presidential primary. Robert LaFollette, who was serving as governor, led the effort to give the party voters a bigger voice in the nomination of candidates. Voters selected delegates who, in turn, chose presidential and vice-presidential candidates. The idea was adopted by Pennsylvania in 1906, South Dakota in 1909 and Oregon in 1910. By 1916, 26 states had adopted presidential primaries.

New Hampshire had its first September primary in 1910 for governor and other state offices, replacing the caucus and convention nomination process. It did not include a presidential primary. Republican Governor Robert Bass unsuccessfully supported legislation in 1911 to establish a presidential primary. But even without the new law, the New Hampshire Republican Party decided to conduct something like a primary. The state government played no role in this delegate-selection process.

The Manual for the General Court #15, published in 1917, noted: "In 1912 a presidential primary was conducted under the auspices of the Republican Party organization, and only the Republican Party participated in the voting." This hybrid primary-convention was a precursor of things to come.

Given New Hampshire's rich tradition of independent governance, it was perhaps no surprise that in 1913 a Richmond, New Hampshire, five-term Democratic representative named Stephen A. Bullock introduced House Bill 430 in the legislature, providing for the state's first presidential primary to be held on the third Tuesday of May in 1916. It was "An Act to provide for the Election of Delegates to National Conventions by Direct Vote of the People." It passed on May 21, 1913 in the term of Democratic Governor Samuel D. Felker.

Bullock was a working farmer, fire warden and tax collector who provisionally cached collected funds in a box in his farmhouse basement, according to his granddaughter Edith Atkins. He was motivated to open up the election process by giving all citizens the opportunity to participate in selecting party leaders. In the dead of winter he made the 65 mile trek to Concord with his wife, Emma, and Edith, in a buggy pulled by "old Jerry." The women sat in the legislative gallery during the day observing Steve's activity on the floor and all spent their nights at the Eagle or Phoenix Hotels. At no time during Bullock's life was he given any credit for the significance of the law he had sponsored.

Two years later and before the scheduled 1916 primary, John W. Glessner, a Republican representative from Bethlehem amended Bullock's law to change the date from the third Tuesday in May to the second Tuesday in March. It was enacted on April 15, 1915.

Glessner moved the primary to coincide with New Hampshire's traditional town meeting day. The March date was an attempt to save money by combining the two elections. Thus a Democrat came up with the idea and a Republican found a way to do it better, saving money by not heating the town hall twice.

Glessner was a wealthy businessman and vice president of the International Harvester Company in Chicago. He came to Bethlehem to mitigate the health of a son who was stricken with asthma and other respiratory diseases. The area was nationally recognized for its clean air and was the home of the National Hay Fever Association. His farm was also used to test his company's farm equipment and agricultural technology.

Glessner was identified in the *Manual for the General Court* as the "owner and manager of a country estate" which is known today as "The Rocks." Very community minded, he was a major benefactor of the Littleton Hospital. He wrote that the farm was cleared with "sweat, and profanity and with oxen and great skill." In the winter when the roads were bad and the towns lacked the resources to repair them, he would use his own crew of 40 or 50 men to maintain them.

When the primary was finally conducted on the second Tuesday of March in 1916, it was not the first-in-the-nation. Indiana had held one a week earlier and Minnesota on the same day. But by the time of the next presidential primary, in 1920, Indiana had moved its date to May and Minnesota returned to a caucus rather than a primary. Several states, after having a primary or two, opted to return to the old caucus system, much to the delight of the party leaders who wanted the power to choose delegates

Democratic State Representative Stephen A. Bullock of Richmond. His legislation, signed into law May 2, 1913, created the first New Hampshire presidential primary.

State of New Hampshire.

In the year of our Lord one thousand nine hundred and thirteen.

An Act to provide for the Election of Delegates to National Conventions by Direct Vote of the People.

Be it enacted by the Senate and House of Representatives in General Court convened:

Section 1. On the third Tuesday in May in the year 1916, and in each year thereafter when a president of the United States is to be elected,

Copy of the handwritten legislation, the Bullock Act, creating the first New Hampshire presidential primary, to be held in 1916.

themselves rather than the general voters. The position of the party leaders was that primaries were too costly and, since the turnouts were low, the voters wouldn't mind giving up their right to vote directly.

As a result, since 1920, New Hampshire scheduled an earlier date than that of any other state and it has been consistently at least a week ahead ever since. Richard Brookhiser commented in the *Wall Street Journal* that "so long as the all-primary system remains, the first ballot will always be the last," which we interpret to mean that New Hampshire's first primary tradition will always be retained. The first real primary ballot has been cast in New Hampshire for over three-quarters of a century.

By fortuitous coincidence, also in 1920, women's suffrage was initiated with the passage of the 19th Amendment to the U.S. Constitution. The two new concepts have had a good relationship and have worked well together ever since that time. Presidential candidates would never have made it without the women who spent endless hours doing much of the grunt work for which the men took the credit.

During the primary's first 32 years, delegates were listed on the ballot as being pledged to a particular presidential candidate or uncommitted, thereby giving the voters the option of selecting their choice of delegates. But voter turnout was not great. Consequently, the 1949 legislature, under the leadership of Speaker Richard Upton, amended the law to provide for a further option. It added the names of the presidential and vice presidential candidates to the ballot, thereby permitting the voter to register a direct preference for the choice of the president and vice president.

The amended law took effect in 1952. It immediately caught the attention of national media as "New Hampshire's Beauty Contest." While voting directly for a presidential candidate had no effect on the mechanics for selecting the eventual choice of party nominee, it served as an early test of public sentiment. It also gave impetus to nationwide election "polling."

Before 1952, the country took little notice of New Hamp-

Republican State Representative John W. Glessner of Bethlehem. His legislation amended Representative Bullock's legislation and saved money for the state by setting the date for the primary back to town meeting day.

Be it enacted by the Senate and House of Representatives in General Court convened:

Section 1. Chapter 167, Laws of 1913, entitled "An act to provide for the election of delegates to national conventions by direct vote of the people", is hereby amended by striking out the words "third Tuesday in May" in section 1 of said act and inserting in place thereof the words, second Tuesday in March, so that said section as amended shall read: Section 1. On the second Tuesday in March in the year 1916, and each year thereafter when a president of the United States is to be elected, a primary shall be held for the election of delegates at large, alternate delegates at large, delegates, and alternate delegates to the national conventions of

Copy of the handwritten 1915 legislation amending the Bullock Act of 1913 by changing the date of the presidential primary from the third Tuesday in May to the second Tuesday in March.

shire's presidential primary. New Hampshire voters went about the process of choosing their national convention delegates as did the voters in a few other states. The primary was not conceived, in 1920, as a plan to gain economic benefit or publicity for the state. The changes of 1952 were the natural extension of the Granite State citizens' extraordinary pride in a valued heritage of direct citizen involvement in government and keeping it ever closer to the people.

Since 1952, a number of administrative changes have been made to the primary process. The most significant was after the primary of 1976, when, in addition to the presidential candidates, there were 391 names on the ballot of persons vying for delegate seats. In the cities using lever voting machines there was barely enough space for the increasing number of delegate candidates. As a result, the delegate names were removed from future ballots and instead had to be submitted prior to the primary by the candidates, but were not printed on the actual ballot.

The Republican National Party and the Democratic National Party rules differ with respect to the selection of delegates after the presidential primary. Republicans adhere to New Hampshire law that requires each candidate before the primary to furnish the secretary of state with a list of proposed delegates. After the primary, the winning presidential candidates choose from the delegate names previously submitted, in proportion to the percent of votes received. A candidate must get at least 10 percent of the vote to be eligible for delegates. They become the elected delegates to represent the victorious candidates at the national conventions. The candidates pick their own teams. The Democrats select their delegates according to a formula that reflects the votes cast by the party's voters at the presidential primary. Their rules require equal numbers of male and female delegates and allow some delegates to directly choose other delegates.

The 1949 amendment to the law has drawn such attention to the primary that today, when most people discuss our presidential primary and its procedures, they are relating only to what has occurred since that time. This is especially true for some in the media, who frequently imply we've held our first place position only from 1952, not 1920.

Reflecting on New Hampshire's history, one recognizes that it did not achieve independent statehood until 1776, meaning that it was 225 years old going into the new millennium of year 2000. The primary has played the key role in its politics for the last 80 years, which is more than one-third of the state's existence. Jere Daniell, Professor of History at Dartmouth College, apparently overlooked this rapidly developing trend, as he teaches, "New Hampshire is not attracted to the 19th century. It's part of the 18th century."

During this period, it has sponsored twenty consecutive successful quadrennial presidential primaries. There can be no question that future writers will agree about the very significant power the primary has exerted in all phases of the state's growth. Further, as this book is written, it continues to be a major influence in the recognition and credibility New Hampshire has earned on the national and international scene.

Looking toward whatever may happen to the presidential primary system in 2008, we are honored that the former Republican National Chairman Marc Racicot recognized that New Hampshire should continue to lead off the presidential primary and agrees with former President Carter in commenting, "It's an institution in this country."

Fashioning a model national political calendar for the scheduling of primary dates, Robert D. Loevy, professor of political science at Colorado College, William G. Mayer, professor of political science at Northeastern University, and Thomas Patterson, professor at the Harvard Kennedy School, take the position that New Hampshire should not be forced to relinquish its traditional position of being first. Their view is that any undue influence which the Granite State might have can best be adjusted by changing the balance of the primary calendar. Mayer further comments that New Hampshirites think of their early primary as if it were "the very Pillar of American Democracy" and he's right.

Jon Margolis, political writer for the *Chicago Tribune*, once wrote of the primary that it was innate "to have things start in New England, which is, after all, where things started. There is nothing rational about this. It is an aesthetic, even mystical notion, that democracy's most vital function should start where democracy began, where towns have town meetings, in places where the Revolution was fought. But maybe what we need is to recapture the aesthetic and mystical in our politics. What politics needs now is some poetry. The New Hampshire primary, simply because it is traditional, because it does not entirely make sense, is the best political poetry we still have." He might have added, "for those who like it unrhymed."

A British scholar, Dr. Niall Palmer, who had done an in-depth study of New Hampshire's primary history, published a scholarly textbook in 1997. During the course of his research, he got caught up in the "sheer exuberance" of the primary and concluded that New Hampshire's first-in-the-nation primary "must be preserved if the legend is to survive that all Americans, whatever their financial or political status, have a chance to be elected president of the United States." As the *Concord Monitor* commented editorially, "It's good to see someone from the outside agrees."

Thus, perhaps, New Hampshire preserves the last vestige of hope for carrying on the spirit of democracy by personalized campaigning, which has been the tradition of its electoral system. It represents democracy as our forefathers intended.

※

Chapter 3

The Three Fathers

RICHARD F. UPTON OF CONCORD, a distinguished lawyer and public servant, was designer of the Presidential Preference Ballot. When he served as Speaker of the House in 1949, he sponsored it with the introduction of House Bill 210. He was its *father*, and it became known as Upton's Law. "My objective was to make the primary more interesting and meaningful to the New Hampshire voters of each party, so there would be a greater turnout at the polls and the delegates would receive advice more truly representative of public opinion." Little could he have imagined how it would revolutionize the electoral process.

Upton was a scholar, born in New Hampshire and graduate of both Phillips Exeter Academy and Dartmouth College. His pioneer work in revising the ballot was not motivated by wanting to bring national fame to the state, rather, as he later said, "The publicity which has come to our state as first, the recognition given to New Hampshire political leaders, the opportunity for New Hampshire to have a greater influence in national affairs and the resulting economic benefits were simply byproducts."

Upton felt the nomination of presidents was too much of an insider's game. The new law introduced the concept of the candidates personally meeting the voters one-on-one and not relying solely on their followers to perform that duty for them. Former editor of the *Manchester Union Leader*, James Finnegan said, "He had the vision—he had the foresight to see what it could do." His foresight inaugurated the beginning of grassroots campaigning by presidential candidates.

The late Richard F. Upton, former speaker of the House (1949–51) addresses a joint convention of the General Court on June 13, 1996, on the occasion of a tribute to Representative Daniel J. Healy of Manchester, the longest serving member of the House in state history— 52 years. In 1949, Upton, while speaker, authored an amendment to the presidential primary law that allowed voters to vote not just for delegates but also directly for the presidential and vice presidential candidate of their choice.

New Hampshire law sets the hours when the polls must be open and closed on primary day. Yet there's a unique provision in state law which allows any town of less than one hundred voters the right to conduct and complete its election at any time during the day, as long as all voters on the checklist have actually voted either in person or by absentee. Obviously only the very smallest communities, where everyone knows everyone else, can take advantage of this provision.

The tradition of early-morning voting originated long before the presidential preference primary, at the Crawford Notch village of Hart's Location where its only five year-round families made up the state's smallest voting population. Everyone's livelihood was dependent upon the Maine Central Railroad whose trains ran through the notch, and the employees didn't want to give up a day's pay to vote. The town had no school, post office, church, town hall, police or fire station. Early-morning voting was a matter of convenience. Ballots were cast at the Willey House railroad station. Later, town meetings and elections were held in the home of the town clerk.

Once every 10 years Hart's Location was entitled to send a representative to the state legislature. Florence Morey so served in 1929, but Concord forgot about the place until 22 years later when she served again in 1951. She was also the owner of the Inn Unique, a summer facility, and sometimes invited the voters for breakfast as, "The men-folk decided to do it early (vote) and get it over with." Before Morey, "in the roaring lumber era" when registration was not required for voting, it is reported that a lumber company imported enough lumberjacks to turn a state election. Fortunately for Gregg, he knew "Flossie," and knows she'd never have allowed it.

In 1952, when the "Presidential Beauty Contest" was introduced, it was perhaps Morey's idea that the first ballot results sent around the world would emanate from the White Mountains. She was a dedicated supporter of General Eisenhower. The citizens of the community saw the opportunity of gaining national fame, so they stayed up until midnight Monday evening to complete the vote count by 12:01 am on Tuesday morning, March 11. Seven votes were cast, six for Republican Ike Eisenhower and one, by a courageous citizen, for Democrat Estes Kefauver. There was also a vice-presidential vote for Republican Harold Stassen.

The media took note, and in later primaries came in droves to "Hart's Location, First in the Nation."

The hardy Hart's citizens continued their midnight layover every four years until 1964, when they got tired of all the media attention. As Les Schoof said, "A couple of the old-timers got so tired they couldn't go to the outhouse without someone sitting next to them asking questions."

But in 1996, the tradition was revived. Thirty voters stayed awake to join Dixville, which also had 30 voters for the early hour activity. Hart's Location's checklist supervisor, Marilyn Dowler, reported, "We're just country folk. I don't care if Dixville gets their tallies 30 seconds ahead of us. This is not a race with them. This is about bringing back a tradition. If every town in America brought back tradition, then we would have a lot better country for everyone."

Dixville began as an unincorporated place. Its citizens previously had been obliged to go to a neighboring town to vote in any

---

Fun along the Campaign Trail

After the outpouring of flowers and welcoming accolades on his drive through the streets of Warsaw in 1959, President Nixon came to New Hampshire to dedicate the federally funded Hopkinton Dam, in the company of New Hampshire Congressman Norris Cotton. As they were driven in an open car, the crowds were sizable, but there was no cheering—though maybe a polite "good morning" here or there along the route. When the day was over, Cotton congratulated the president on the tremendous reception he'd received. Nixon thought the senator was joking. "Not at all," replied Cotton. "A 'good morning' in New Hampshire is the same as hurrahs and tossing flowers in Poland."

election. But in the 1960 legislative session it received special recognition to incorporate, solely for voting purposes. Unfortunately,
the authorizing enactment was not passed until after the March
8 presidential primary election. Thus, it was not until 1964 that
its residents had their first opportunity to participate in the state's
presidential primary, which they have consistently exercised since
that time.

Even today, Dixville, or Dixville Notch, as it's sometimes called,
is organized only for voting purposes under New Hampshire law.
It should, in fact, be more appropriately identified as the home of
The Balsams, one of the nation's premier resorts, where the elections are held and where most of the voters are employed. Steve
Barba, president and managing partner of The Balsams has been
a voter and selectman for elections in Dixville since 1972. He and
his staff organize the quadrennial midnight spectacular. Their
famous ballot box which is featured every four years on national
television is emblazoned "Town of Dixville." Presumably that's
because the word "unincorporated" was too long to fit on the box,
or the governor who donated it to them couldn't spell it.

For both communities, the late-night duty is also a social occasion, with refreshments provided. At the Notchland Inn, where
Hart's Location balloting has recently taken place, each voter has
had his or her own individually-identified booth. At The Balsams,
individual booths have been provided for the precise number of
people voting, but without proprietary rights. In both situations,
this convenience allows swift action. It avoids the long waiting lines
their handful of voters and the media might otherwise suffer.

Neither place, still, where the clock has struck midnight all
these years, has qualified as a bellwether, with a consistent record
of picking the eventual nominees. As the Associated Press writer
Rachel M. Collins described these episodes, "voting could be considered two parts democracy, one part sport."

Dixville's most revered citizen, and owner of The Balsams,
Neil Tillotson, died October 17, 2001 at the age of 102. Neil had
cautioned others to "beware of your 100th birthday. It starts early

Dixville Notch election moderator and owner of The Balsams Grand Resort Hotel, Neil Tillotson, at age 100. Between 1964 and 2000, he cast the first official New Hampshire vote for president—at midnight—in every presidential primary and national general election.

and goes on for about three months." He is remembered as the *godfather* of the primary. He was a remarkable man, with a Horatio Alger life experience of growing up in the north country of New Hampshire and Vermont and becoming an international industrialist with a multi-million dollar businesses making latex products.

In the 2000 primary, he set an all-time record. From 1964, as moderator of Dixville Notch, Tillotson had been the first person in the world to vote for the president of the United States in both its primary and general elections. Further, from the age of twenty-one in 1919, he had voted in all elections wherever he was transiently resident. Thus his dedicated participation in democracy dated even before New Hampshire achieved its 1920 first-in-the-nation status.

"Mr. T," as he was affectionately called, exhibited a boundless love and loyalty to the country north of New Hampshire's "notches." Logically this generated from the heritage of his great grandfather, who married a North Country Indian. The couple were the original homesteaders of Dixville Notch.

In 2001, at a ceremony sponsored by the Library and Archives of New Hampshire's Political Tradition, a mock pre-enactment of the year 2004 primary took place under the supervision of the secretary of state. Tillotson again cast his ballot as the first voter in the nation, in the Dixville box brought down from The Balsams by Steve Barba. It would have been his eleventh time to do so! Fortunately, as he remarked, no one asked for whom he would have voted.

At the same event, on behalf of the New Hampshire Legislature, Tillotson was presented a scroll signed by New Hampshire House Speaker Gene Chandler and Senate President Arthur Klemm which read in part: "Neil Tillotson has been a staunch and proud supporter of the electoral process, having campaigned as a young man for Teddy Roosevelt and the Bull Moose Party."

The *grandfather* of the primary is Harold E. Stassen of Minnesota. Stassen became the "boy wonder" of GOP politics when he was elected governor of Minnesota in 1938 and was only 31 years old. In 1948, in a winter as snowbound in New Hampshire

*Former Minnesota governor and U.S. delegate at the founding conference
of the United Nations, Harold Stassen, files his 1992 presidential
candidacy papers at the Statehouse in Concord.*

as in his home state, he joined New Hampshire's primary, before the introduction of the "Presidential Beauty Contest" four years later. Ballots were cast for eleven Republican delegates at large, some pledged and some not pledged to a certain candidate. Earl S. Hewitt, of Hanover, was the only one pledged to Stassen. Four delegates were elected. Hewitt came in eighth with 17,227 votes or .09 percent of the total votes cast, and didn't make it.

In the general election that followed, Stassen challenged Thomas E. Dewey to a debate "any place at anytime." Physically, Stassen was a big guy, full of self-confidence; he figured he would outshadow Dewey, a man of small stature on the platform. Unfortunately, Dewey consented only to confrontation on the radio, so Stassen lost the debate and Dewey won the Republican nomination; not that Stassen had any chance anyway.

The Minnesotan liked the Granite State so much, he ran six times thereafter, earning the distinction of being the national candidate whose name has been on the New Hampshire ballot the most. In 1952 he ran against Eisenhower, though he, himself, had encouraged Ike to run. "He (Eisenhower) was in Europe at the time," Stassen recalled, "so I filed for myself but ran a campaign to elect him." He received only 7 percent of the votes cast for president, but he cornered 28 percent of the "write in" votes for vice president. That year was his best effort.

His subsequent votes dwindled from .01 percent of votes cast to just 130 votes or .0008 percent. When he filed in 1992, Theo Lippman of the *Baltimore Sun* commented: "Of all the unrealistic candidacies in New Hampshire's presidential primary this year, none is more of a joke than Harold Stassen's. He is almost 85 years old. He hasn't won an elective office in 50 years."

Stassen did not run in 1996, but in 1998, after Hugh Gregg asked him if he would try again in 2000, he said, "If I am blessed with good health in the year 2000, I will add another year." He didn't file in 2000, saying, "I think I'll let the others be active this year." At 93 years of age, we forgive him for forgetting. When he passed away on March 4, 2001, he had the record of longevity on the New Hampshire ballot.

John Mongan, who was mayor of Manchester when he served as Stassen's chairman, tells of the day they were towing a platform trailer behind their car to be used as a speaker's podium, and pulled up in the center of Wolfeboro. There were only a couple of people standing around and Stassen said, "Introduce me." Mongan thought to himself, "to whom?" Nonetheless John gave the full pitch for his candidate Stassen, who was an effective speaker with a commanding presence. Soon there was a reasonable gathering. A couple of days later there appeared a newspaper editorial commending Stassen for his down-to-earth manner and for speaking to such a sparse crowd.

Stassen told Gregg he liked to run in the primary because he did not want "to leave someone that I did not favor have an unopposed primary, so at various times I would try to see to it they weren't left totally without opposition."

Albert R. Hunt, writing in the *Wall Street Journal* after Stassen's death, referred to him "as a laughing stock of the political world with his quixotic campaigns and ill-fitting toupee." While such an assessment may be true, Hunt took a more rightful measure when he admitted that Stassen "was a thoroughly decent man who cared a lot about his country." And he might have added, "he loved the New Hampshire primary."

It's a great tribute to the Granite State that, while Stassen knowingly suffered beating after beating, he kept returning for punishment. He told Gregg it was well worth it because, "I've always found and believed that the best way to focus on an issue is to state it in a primary where people get a chance to vote; that you get coverage on it, and then you get a chance for the people to express their reactions. I felt that New Hampshire was one of the most open states as far as their electorate coming out to forums and listening and questioning. I believe I at one time called it the Town Hall of America, or something like that. They had that openness and consideration by the people, on the issues of those years."

*

Chapter 4

From White Steeples to High-Tech
The New Hampshire Political Culture

E VERY PRESIDENT SINCE THE INTRODUCTION of the "presidential preference" has been on New Hampshire's first-in-the-nation primary ballot. Maybe it was a harbinger of the political significance of this small state that, as reported by Shirley Barker in *New Hampshire Profiles*, of the thirty-three men who had previously served as president before Eisenhower, fourteen had visited the state while in office and five others came before being elected, along with the state's Franklin Pierce, who was a resident. Vice President Henry Wilson, in Grant's administration, was also a native, born in Farmington.

In 1789, George Washington spent five days, from October 31st to November 4th, in Portsmouth, Exeter and the seacoast region. He met with state leaders John Sullivan and John Langdon, among others, and old friends and fellow soldiers of the Revolutionary War years. He took a boat tour of Portsmouth harbor and did some cod fishing. Following his visit, in deference to him, state leaders agreed there should be only one president and the title of New Hampshire's chief executive was changed from president to governor.

"Teddy" Roosevelt came in 1902 for a visit to the Weirs and Cornish, where he was hosted by New Hampshire novelist Winston Churchill. (Two years later he helped mediate the Peace Conference ending the Russo-Japanese War, the delegates to which stayed at New Castle's Wentworth by the Sea Grand Hotel, just recently reconstructed.)

Abraham Lincoln came to see his son, Robert, who was a student at Phillips Exeter Academy. He gave speeches at Exeter, Concord, Dover and Manchester. Before he spoke in Manchester, during a rainy evening on March 1, 1860, he was introduced to the overflowing crowd as the next president of the United States. It was the first time he had been introduced that way and he was caught by surprise.

Presidents Ulysses Grant, Grover Cleveland and Woodrow Wilson were summer vacationists. We're proud that the media so frequently notes the beauty of the Granite State as a holiday destination. It is blessed with a collection of small towns bonded by winding roads through covered bridges over trickling brooks, with white church steeples and sparkling lakes or user-friendly mountains as backdrops. Why not? In few places elsewhere can these wonderful qualities of life, plus a seacoast, be found.

Sometimes though, this flattery doesn't catch up with the social change which at the same time has furthered New Hampshire's leadership in the modern industrial age. As R.W. Apple wrote in the *New York Times,* the state is changing. "Journalists and politicians spend wintry weeks trekking from town to town, scarcely noticing that the state they have known in past campaigns—the

---

Fun along the Campaign Trail

Texas Governor George W. Bush was having a great day shaking hands with everyone in sight on the Main Street of Colebrook when a monstrous logging truck came crawling down the street. Bush quickly hopped onto the running board of the cab to greet the driver with a friendly, "Hi, I'm George Bush, running for president." Getting an empty-headed response from the operator, the governor repeated the happy message to the vacuous face at the wheel.

"Hey governor," called out one of the sidewalk observers, "try your Spanish on him; he's French Canadian from Quebec and doesn't understand English."

New Hampshire of village greens and white steeples, of grubby mill towns and taciturn Yankees—is disappearing."

No longer is our economy in the larger population centers dependent on textiles. The vast cotton mills along the Merrimack River in Manchester or the Nashua River in Nashua are now spinning out cyber-age products. Tucked away in our small towns are spin-off companies creating software and devising computer programs marketed throughout the world. We've shifted from producing blankets to becoming a major player in the high-tech industry.

From as far away as Texas, the *Dallas Morning News* noted: "Once a struggling, insular and rural state, it now draws outsiders to a booming high-tech, evolving economy . . . the state has real clout in determining who will become the next president."

In the 1800s, native "Yankees," who were mostly of English and Scotch-Irish lineage, were the governing citizens. Eighty years ago, when the presidential primary began, the French Canadians who had immigrated from Canada to work in the mills shared the political reins, and they tended to be Democrats. French was a common second language. Today all that has changed. French is no longer frequently heard in public places and voter registration is split between the two major parties, as is that of most of the other nationalities who have located here.

Though still very small minorities, Hispanics and Asians are now a new population showing up on the voting roles, particularly in southern New Hampshire. As when the Franco-Americans initially appeared here, the Hispanics still tend to use their own language, with Spanish spoken in shopping malls and on the streets.

A Latin American Center has been established in Manchester and companies such as the state's largest utility and other businesses have appointed people to serve the community's needs. As it was with the textile workers, they are more inclined to register, when they do, as Democrats rather than as Republicans.

Tied in with this rapid increase of overall population is the statistical fact that the elections of the year 2000 disclosed that more

Vice President Al Gore and wife Tipper don't let New Hampshire's typical wintry weather slow them down on their way to greet voters at a Dunkin' Donuts in Manchester's Granite Square.

citizens had registered without a party affiliation than as either Democrats or Republicans. This was the first time in the state's presidential primary history that party dominance has not been held by the Republican Party. Undoubtedly this bulging trend will unpredictably and tangibly influence the alignment of candidates and their issues in 2004 and 2008.

Although few African-Americans are residents, Jesse Jackson has been a frequent campaigner. He has never done well, finishing fourth in both the 1984 and 1988 primaries. He returned in 1999 to consider being a candidate again in 2000. Even though he didn't file a third time, perhaps the state should nonetheless reward or denounce him for continuing to press the most passionate issue of his previous campaigns. It was Jesse's view that, "New Hampshire likes to be seen. It likes to have a first primary. Why, then would it want the dubious distinction of being the only state that doesn't have a Martin Luther King day?"

Shortly thereafter our legislature passed one, thereby doing away with another of our wondrous claims to fame. So who can honestly say presidential candidates don't affect our way of life? We hope no one threatens our blessing of being the only one of two states without either an income or sales tax or the unique right to ride a motorcycle without a helmet even though we may register more motorcycles per capita than any other state.

Integral to this cultural change and new ethnic diversity is the inclusion of ambitious entrepreneurs. Many are highly skilled engineers from other countries. In resettling here they are joined by talented retired individuals from a wide variety of professions who also seek the New Hampshire advantage. They bring a fresh focus to our unique government and the presidential primary, as their concern is based on life experiences elsewhere.

The newcomers are forever making adjustments to live here. In relation to politics, some fail to understand why we esteem our large legislature, treasure our first-in-the-nation presidential primary or why undeclared voters are allowed to become party members on primary day.

Another development for 2004 attention is the increased potential for women entering the presidential primary race. Elizabeth Dole's candidacy gave it impetus when she said, "The time is ripe for a woman president. There are many women who are prepared." Quite aside from the prominent women serving on the national scene, New Hampshire would be the perfect place for a lady to break the glass ceiling. In 1999, the state had a woman governor, a woman president of the state Senate and a woman speaker of the House.

It's also unfortunate there's a misconception that the first-in-the-nation primary is a selfish money maker. Nothing could be further off the mark. A detailed study was commissioned by the Library and Archives of New Hampshire's Political Tradition of the primary's impact on the state's economy. It was conducted by the state's leading economists and business association. They concluded that in the 2000 cycle the primary contributed "about six-tenths of 1 percent of the state's $42 billion gross state product."

The annual motorcycle week at Laconia, a NASCAR auto race weekend in Loudon with its normal attendance of over 100,000 fans, or a couple of good snow days at our ski resorts brings the state as much or more revenue.

Of greater consequence was the flip side of the same report, which disclosed that media coverage exposed a potential audience of 220 million people to the primary. Visiting reporters wrote that we were informed, supported a serious voting electorate, and had earned our justifiable reputation.

"The New Hampshire primary today is the country's most vivid example of democracy, with the voters fully participating. At least in one small northeastern state, American voters are actually engaged and excited" was the 2000 view of the *San Antonio Express-News*.

Some make the mistake of equating the Iowa caucus to the New Hampshire primary. Although the voters of both states are generally conservative, otherwise they are politically dissimilar. Not only is the Iowa event sponsored by the political parties, as opposed to government sponsorship in New Hampshire, but the Granite State percentage turnout of total registered voters far exceeds that of the Hawkeye State. This is an inherent difference between a caucus and a primary.

Iowa is primarily concerned with agricultural issues, whereas here the major emphasis is on taxes and education. Senator Bill Bradley found out that: "New Hampshire is a bastion of independent thinking. Nobody tells them what to do. They make up their own minds."

Then there's always the proverbial question: Does New Hampshire have a disproportionate influence over the choice of the president? In 2000, Harvard's John F. Kennedy School of Government conducted a poll on this question, the Vanishing Voter Project, under the stewardship of Marvin Kalb. It concluded that Americans have an inflated view of the importance of New Hampshire's role. Residents of larger states were almost twice as likely as small states to think New Hampshire has too much influence. Co-director of the project, Thomas Patterson, concluded

Cartoon published in the Omaha World-Herald, *January, 1992 (Courtesy of political cartoonist Jeff Koterba)*

that our primary "will always generate some resentment or controversy, at least as long as it remains first."

At least it's encouraging to note that Harvard professor Patterson also wrote that New Hampshire had a better claim to being first than the Iowa caucus, because "the turnout rate in New Hampshire is twice that of nearly every other state and its residents take their role seriously in other ways. . . . One study found they were 100 percent more likely to have particular knowledge of primary election candidates and issues than other Americans." Fortunately, the author understood and appreciated the flexibility of our election-day ballot choices for new voters.

It's a good thing that Governor Nelson Rockefeller, a candidate in the 1964 primary, and a Dartmouth alumnus, was not around in 1999 to read a study presented by Dean Spiliotes, a faculty member connected to the Rockefeller Center at Dartmouth College. It gave "scholarly attention," using "unique survey data," from the 1996 primary to conclude that the national media has undue influence over New Hampshire voters and that "retail politics is consumer driven—not supplier driven—and, as good consumers, voters are seeking out contact with candidates they already know a lot about and for whom they tend to have high favorability."

Jeff Woodburn, former Democratic state chairman, was critical of the Dartmouth report, alleging that the authors had not been at factory gates watching workers being greeted by the candidates. He believes that such one-on-one context tells more about the candidates than about the voters, as it brings "big shot politicians" down to earth and exposes their real character. Jeff believes, "Grassroots or retail politics is not a tool, like television commercials, direct mail or polling. It is a process that gives us a peak at the personality of our potential leaders."

Having served as Governor Rockefeller's chairman and having accompanied him on each of his frequent visits to the state in his campaign, Gregg attests that the vast majority of the many who came to greet the New Yorker were motivated more by curiosity than by any preconceived thought of voting for him. Inasmuch as he drew larger crowds than his opponents, the additional fact that he finished third after Henry Cabot Lodge, a write-in, and Senator Barry Goldwater, would tend to discredit the professors' theory that celebrities have higher "favorability."

The authors, who hold the utmost respect for Dartmouth, are somewhat reluctant to refresh recollections about its teachings in earlier days. Although the college was only established in 1769, in 1778 its then negligible faculty triggered the state's Constitutional Convention. The Hanover teachers were angry that the Exeter-based wartime Legislature in 1776 had passed a temporary state constitution without getting statewide voter sanction, and also thought the seat of government should be moved from the sea-coast to a more convenient venue for better service to the central and Connecticut River valley populations.

Historian G. Parker Lyon records that when the 1778 Constitutional Convention was held "it was boycotted by Hanover, Lebanon, Haverhill and all the other far-inland towns it was designed to placate." The Dartmouth faculty was recognized for its lack of political sophistication by the following language which appeared in the constitutional document: "No person holding the office of professor, or instructor of any college, shall at the same time have a seat in the Senate, or House of Representatives, or council." Fortunately for the "Big Green," this restriction was removed prior to the constitution enacted in 1783.

Could it be, though, that Dartmouth professors nonetheless sometimes regress to their ancestral heritage when attempting to understand and thus teach the state's unique political philosophy?

Fun along the Campaign Trail

In New Hampshire, Governor Reagan preached his Eleventh Commandment, " Thou shall not speak ill of a fellow Republican." Candidate Bush subsequently proposed a Twelfth Commandment, "Don't make any foolish promises."

In our view many of the candidates who participate in the primary are celebrities, who get the most personal attention from the voters and yet don't win. To put it in another way, our citizens are curious enough to check out everyone on the ballot and do not restrict their analysis to someone whom they thought they might favor before the campaign began.

Perhaps the popular writer E.B. White best describes how many of New Hampshire citizens make their choices on election day. He was told that the reference library of the House of Commons stated that qualifications for voting in England say, "any adult twenty-one years of age or over may register and vote except peers and lunatics. The latter, if they have a moment of lucidity, may register and vote."

White's comment, "When we step up to the polls next November we will feel like one of those British voters—daft as a coot, but praying, as we draw the curtain behind us, for a moment of lucidity."

The International Institute for Democracy and Electoral Assistance study disclosed that the United State's average turnout for general elections is 45 percent. When there is a spirited race in its presidential primary, Granite Staters jump in. Our tradition of political vitality goes way back to 1888 when 91 percent of the state's 99,432 registered voters cast their votes for governor.

New Hampshire is a state where citizens have always demonstrated their interest in picking presidential primary candidates. In 2000, for example, 86 percent of its registered Republicans voted in the McCain/Bush race and 75 percent of registered Democrats, twice the national average, did the same thing in the Gore/Bradley contest. In 1992, when Senator Paul Tsongas ran against Bill Clinton, 89 percent of the registered Democrats showed up at the polls.

Our election counts have consistently been smooth-running and never with controversy in presidential primaries. Nor have there been serious charges of fraud. The office of the secretary of state produces all the ballots used throughout the state, supervises voting procedures and certifies the results. It's backed up by a Ballot Law Commission authorized to hear and decide on any appeals relating to election procedures from rulings of the secretary.

Today New Hampshire communities can select any one of three approved methods of balloting, two by machine and one by hand, with each community responsible for its own checklists. Fortunately, in 1986 the Ballot Law Commission outlawed the controversial butterfly ballot where voters punch out holes to select their candidates. This method created the hanging chads and dimples which led to the Florida debacle in the 2000 presidential general election.

Former Florida Secretary of State Katherine Harris has suggested a plan whereby the voters of her state, by use of optical scanners, would cast their ballots from any precinct in the state based on a centralized statewide data bank which would be currently updated with registration information. This would be a big

This cartoon by New Hampshire cartoonist Mike Marland appeared in 1988 in the Concord Monitor. *He also contributed the cartoon on the cover of this book.*

step forward after their "chad" failures of 2000. Oklahoma has a somewhat similar system. New Hampshire does not yet have a statewide data bank in the secretary of state's office. Checklists are made and retained in the local precincts.

All three New Hampshire voting procedures require the voter to mark an individual ballot which is then counted by hand or by machine. The time-tested paper ballot which is executed in a polling booth and then placed directly into the old fashioned wooden ballot box continues to be used in smaller communities. These votes are then hand-counted after the polls close.

Larger precincts prefer to have the executed ballots passed through an electronic optical scanner which counts either a filled-in circle or extended arrow on the ballot. The state approves use of two different types of such scanners. The electronic machines offer the advantage of an instant vote tally when the polls close.

Political scientist Walter Dean Burham, has said United States election procedures are "the sloppiest in the industrial world." New Hampshire state law requires cities and towns to update their checklists by a statewide purge every ten years, thereby somewhat obviating the chances of registration fraud which has so bedeviled elections in many American polling places.

Our younger generations appear to be very cynical of the present system. A National Association of Secretaries of States' New Millennium Project report states it well: "Young people today lack interest, trust and knowledge about American politics, politicians and the public life generally. In these and other respects, the future of American democracy seems gloomy, indeed."

Looking ahead to what may happen by 2008, it seems to us that these cyber-age adults would be enthused if voting were made more accessible to them. There are several such options currently under consideration in New Hampshire by interested protagonists. Perhaps the least discussed possibility is for mail-in ballots. New Hampshire's only experience with this method is a very restricted right to use an absentee ballot. To use one, a potential voter must be physically unable to go to the polls or be "out of town" on election day.

A number of states permit casting of absentee ballots for any reason. Oregon has done well with its experiment of permitting any voter to use one. After years of holding local and statewide elections by mail, in 2000 it conducted its first fully postal general election. Ballots were mailed out statewide two weeks before election day. Both major parties pushed supporters to return them before election day. Volunteers even offered to pick them up. We don't believe this idea would ever catch fire with Granite State lawmakers who would question the security of the system.

Nor do we believe that the establishment of early voting days, as some states have done, would have much appeal in a state which has traditionally established its polling places for a single-day spectacular. It's doubtful that it would be willing to extend for several days of repeat performances. One day in an election cycle is enough for most ward workers, not counting the additional expense.

Besides, with the state's same-day registration opportunity it has already gone well down this road of making the polls more accessible. Weekend voting, another alternative practiced elsewhere, wouldn't work either unless the candidates could bring greater revenue to the state than the skiers who stay at the state's resorts over weekends during the primary period.

With the new millennium, the presidential primary of 2000 exploded politics big time on the Internet. Not surprisingly this applied particularly in New Hampshire, which has the nation's third highest employment on a per capita basis in the high-tech industry and where schools are being wired faster than in most other states.

The New Hampshire High Technology Council reported that slightly more than half of the Granite State's population of 1.2 million people were online. The overwhelming percentage of the computer wizards who design and operate these electronic systems are under the age of 45.

During recent campaigns, the Internet has served several purposes. Every major candidate and even a number of the fringe candidates had an established website. These sites were an innovative means of spreading the word on issues, itineraries, where to get bumper stickers, and provide biographies and information on how to volunteer.

Wall Street Journal staff reporters, Glenn R. Simpson and Bryan Gruley, wrote a story about a college student, Joe Burns, who from his fraternity house sent e-mails to voters he did not know urging their support for Steve Forbes. As this young man said, "I think the Internet is the future of political campaigns." The Internet is a logical vehicle for attracting new voters, particularly younger ones.

More important, for some candidates, the Internet is a quick way to raise money. As reported by Dan Touhy, at that time of the *Foster's Democrat*, after Senator John McCain won the New Hampshire primary, in addition to picking up a substantial number of volunteers, he took in over one million dollars in online contributions within forty-eight hours. Sheila Krumholz, a research director of the Center for Responsive Politics said, "The rate at which it (money) pours in is phenomenal. It's such a cheap way to raise money." In 2003, former Governor Dean brought this medium to a new high level as a fundraising mechanism, even in the primary.

Lots of arguments are advanced for the concept of direct Internet voting, such as no hassle in losing time at work, avoid-

> *Fun along the Campaign Trail*
>
> **At the University of New Hampshire on the day of the November 2002 mid-term elections, all students received an e-mail entitled "Do it in the voting booth." The e-mail pictured a voting booth with two sets of legs appearing below the curtain. The voting booth was rocking from the movement of the voters inside. This was intended to gain the students attention and get them to vote. It was the main topic of conversation on campus that day.**

ing long lines at polling places and long hours for ward workers, comfort of clicking a button from an easy chair in the living room, elimination of exit polls, saving government money, weather not being a factor, everyone everywhere would vote in the same time frame, absentee ballots are reduced or eliminated, voting made easier in remote areas, and instantaneous results when the day is over.

The candidates are now well aware of these opportunities. That's why their website addresses are crafted into their literature and constantly publicized on the stump. Up to this point all is well and the Internet is a great new tool for widening interest and participation in primaries.

But is the Internet just the beginning of a process which will obviate the time-tested paper ballot? Will Granite Staters be voting by computers from their homes, places of employment or publicly placed ATM-like kiosks rather than casting their ballots at the traditional polling place? Are people going to vote for the best website? Could a hacker change election results?

Louisiana Republicans flirted with the idea of voting on the Internet. In Alaska, Republicans took a straw poll on the web from three distant districts which normally had low turnout where snow and darkness limited travel largely to dog sleds. Arizona Democrats in 2000 actually experimented with it. As described by Thomas E. Weber in the *Wall Street Journal*, personal identity numbers were mailed to more than 800,000 Arizona party members, voters could surf a special web address, identify their number and then be queried for further ID information before clicking their vote from a candidates' list posted on their screen.

The Arizona Democratic Party claimed the test caused a 600 percent increase in voter turnout. But questions of security, privacy and possible fraud triggered a lawsuit against Arizona, alleging violation of the Voting Rights Act of 1965. However, in the opinion of John Chambers, the CEO of Cisco Systems, whether we like it or not, it's coming anyway. "The Internet will do to democracy what it did to business." Chambers believes the country should be planning for it.

Rebecca Mercuri, computer science teacher at Bryn Mawr College, points out a major deficiency in planning for an exclusive computer solution. She believes "Electronic voting systems are fine as long as they produce a paper record that can serve as the true ballot. Voters might enter their choices on a computer, which could then print out a slip of paper. The voter would then inspect the paper record to make sure it was accurate and put it into the counting box. The paper would remain as a permanent record, always available for recounts."

New Hampshire has already taken action with the appointment of a legislative committee to study online and other forms of electronic voting. Vice president for research at the Internet Policy Institute, Gerard Glaser, supports the state's study, commenting, "Internet voting is certainly an attractive thing to consider and has a lot of promise. It's reasonable to pursue what the voting options are, for New Hampshire or any state."

No question that Internet voting depersonalizes the electoral process. Rick Valelly, a Swarthmore College professor, says its somewhat like Internet shopping; "you feel more like a consumer

---

Fun along the Campaign Trail

When Donald Trump was considering joining the fray in 2000, Clare Kittredge of the *Boston Globe* reported that many of his British supporters called the White House, "The Oral Office," and the *Daily Telegraph* asked, "Will he have his name erected above the White House as he does on all his buildings?"

After Warren Beatty had also expressed interest in being president, the *Globe* reporter quoted the *South China Morning Post* as commenting he, "seems to be toying with the idea of running, the way he once toyed with many of Hollywood's most famous women."

than a citizen." It would not be unrealistic for the retail market-place to serve both purposes.

The *Conway Carroll County Independent* sounded its warning with an editorial: "The Granite State primary may also be the last time for the average voter to actually get a feel for a candidate as a human being as opposed to a talking head on the tube." Also, via the Internet there's always the possibility of a virus invalidating an entire national election."

In our opinion, the dot-com revolution is a perilous potential threat to the wellbeing of our system of electing government officials. We have always taken pride in our right to vote. Using an hour or so on election day to go to the polls has always been a voluntary civic duty eagerly performed. It offered citizens the opportunity to guide local, state and federal governments without being directly involved in them. By insuring that our names were on the checklist and by our annual and/or biennial casting of a ballot we have proved our concern for the society in which we live.

The New Hampshire Legislature, in 1994, enacted election-day registration. It was the only option to avoid complying with the federal motor voter law passed by the United States Congress. Some think voting "made easy" has already gone too far. Democracy wasn't designed to be convenient or easy. It takes an effort to be informed on the issues and the candidates. And it should generate a sense of pride to participate by showing up at the polling place when due.

There are those who say that whether a person marks his ballot via a television set or walks to a polling place to do the same thing, it won't cause any change in New Hampshire's grassroots approach to campaigning. In fact, they believe the handiness of voting at home or elsewhere will increase voter participation. Quite true, perhaps more people would vote. Question is: Would they vote as intelligently?'"

It is personal exposure to the contestants which separates the winners from the losers. Tami Buhr, a Ph.D candidate at Harvard, points out that candidates constantly visit and revisit New Hampshire, "thus giving residents more opportunity than residents of other states to meet them. It benefits from a 'gold standard' of campaign information. Campaign workers go door to door or stand on street corners and hand out fliers. Voter solicitations are made by regular mail, e-mail, telephone, fax and many candidates send out videos or even Christmas cards."

According to Professor Emmett H. Buell, Jr. of Denison University, as the candidates were preparing for the 1996 primary, "Alexander made twenty different visits to New Hampshire. Dole logged fifteen visits, and Buchanan made eleven." He concludes that maybe so much tourism doesn't always win, but it does prove that "retail politics is no myth in New Hampshire."

What incentive would remain for the candidates themselves to take the time to shake hands with voters, as they do now, on their one-on-one visits to the state if their promos were limited to the electronic media, especially TV? Imaginative production could create such images on the screen without the candidate ever having had to actually meet voters face-to-face. The voters would never have had the chance of really getting to know the true persona of the person for whom they are voting.

If such technology supplants traditional campaigning, so goes another vestige of what our nation's forefathers designed as the democratic elective process.

Whatever has happened to the responsibility we used to feel for making at least a modicum of effort to support the freedoms bequeathed to us? Even if, in the next several years, the downside of privacy, security and fraud get worked out for safe Internet voting, we hope New Hampshire won't ever adopt it!

※

Chapter 5

The Primary Isn't For Sale

THE INFLUENCE OF MONEY ON THE presidential primary has accelerated substantially since 1952. Gregg well remembers that the governor's office in those days relied on the manual typewriter and mimeograph machine for correspondence. General mailings were first prepared on nonelectric typewriters, then sent to the printer for typesetting and reproduction. There were no computers, laser printers, or copy or fax machines. Radio was the staple for news. There were no satellite trucks, as television was struggling through its infancy. In fact, if the governor wanted to send a quick message to UPI in Boston he used a couple of Democrats who kept a fire burning on the front lawn of the Statehouse, always available for smoke signals.

It didn't cost much to run for office in those days. Radio and the local newspapers were the bulwarks of political advertising. Not just the few dailies, but every weekly in the state got a piece of the action. Today even the dailies are lucky to get an occasional full page. Candidates' staffs only read the weeklies for learning where letters of congratulation or sympathy should be addressed. Today a few minutes of television advertising, with its attendant price for production, costs as much as an entire press budget fifty years ago. Cell phones had not been invented.

If a person is considering a run in the 2004 primary, it's also worth noting that long before filing here he has important decisions to make. He perhaps should visit the state, maybe several times, during one or more of our local campaigns for state office.

The purpose will be to identify those contestants who would make the best supporters for his own eventual national campaign, and to seek their help. This process will probably result in preliminary financial investment even before he definitely makes up his mind to run. It will be an add-on to the burden of those traditional expenses which will be incurred later, after becoming a candidate.

In recent years, to soften up the terrain even before getting into the New Hampshire presidential race, many potential hopefuls send cash from their PACs or personal funds to the New Hampshire branch of their party, or directly to aid New Hampshire aspirants to local contests. Although they are not qualified to vote here, there has been a recent trend for many of these out-of-staters to publicly endorse politicians running in our state primaries, both before and after presidential elections. The anticipated *quid pro quo* is return of support to the donor in his quest for presidential office.

As recorded by the *Manchester Union Leader*, in 1998 Quayle's PAC, Campaign America, gave nearly $60,000 to the state's GOP and Republican senatorial candidates; Bauer's PAC, Campaign for Working Families, spent more than $45,000 for similar purposes, as did Kasich's PAC, Pioneer, to the tune of $25,000. Alexander, Ashcroft and Forbes all took similar action.

Tom Colantuono, a candidate for our Executive Council, got dollars from Quayle, Forbes, Ashcroft, Bauer, Alexander and Smith. Fortunately, only Forbes and Bauer remained in the Republican presidential race, so Tom only had to choose between two candidates on presidential primary day. But that outpouring of confidence paid off big for him. He not only got elected but now has moved up and serves as an appointed federal district attorney.

On the Democratic side, the National Committee put up $100,000 to assist in the election of Democratic state senators. It was well spent, as the GOP lost its control of the body, after the 1998 election. Steve Jarding, a Democratic fundraiser said, "One of the reasons you give more to New Hampshire than other places is that people in New Hampshire ask." Gore, Bradley, Kerrey, Kerry, Wellstone and Gephardt also assisted in raising money for their Granite State compatriots.

But these advance payments are only the warmup for the big dollars needed to underwrite what's needed later. Lamar Alexander, after gaining a strong third-place finish in 1996, joined the race a second time in 1999 but pulled out before the filing period for 2000. He withdrew partly because of the strain of spending time raising money which otherwise could have been more profitably used soliciting votes. Elizabeth Dole did the same thing.

Lamar told the *Wall Street Journal* that because of the 1974 federal election reforms, such as the $1,000 limit on an individual's contribution, "The election is longer, there are fewer choices, and money is more important, not less." As the paper pointed out, "It puts a premium on money-grubbing. All kinds of good potential presidents are out of the running simply because they won't, or can't, spend eight hours a day dialing for dollars."

Alexander believes that as long as there's a limit on the amount which an individual contributor can give to a candidate, then the system is forever going to give an unfair advantage to the contestant who can furnish his own money. He asserts that "this trend has encouraged the rise of celebrity candidates, who never need host a fundraiser. Because the Supreme Court has rightly ruled

Fun along the Campaign Trail

In every presidential primary, the newspapers run a plethora of "issue advocacy" advertisements for pet causes by dedicated sponsors for all kinds of special issues. Some deliver unusual messages, such as the ad sponsored by the Pro Tem Committee for Decency in Government which accused Bush, Gore, Bradley and McCain of policies encouraging homosexual conduct, thereby increasing disease, early deaths and health care problems.

that using your own money to advance your views is constitution-
ally protected speech, nothing stops them from spending all they
want."

At the same time the former senator took cognizance of the
fact that special interests like teachers' unions, abortion-rights
groups and industry associations have the same opportunity to
underwrite their own self-seeking causes.

Alexander also thinks that the reason Bill Bennett, Jack Kemp,
Dick Cheney, Governors Campbell and Thompson, and maybe
even Colin Powell didn't run in 1996 was, "largely because they
could not or would not devote the time to raise the money."
Meanwhile Alexander attended fundraisers at a rate of nearly
one every working day for a year. If one accepts his conclusion,
the New Hampshire primary would be realistically restricted to
only the wealthy and/or those fringe candidates who make little
or no effort to raise money.

It is required by the system that if a potential presidential
primary candidate wishes to participate in public funding by
receiving matching funds from the federal government, he must
first raise in excess of $5,000 in each of 20 states. Although an
individual donor can contribute up to $1,000 to a candidate, only
a maximum of $250 per donor can be applied toward the total
threshold of $5,000. In return, the government will match up to
$250 of each donor's $250 contribution.

In addition, the candidate must agree to cap his campaign
spending to a figure arrived at by the Federal Elections Commission (FEC) which sets a campaign expenditure limitation per
state for each presidential primary. It is determined by using a
formula based on the voting-age population of each state plus a
cost-of-living adjustment. In 2000, New Hampshire's limit was
$675,600. For 2004, this limitation will increase to approximately
$729,600.

By contrast, Massachusetts was allowed $2,544,039. Ex-
empted from these limitations are $50,000 of the candidate's
personal funds and certain fund-raising, legal and accounting ex-

penses. Customarily candidates register with the FEC to receive the matching funds benefit. In 2000, Forbes and Bush didn't, thus allowing them to spend as much money as they could solicit.

Candidates in the New Hampshire contest who sign up for matching funds normally get around the strict limitations of the law by passing off much of their expense for such things as TV, radio and print advertising to media markets in adjoining states which also serve New Hampshire. The same procedures are applied to telephone polling, along with purchases of equipment or other out-of-state services, as long as they don't exceed the limitations in those other states for whatever campaigning may be planned there. Also, candidates generally raise more money than they receive with matching funds from many nonmatchable contributions, such as from political committees.

Susan B. Glasser, *Washington Post* staff writer, came up with a scenario whereby a candidate could spend $6 million and legally still come within the New Hampshire FEC limit of $675,600. Overall, her objective would be accomplished by flooding the state with direct mail, providing it reached voters 28 days before the primary, and advertising heavily over Boston television. The details take into account allowable deductions and hiring of personnel exclusively to work in New Hampshire.

The *Wall Street Journal* had predicted in 1998 that "unless a candidate can bankroll at least $20 million before New Hampshire, he's got little chance of competing afterward." The primary of 2000 tested that theory when George Bush entered the contest with so much dough already in his money bags that he didn't need to take federal matching funds. He probably wanted to be competitive with Steve Forbes, who was a threat with his own personal fortune and certainly didn't require federal financial assistance.

Not so with Senator McCain in 2000. He proved that money is not necessarily a requirement. He skipped Iowa, thereby conserving his funds and energy for the first primary race in New Hampshire, where the voters do not signify their preferences in private party caucuses, but rather in public polling places administered by the state. The senator demonstrated that with the right kind of grassroots campaign there is life after New Hampshire. Although the Iowa caucus has not been a bellwether, any candidate skipping it does so at his peril.

In fact, it was McCain's victorious effort in the state that filled his treasury and allowed him to move forward to the big states thereafter. Had Bush given more attention to the sometimes so-called idiosyncrasies of the New Hampshire voter and met them one-on-one, then perhaps Bush would have been as good as the elected president of the United States when he departed the state. But he didn't. Even Bush's overflowing cash did not impede McCain.

The lesson learned is that it's a fair conclusion money in the pocket before arriving in the Granite State is an obvious advantage—but don't count on it to carry the day. Steve Forbes learned that the hard way in 1996. Dollars by themselves don't win the votes of New Hampshire citizens. In fact, the candidate doesn't need $20 million to get in the game. If he plays his cards well, the $20 million jackpot will accrue because he did. Thereafter it's up to him to spend it wisely elsewhere if he expects to be president.

Senator Hart went through this exercise in 1984 when, with limited funds in New Hampshire, he topped Vice President Mondale's extensive assets. After Hart's upset victory the money rolled in and he stayed all the way to California in June. However, his untimely philandering after he left the state fogged his otherwise clean shot at the Oval Office.

Bradley Smith, a member of the Federal Elections Commission, in his book, *Unfree Speech,* curiously, for a member of the commission which oversees the spending of candidates in presidential elections, agrees with Alexander. Smith's view, as summarized by Gerald F. Seib in the *Wall Street Journal,* is that, "money is good for politics, and more money would be better; restricting campaign contributions undermines the right to free speech; and there's no evidence that campaign money corrupts the legislative system."

If this view prevails, maybe we'll hear more from those multi-millionaires who have been rumored to have considered political campaigns, such as Donald Trump and Warren Beatty.

As an aside, the outpouring of money to finance politics has antagonized some New Hampshire citizens to the point of alliances being formed to combat the trend. David Diamond of Dover established The Real Democracy Project to address the question of financial reform for the entire political process. While supporting democracy as it is commonly understood, the Project's oxymoronic solution to the problem called for boycotting of the state's 2000 presidential primary.

By encouraging people not to vote, this group's objective is to bring about "real democracy," which they believe is now under the control of wealthy individuals and corporations, thus ignoring the legitimate expression of the peoples' will. Fortunately, their program of destroying the ballot box, rather than using it for the purpose for which it is provided, did not prevail. New Hampshire had a record-high turnout for the 2000 presidential election.

The funding requirements for a successful campaign vary widely from primary to primary, depending on the competition and when it occurred. Before the Federal Elections Commission was established, there was little public awareness or public record of how much money was spent. Today, with fundraisers a critical part of any candidate's agenda, there's always the question of what part dollars play in a person's motivation to enter the presidential race or, perhaps more importantly, his or her exiting it.

Lack of sufficient funds is obviously a good reason for a candidate to get out of a race where the results look bleak anyway, with or without the cash to go forward. It can be a convenient face-saving device. The 2000 New Hampshire primary offered a perfect opportunity to test this question, as there were so many candidates who initially entered the race. Some stayed it through, others didn't, as will be discussed in chapter 8, 9 and 10.

❊

Chapter 6

On the Fringes

I F ANYONE WANTS TO BE PRESIDENT, he or she has to start somewhere. The New Hampshire presidential primary is the logical entry point. As David Nyhan explained it in the *Boston Globe*, "The road to the White House has to go through New Hampshire, the Panama Canal of the process."

Article 11, Section 1 of the Constitution of the United States provides: "No Person except a natural born Citizen, or a Citizen of the United States, at the time of the Adoption of this Constitution, shall be eligible to the Office of President; neither shall any person be eligible to that Office who shall not have attained the Age of thirty five Years and been fourteen Years a Resident within the United States."

In addition to meeting the foregoing Constitutional requirement, every presidential candidate must first register his or her candidacy with the New Hampshire secretary of state between the first Monday and the third Friday in November of the year preceding the presidential election. It may be done in person or by mail, and the filing form must be accompanied by a $1,000 cash or check filing fee. There is also a provision in the law for an indigent person to file without paying the filing fee; however no one has ever made it to the ballot by use of this provision.

It should be noted that although most lesser-known, darkhorse or fringe candidates are totally obscure self-starters, most of them are sincere and have serious concerns or missions to foster. They are a welcome part of the political landscape. The majority know they're probably not going to be elected, yet each allows for the chance of a miracle to put them in the White House. They are treated with full courtesy by the secretary of state because their hearts are in the right place. Every American child is taught that he or she can grow up to be president. The New Hampshire primary honors that tradition. We listen to people you've never heard of.

In 1992, there were 64 candidates listed on the ballot. Added to the "write-ins" not listed on the ballot, there was a record number of so-called fringe or lesser-knowns who paid the $1,000 to participate. In that group were ten authors, three lawyers, two businessmen, two software programmers, two mayors, two registered nurses, a minister, a doctor, a certified public accountant, an aircraft mechanic, an anti-AIDS activist, a former FBI agent, a professional comedian, a building contractor, a public relations counselor, a former nun, an investment consultant, a real estate broker, a process server and a sign language interpreter.

Who actually qualifies as a lesser-known or fringe candidate? In most cases, it's easy. It is the one-of-a-kind who is totally unknown and would be totally unqualified to serve as president. Usually he or she is an unconventional person who may or may not recognize their unorthodoxy. If they recognize it, then chances are they are in the game for the publicity or self aggrandizement. If they don't recognize it, they are probably serious contenders who want to emphasize a particular message. Most of them in this class seem off-the-wall to the electorate, yet are seriously dedicated to their cause, however fanciful it may be.

In the borderline cases it becomes more difficult to quantify. Clearly the media plays the key role in making that determination. Its decision is primarily based on four factors. First: has the candidate held a major elective office such as governor or congressman? He could also be a nationally recognized celebrity. Second: does he have the facility to raise the necessary campaign funds? Third: do the party professionals consider him to be a feasible choice? Fourth: is there a consensus among media confreres that he has at least an outside chance of winning?

Somehow it doesn't seem right that the media should hold so much power over which candidates are going to receive maximum coverage, yet as a practical matter there probably is no other way of assessing what is both fair and practical. The national media can only afford the staff and crews to trace the activities of a minimum number of the candidates in the race, thus no matter what selection procedure is used it'll soon break down to a national media choice. The ones they don't pick will probably be branded as lesser-known, dark-horse or fringe.

This "following of the pack" does not necessarily apply to the local media, at least not in New Hampshire. Because we have the singular opportunity to see all the candidates up close, our newspaper interviews may discover a candidate rated as fringe who deserves further analysis. Though properly such a person may not be judged as a significant candidate, yet he rises above the insignificant rating conferred in the national press. In addition to having presidential qualifications, such a candidate may expound views which are innovative and have considerable public appeal. The voters want to know more about him and regret his not having the right to participate in debates with the "so-called" majors.

The case of Larry Agran is an example where perhaps the system of media judgment could have been better. He was a longshot Democratic candidate who ran in 1992. Larry had served as mayor of Irvine, California. The national media recognized the major candidates that were his opposition: senators George McGovern of South Dakota, Tom Harkin of Iowa, Paul Tsongas of Massachusetts and Bob Kerrey of Nebraska, along with governors Bill Clinton of Arkansas, Douglas Wilder of Virginia and Jerry Brown of California. Agran did not receive equal treatment with any of them.

Yet Agran was a Harvard Law School graduate, an author, had a twelve-year record as an elected public official, qualified for federal matching funds, sponsored reasonable progressive position papers, had the staff to get his name on a substantial number of primary and caucus ballots, had three delegates elected to the Democratic National Convention, visited schools, held rallies, participated in some of the debates with good audience response, and made the *Larry King Show* and *MacNeil-Lehrer News Hour.*

Agran's lack of recognition was justified by journalist Roger Mudd, "It does stretch credulity to think that a Jewish ex-mayor of a small suburban California town can make it."

Mudd was probably correct in his assessment; still, because the mayor had not held a major office and was otherwise unknown he was excluded from most of the debates. His campaign activities were largely ignored in the national press though frequently well and favorably reported at the local level.

Foster's Daily Democrat, for example, while admitting Agran had little chance of being president editorialized "but then Jerry Brown and Paul Tsongas do not have much better chances." The newspaper did not consider him a fringe candidate, rather perceived him as "a serious candidate, addressing a number of important issues."

Professor Joshua Meyrowitz of the University of New Hampshire wrote an excellent detailed treatise detailing Agran's difficulties in attracting national coverage of his campaign as opposed to the picture generally presented by the New Hampshire media. He said Agran had "an anomalous status which made him less than a 'major' candidate yet more than a 'minor' candidate."

The professor also noted that national journalists appear "to hide the arbitrariness of news judgments (of whom to cover) and the impact of such judgments on the outcome of campaigns."

Alvin Sanoff, a senior editor of *U.S. News & World Report,* probably was closer to the truth in writing, "it's always safer to stay with the pack and be wrong than to risk going out on a limb and covering someone who then turns out to be not that important."

The "Fringe Candidates Debate" and Other Fringes Who Filed in 2000

While debates have traditionally been standard fare for the major candidates in presidential primary campaigns, it wasn't until the 2000 primary that there had been any formalizing of debates for the fringe or lesser-knowns who also had actually filed in the contest. In that year the New Hampshire Political Library organized what it planned as the beginning of a quadrennial event of offering public exposure for such participants to compare their qualifications and programs against each other, with widespread media coverage.

Five days prior to primary day a forum for fringe candidates was arranged, to which all of them were invited. Unfortunately, the program was so late in being organized it received little public notice or audience. Although all who had filed were invited, only eight of the potential 22 who had filed for president and one of two who had filed for vice president were able to make it.

The format was similar to the national debates produced for the major contenders. Interrogators from the Political Library were: Bill Gardner, secretary of state; Sean O'Kane, general manager of the Holiday Inn/Center of New Hampshire; Rich Ashooh, communications director of Sanders, a Lockheed Martin Company and Michael York, state librarian. It was Gregg's honor to serve as moderator.

The event was well covered by the national media including C-Span, CNN and MTV. Sarah M. Earle and Ken Williams of the *Concord Monitor* prepared a full page spread with individual photographs of each participant. Laura A. Kiernan of the *Boston Sunday Globe* wrote a detailed review. There follows an abstract of each candidate and his or her positions.

Republican Timothy Lee Mosby, 55, from Red Bluff, California. He said he was an out-of-work, self-taught scientist who favored advancement of science and teaching of the Gospel. He told the media he was currently in love and needed a job. Would like to see world government and colonization of Mars. Wanted hybrid cars that run on gas and electricity. He had run a newspaper advertisement in the *Manchester Union Leader* advocating monies for the space program. "I want to get social problems figured out and have people love the Lord." Mosby received 41 votes.

Democrat Jim Taylor, 35, from St. Paul, Minnesota. He claimed to be a writer/director/filmmaker/performer, arrived with his own TV crew plus a guitar and Hawaiian leis to sing his campaign theme song. He recorded his campaign activities for a Minnesota TV station and planned a documentary *Run Some Idiot, One Schmuck's Odyssey.* "I'll do whatever it takes to get attention, no matter how ridiculous." Once he got attention, he then talked about national health care for all at a living wage, 30-hour work week, ending corporate welfare and financing election reform.

Taylor raised money by charging $2 to hit him in the face with a pie and sold ambassadorships. "If we get a higher bid later for the same ambassadorship, we just replace them." "My show is a little song, a little dance and a little seltzer water down my pants with an important political message you won't get any other way." His slogan: "Everything is Crappy." Taylor received 87 votes.

Democrat Edward T. O'Donnell, Jr. From Wilmington, Delaware. O'Donnell had run three times previously in New Hampshire with total votes ranging from 24 to 74 and hoped to get enough publicity from New Hampshire to form a third party. Ran ads in the *Man-*

Fun along the Campaign Trail

Dan Quayle learned local politics the hard way with the statement, "You cannot come to New Hampshire without avoiding politics." While here he backed that up with, "I believe we are on an irreversible trend toward more freedom and democracy. But that could change." Richard Cohen, writer for the *Washington Post*, also had a few words about the vice president, "An expedition that set out in search of a Quayle accomplishment would never be heard from again."

chester Union Leader stating he was graduate of Colgate, president of a charitable foundation and a Rockefeller Fellow at Harvard Divinity School. Supported four-day work week, mental health courses in schools, no private ownership of guns, promoted Christianity and would cut his presidential salary to $25,000. Further, O'Donnell would work for a Constitutional Convention "to start the whole government over again." O'Donnell received 35 votes.

Democrat Anne Heather Harder, 51, from Crown Point, Indiana. Harder was a Ph.D. professor/author/businesswoman who had previously entered the 1996 primary and finished sixth with 369 votes. She had better campaign materials, from lapel pins and bumper stickers to brochures and position papers, than most of the major candidates. She ran a full schedule of addressing educational groups, particularly school classes. Boasting she was a true "outsider" who had never been tainted by politics and owed no political favors, Harder didn't expect to win, but planned to keep trying until she does, saying, "It took Ghandi decades to wake up India."

Harder, who campaigned with her daughter, opposed federal encroachment on private lives, would allow only one law per bill written in standard English. She would institute a national referendum for important and/or sensitive issues where the voice of the people should be heard. "I stand as a living model for every American. If I can run for president, giving up my job, life as I knew it, and normalcy, for this country, then every American can do something." Harder received 192 votes.

Democrat Mark Greenstein, 35, from Culver City, California. He addressed diverse issues, concentrating on education as he was reported to be a Dartmouth graduate who owned a company which prepared students for college entrance exams. Mark proposed a military-trained, airborne service corps which from helicopters would rappel to disabled cars in traffic jams and haul them away to service stations. As president he would remove "dumb laws" and abolish Social Security that "penalizes African-Americans and steals from younger workers without paying it back." Greenstein would also sell a third of the interstate highways and proportionately reduce gasoline taxes. One of the lessons he learned from campaigning was that, "Ideas that just might change the world are less important than the car you drive." Greenstein received 75 votes.

Democrat John B. Eaton, 77, from Oak Bluffs, Massachusetts. Eaton admitted his previous political experience was limited to running for homeroom representative in high school when he competed against three other candidates who gave speeches. "I invited the three friends in, we sang and that seemed to put us over." He was surprised to find so many Democrats on the ballot because he thought it would only be Gore, Bradley and himself. Said he had distilled about 320 issues into 15 themes. Eaton claimed to be a marketing man who had secret plans for a big campaign event, but not yet ready to give details. "It is so different, I just don't want to spill it before I do it." He never did! Eaton received 134 votes.

Republican Kenneth A. Capalbo, 56, from Wakefield, Rhode Island. Capalbo was a retired state prison employee who had lost local elections for both school committee and senate but said it would

---

Fun along the Campaign Trail

When Eisenhower supporters in 1952 were trying to determine to which party he belonged, New Hampshire Attorney General Gordon R. Tiffany wrote the county clerk of Abilene, Kansas for information about Ike's voting record. To everyone's surprise, the answer came back that there was no record of Eisenhower ever having voted in the precinct of his domicile.

The clerk wrote: "Dwight's father was a Republican and always voted the Republican ticket up until his death; however that had nothing to do with the son, as many differ from their fathers of which I am sorry to see . . . I don't think he has any politics." This was a lucky strike for the Eisenhower fans who were all Republicans and thus were able to so commit him on the New Hampshire primary ballot.

be "almost un-American" to count him out of the presidential race. He thought it was worth paying $1,000 to New Hampshire for the opportunity of talking about eliminating the income tax, which he'd replace with a flat tax on wealth, and he'd substitute a "living wage" for the "minimum wage." Capalbo was also upset with foreign policy which "is not based on right or wrong, good or bad or unjust. It is solely based on what is perceived to be in our best interests. In the long term, it seldom is." His humility was best expressed in admitting, "even if I'm not worthy of discussion as a candidate, the issues are." Capalbo received 51 votes.

Democrat Jeffrey B. Peters, 51, from Jackson, New Hampshire. Peters, although filed as a Democrat, was the spirit and founder of the We The People Party. Said he'd run as a Democrat for Congress in the 1986 Connecticut election. "Granny D," Doris Haddock, was a 90 year old Granite Stater, who walked across the nation in support of her interest in tax reform, and had been joined in the trek by Peters. His main concern was to secure public financing and free media exposure for candidates unable to raise sufficient funds for themselves. He described himself as worried about the perishing of our democracy and as "a citizen leader and populist alternative to the professional politicians." Peters received 156 votes.

Also in attendance was *Democrat Michael Skok from Cheektowaga, New York* who was nervous about speaking on the program, but with encouragement from questioner Gardner took a position against partial-birth abortion and favored a manned mission to Mars. Skok received 18 votes.

An uninvited guest who showed up was "Vermin Supreme." He was not allowed to address the audience because he was a write-in candidate as he had been in 1992. His costume was a long boot for a hat, faux-fur-covered jumpsuit and flipper shoulder pads, and he carried a huge toothbrush to emphasize dental hygiene with free dental care for all.

Democrat Wladislav D. Kubiak from Kennebunkport, Maine. Kubiak was one of the two Democrats who had filed for vice president. He said he was a former teacher and journalist. Claimed he had spent the past several years in Japan, having been the "virtual" mayor of Kyoto. Kubiak had filed for vice president as opposed to president on the theory it would get him better media and a better chance to win. He would abolish mega-corporations, enthusiastically supported the New Hampshire primary, feeling, "there's been a great preternatural understanding here in New Hampshire of the issues." Said if he didn't win he might declare himself the "virtual" president and rule from the Internet.

Kubiak got 21,275 votes and won the Democratic vice presidential nomination. He defeated the other Democratic vice presidential contender, *Sam Costello of Berwick, Pennsylvania.* Costello, who received 16,726 votes, did not participate in the debate.

Costello had written the "Board of Elections" a classic letter prior to his filing as a vice presidential candidate: "I've got a problem! I want to run in the NH democratic primary for vice president, but I don't have any delegates or alternates. I don't even know how many I need. Since I probably won't win the primary, why do I need them? And if I do WIN, everyone will want to be my D & As! Can't I just pay the filing fee, run my newspaper ads and try to get 15 percent of the vote? . . . Must I skip the NH primary and deny its citizens a chance to re-kindle the Spirit of '76?" Costello paid his $1000 filing fee but never came into the state. If he had, maybe he would have beaten Kubiak and won the Democratic vice-presidential nomination.

The repartee between the inquisitors and the candidates, between the candidates themselves and media interviews was an interesting and entertaining initiative for the presidential process and well worthy of repetition in future primaries.

On the Republican ballot there were also two candidates who had filed for vice president; neither of them had participated in the debate. *William Bryk, 44, of Staten Island, New York* won with 23,808 votes. Bryk was a columnist and lawyer, graduate of Manhattan College and Fordham Law School who served as a Small Claims Arbitrator for the New York City Civil Court. He had previously been a candidate for the NYC City Council, for the State Assembly and Congress. He described his effort as a "rocking chair campaign."

The second Republican running for vice president was *Russell J. Fornwalt, 88, of New York, NY.* He was a public relations counselor and freelance writer. Fornwalt had run in the 1996 primary for president as the "Republican Alternative" and received 37 votes. A former teacher, he placed numerous ads and issued press releases in 1996 advocating military occupation of high schools to stop violence, plowing under farm subsidies and mandatory fingerprinting of all citizens, but he did not personally appear in the state. The candidate expected to receive "maybe one or two (votes). Thirty-seven came as a shock, actually" and he said he'd love to meet those 37 voters. "This has been a terrific learning experience. I look at this as continuing my education in political science in a practical way." He graciously submitted a book documenting his efforts for the Political Library Archives.

Again in 2000, Fornwalt did not visit New Hampshire. He filed for vice president to "Get the Vice out of the Vice Presidency and put Virtue back in." As the second place finisher for vice president, he got 18,512 votes. He wrote Gregg that, "The 'fringe' candidate proves that democracy is alive and well. He or she gives a much needed dimension to the political process." The 18,512 votes he received in 2000 after the 37 of 1996, probably gave him a heart attack. Fornwalt said he was "honored to have become a part of New Hampshire's political history."

Although they had been invited to participate in the debate, there were thirteen others who filed as candidates but were unable to attend on the day of the event. This group included the following:

Democrat Charles Buckley, 57, from Whitefield, New Hampshire was an immigrant from Massachusetts. He was a Boston College graduate and a Massachusetts lawyer. While admitting one has to be a "little nutty" to run for president, he claimed to have been a clerk of court, probation officer, teacher, bank examiner, and navy veteran. He offered a six-point plan on education, defense, environment, social concerns, Social Security and housing. "At the risk of sounding obnoxious and self-righteous, I am more qualified than Gore or Bradley." Buckley told the *New Hampshire Sunday News* he would solve the lack of affordable housing in the east by irrigating vast tracts of land in the west. He was also concerned with road rage, saying there are a lot of angry people looking for direction. Presidential Inauguration Day in 2001 was scheduled for his birthday, so he looked forward to celebrating both events at the same time. Buckley received 322 votes.

Republican Tom Oyler, 54, from Wichita, Kansas. He was an industrial engineer, had two unsuccessful U.S. Senate runs in Kansas, once as a Republican and once as a Libertarian, and had a slogan, "Better than none of the above." Oyler told Matt Stearns of the *Kansas City Star* it was kind of "neat" running for president because his boss whistles, "Hail to the Chief" when he passes the candidate's desk. Oyler campaigned on the Internet from his spare bedroom where he sent sarcastic editorials nationwide about his upset with government, education, environment, entitlements and taxes. "I sent a letter to Clinton about nine months ago. He was giving away money right and left. I asked him for $243,000 as long as he was giving money away. That was the first estimate on the house I wanted to build. He never answered." The candidate realistically estimated his chances as "probably a little less than zero." Oyler received 14 votes.

Democrat Willie F. Carter from Fort Worth, Texas. He was a certified aircraft mechanic, who had run in 1996, receiving 85 votes. A deeply religious African-American who sought God's guidance in entering the presidential race, he quoted the Bible and supported decent wages, health care for everyone, stopping rampant crime, fair taxes and a strong military "to insure that this nation under God shall not perish from the earth." Carter asked God for help and "after I prayed, the Lord opened the door and I was blessed to

---

Fun along the Campaign Trail

Overconfidence doesn't seem to get you anywhere in New Hampshire primaries. Senator Orrin Hatch was convinced, "If I did not believe I would be a better president than anyone running, I would not be in this race."

---

get on the ballot in the state of New Hampshire." Carter visited the state in 1996, but didn't in 2000 and received only 30 votes.

Democrat Randolph "Randy" Crow from Wilmington, North Carolina. It was noted in the *New Hampshire Sunday News* that he had run in his own state to promote anti-Semitic and anti-government views. It was reported that he believed the FBI blew up TWA Flight 800 with a laser and that free enterprise is being destroyed by Wall Street. "When I hear somebody in power is Jewish, I raise my eyebrows and I try to investigate it." Crow received 29 votes.

Republican Richard C. Peet, 71, from McLean, Virginia. Peet claimed to have had considerable background in serving on Congressional staffs and drafting legislation which would qualify him for winning. "I'm disappointed about what I've seen and not seen and that's why I got into it." Peet received 23 votes.

Democrat Vincent S. Hamm from Golden, Colorado. A businessman and computer consultant, he had run in 1996, receiving 72 votes and finished 13th out of the 21 Democrats on the ticket. While he had ten major issues, including technological accessibility across class lines, better distribution of food to Third-World countries and prevention of disease worldwide, his principle focus was on a plan for the decriminalization of drugs. It would levy a heavy tax on them, using the money for substance-abuse programs and for the reduction of the federal deficit. "The money that now goes into the pockets of the drug lords would go into the pocket of every American." He said he was running because most politicians don't fit the profile of a typical American and he does. "Everyone needs to be a part of our political process in order to make a difference." Hamm received 22 votes.

Democrat Thomas Koos from Woodside, California. Koos stated to the *New Hampshire Sunday News* that he worked at Stanford University and was running because he wanted to get others involved in the political process. "Being a candidate allows me to engage strangers in conversation, and it is amazing to see how so many people just want to talk about their concerns, hopes and ideas about this nation." Because most of his family were in Hungary, he appreciated his responsibilities of United States citizenship while others close to him did not have that privilege. He took serious positions on the issues, yet knew he couldn't win and just enjoyed the opportunity to participate. Koos received 19 votes.

Democrat Lyndon H. LaRouche, Jr., 80, from Round Hill, Virginia. LaRouche was born in Rochester, New Hampshire, and had run in 1980 getting 2,236 votes. Thereafter he called for a recount of his votes from among the 107,911 votes cast for the Democratic candidates for president. He ran in 1988, receiving 188 votes, in 1992 ,with 115 votes and in 1996, with 433 votes. On his fifth try in 2000 he got 124 votes and set the all-time "fringe" filing record for the most attempts. Governor Harold Stassen, not a fringe, was on the ballot seven times.

A prolific author of books, pamphlets and articles, LaRouche is described by his committee as the world-famous economist and former political prisoner. He did five years in the federal pen for conspiracy to commit mail fraud. LaRouche's literature lists 31 New Hampshire legislators who called upon the president and attorney general for his exoneration for the alleged fraudulent conviction.

LaRouche believed the world is in the process of disintegration and implosion of all the leading monetary and financial institutions, including every part of our federal reserve system. "The nation is not only very sick; the nation is terminally ill and we are in the final phase of terminal illness." He advocated creating a global economic summit to develop world economic policy simi-

lar to the one held at Bretton Woods. LaRouche advertised extensively in 1996 but ran an Internet campaign in 2000. He thought
little of the presumed frontrunners, predicting, "The sheep are
going to march into the slaughter pen, which is what Al Gore and
George Bush represent." Though he traveled with a security detail, he told Gregg he enjoyed getting back to the "quaintness" of
his fellow New Hampshire people.

Republican Samuel H. Berry, Jr. from Medford, Oregon, 43, lawyer,
website designer, had run unsuccessfully for the U.S. Senate in
Oregon. He was the first to sign up for the 2000 race and did not
plan to campaign actively elsewhere, saying, "New Hampshire
recognizes the candidacy of an ordinary citizen to a greater extent, probably, than any other state." Barry ran ads in the *Manchester Union Leader* to scrap the tax that discourages hiring, simplify
the complicated tax code and nurture the family. He supported
fiscal responsibility, traditional family values and an economy
free of government mismanagement. "Government may not be
the solution, but let's be sure it's not the problem." As president
he would have regular teleconferences for citizens to press their
grievances. Berry received 61 votes.

Republican Andy Martin, 54, from Palm Beach, Florida. Under the
name of Anthony R. Martin-Trigona he had filed here as a Democrat in 1988 and received 61 votes. Martin was a lawyer who frequently filed suits. He had run unsuccessfully for the U.S. Senate
in Florida. He referred to himself as a "straight Christian" and
the first "consumer advocate in cyberspace." Andy claimed to be
New Hampshire's "favorite son candidate" with four generations
of family from this state. His platform favored gay-lesbian rights
and opposed the death penalty. He ran an ad on WMUR-TV
in which he alleged George W. Bush used cocaine, saying, "his
(Bush's) brain suffered from alcohol abuse. Don't trust Bush with
your vote until he trusts you with the truth about his past." Ironically, Martin was at the same time exhorting Republican candidates not to attack each other.

Martin sued the sponsors of a New Hampshire televised

presidential candidate debate for a million dollars because he was not included. Thereafter he did not show up for the hearing in the New Hampshire federal district court. He had also served a jail sentence in Florida for contempt of court. Martin received 81 votes, 20 more than last time when he ran under a different name.

Republican Dorian Yeager, 50, from Rye, New Hampshire. Yeager was a writer, actress, member of the Screen Actors Guild and operated her own "Blatant Self-Promotion Department." On her Web page she took positions on a litany of issues as fiscally conservative and sociologically Libertarian. "I urge the federal government to return to the role of 'loving parent,' and relax the growing need to behave as would an overzealous baby-sitter." She said she was annoyed with lack of straight talk from candidates and she was a "real person" with yes or no answers. Yeager planned to finance the campaign entirely from donations for her bumper stickers which were to read, "A New Hampshire President: Dorian YEA-GER—You've done worse." Yeager received 98 votes.

Republican Mark "Dick" Harnes from New York City. Harnes was a bodyguard and entertainer, who had previously served as a disc jockey at Manchester's radio station WGIR and WEMJ in Laconia. His special interest was automobile ownership and he believed every employed American should be entitled to a loan for a 100 percent tax deductible car. "We did not become a superpower from World War I or World War II. We became a superpower because of Henry Ford and the Model-T." Harnes planned to take four weeks off from work to talk to people about the issues. Harnes received 34 votes.

Democrat Nathaniel Thomas Mullins from Wakefield, Massachusetts also filed and received 35 votes. He left no trace of his activity, if any.

In addition to the thirteen who were absent from the debate, there were also others who didn't file, yet should receive honorable mention:

One who didn't quite make it was *Jim Carroll of Knoxville, Tennessee.* Carroll issued a release the day after Clinton's election in

1996 that he was running in 2000, claiming to be an author, businessman, educator and philosopher, but he never filed.

Edwin A. Conklin, Jr.,43, of Manchester was surprised to learn he'd need 3,000 petitions, not for the primary, but to file as an Independent candidate for the general election in 2000. His platform called for a mandatory, three-day work week and four-day weekends for his "Adequate Time, Space and Resources" ticket. "Three honest-to-God 10-hour work days; don't burn yourself out, but don't ass-drag either." Guess he had difficulty getting the 3000 petitions as he never made it to the November election.

The *Manchester Union Leader* took some ads and refused some in a series promoting "The *fabulous* team for victory in 2000 of Gov. Claude D. Flunch, America's greatest American, and Sen. Horace B. Mason, Divine choice for number 2." This quixotic pair advocated an eighth day to the week between Saturday and Sunday to be Leisureday and making the abortion laws apply to men. The newspaper reported that the candidates' spokesman-inventor, Doug Payne, said Gov. Flunch would not comment on the ads as, "he was in Washington having a tour of the White House because Mrs. Flunch wanted to get an early start in the redecorating." Their ads contained the tag line, "If you got an *F* in lunch, you can still write-in Flunch."

Laura Kiernan of the *Boston Globe* reminded us that there were also alien impostors like the Cookie Mom who showed up at campaign events in 2000. She gave away cookies with pie charts urging candidates to spend more money on schools and less on bombs. She was underwritten by a business group founded by Ben Cohen of Ben and Jerry's Ice Cream.

Pentagon Pork Pig, decked out in a teddy and shiny jewels, and her date, Contractor Pig with a silver vest, traveling in a white stretch limousine, boasted of their enormous wealth gifted from the federal government. Educational activists planned to have a dilapidated vehicle following, with children inside begging to get some of that money from the greedy pigs.

Captain Climate, a high flier from the year 2050 had "spent

his life fighting the disastrous effects of global warming." He was the brainchild of Ozone Action, seeking to have the issue joined at candidate debates. But the candidates never heard the message.

Considering that some of the fringe candidates never came into the state, probably knew no one here, had no Web page, did no advertising, held no press interviews and probably did no mailings, its amazing that all of them who filed in the 2000 primary scored with vote totals at least in the teens.

A few who visited in person and/or used one or more of the standard campaign tools achieved results in the hundreds. None of them will probably ever make it to the White House, yet maybe it was worth the $1,000 to have a New Hampshire certificate on the wall proving they were presidential candidates!

2004 Should Be a Banner Year for Fringes

Four months before the opening of the filing period for the 2004 presidential primary, the secretary of state's office had already received about 30 requests from potential fringes seeking information on how to register as candidates. Others had let their intentions to run be known through the media or personal contacts.

Among them were two old friends to New Hampshire:

Caroline P. Killeen, a former Roman Catholic nun had run in 1992 and 1996. Known as the "Hemp Lady" because she supported the legalization of marijuana, she traveled the state on a bicycle, sleeping in fields, churches, homeless shelters and college dormitories. She moved to Italy after her 1996 campaign but ran as an absentee write-in candidate in 2000. From Italy in June of 2003, once more this remarkable 78-year old woman contacted the secretary of state's office to announce her intention of being involved in 2004.

Fred Sitnick, the "Messiah," campaigned in 1996 as a Democratic write-in and handed out business cards promising "Zillions for all the world." Since that time he has been in constant touch with the authors of this book, advising he'd inadvertently missed the 2000

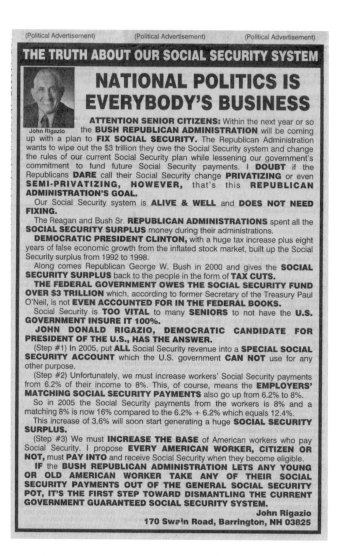
John Donald Rigazio, a Rochester retail grocer and Democrat, has published a series of large ads in the Manchester Union Leader *and elsewhere announcing his candidacy for president, but the New Hampshire Democratic Party would not recognize him as a serious presidential candidate.*

filing date. Meanwhile he has decided the Democrats are corrupt and has changed his party to Republican!

Also among them were two New Hampshire residents making their first pitch:

Kenneth Stremsky of Manchester has set up a website and written letters to the *Manchester Union Leader* expressing his intention of being a presidential candidate in 2004. He writes, "I am looking for a campaign treasurer who will accept contributions from people other than myself."

John Donald Rigazio, a Rochester retail grocer, has published a series of large ads in the *Manchester Union Leader* and elsewhere announcing his candidacy for president. He is quoted in *Foster's Daily Democrat* as saying, "I expect to spend $100,000 of my own money and won't accept donations. I would love to get 10 percent of the New Hampshire vote and send a message.

The Last Word on Fringes

During Gardner's tenure, several hundred fringe or lesser-known candidates have come to his office to run in the New Hampshire primary. One day in the middle of the presidential primary filing period, a man walked into the secretary of state's office and asked if he could hang around to observe. One day led to several. The man was Richard Stengal, the senior editor at *Time* magazine. The following excerpts come from a column he wrote for the December 18, 1995 issue of *Time:*

Look Ma, I'm Running!

During the past week, more than a dozen people perched themselves behind the same tatty 1819 writing table to fill out the Declaration of Candidacy form, which is kept on the shelf right next to the application forms for Notary Public. The registrants include not only Phil Gramm and Bob Dole but also the Rev. Billy Joe Clegg from Biloxi, Mississippi, whose slogan is "Clegg Won't Pull Your Leg". . .

There's also the poet and former seaman Michael Levinson from Buffalo, New York, who proposes a jobs program to build 10,000 clipper ships, and Caroline Killeen of Flagstaff, Arizona, the self-described "Hemp Lady" and ex-nun who advocates legalizing marijuana as a way of enabling Americans to get back in touch with nature. For $2 she'll sell you a bumper sticker that reads *Let Clinton Inhale.* . . .

At 11:10 last Thursday morning, Michael Eric Dass, from Washington Crossing, Pennsylvania, shuffled tentatively through the door to the secretary of state's office and asked where he could register to run for president. Dressed in stiff new blue jeans, work boots and a wind breaker, Dass sat down at the desk to fill out N.H. form 655:47. Out of an empty Mueller's spaghetti box, he plucked a $1,000 check. A reporter from the *Manchester Union Leader* pulled out a pad and asked Dass why he was running. "No one appreciates the press more than I do," said Dass, who is intense and deadly serious, "but I'm not going to take any questions until the day after the primary. I want to talk to the people of New Hampshire unfiltered by the media." Peppered with a few more questions, an exasperated Dass replied, "Look, I'm a regular guy, a working stiff. The money comes out of my savings. I'm going to try something no one else has ever tried, and I'll talk to you when it's all over." And with that, the newest Republican candidate for president walked quietly into the bracing New Hampshire air.

✳

Chapter 7

Third Parties and Independents

Third Parties

A CATEGORY OF THE LESSER-KNOWNS—who are largely ignored by the media—are third-party presidential candidates. Until 1992 when the Libertarian Party first qualified for listing on the primary ballot, the last time any other party had done so was in 1968, when the American Party accomplished formal recognition. Even then, that party never organized sufficiently to present candidates for nomination.

Thus the Libertarian Party is the only one in modern history that has received official party status for the primary. It was on the ballot in 1992 and 1996, but did not qualify for 2000, nor is it qualified for 2004. To qualify and have its party symbol printed on the presidential primary ballot a party must receive at least 4 percent of the total votes cast at a preceding state general election for governor or United States senator.

In 1996 when the Libertarian Party was recognized for the second time in the Granite State, it had two candidates on the ballot, Harry Browne and Irwin A. Schiff. Browne was a financial adviser, author of nine books, mostly on finance, and claimed all of them were best-sellers with one as number one on the *New York Times* best-seller list.

He told Gregg that for 30 years he didn't vote because he didn't see any point in it; "it doesn't matter if Republicans or Democrats have the presidency, or which party has Congress, nothing changes. Republicans campaign as if they were Libertarians but when they get into office they govern as if they were Democrats. Only when someone goes to Washington who is determined to clean the stables . . . only then will the political battle be won. But it's obvious that there is no such person in two-party politics we can look to." In 1994 he registered and voted as a Libertarian.

Browne believed in liberty and self-responsibility on all issues at all times, with the claim that government doesn't work. He advocated repealing the federal income tax and not giving Washington authority in such matters as welfare, education, transportation, social security and crime control. Harry did believe the federal government was necessary to defend the nation.

As a Libertarian he advocated selling off most of the government's assets and legalizing drugs. Though he claimed he'd qualified for federal matching funds, Browne turned them down. "I don't believe in welfare for politicians any more than for individuals or corporations," he said. He never expected to win, but figured a 10 percent favorable vote would send a strong message to the nation. On primary day he received 653 votes.

Schiff, the other Libertarian candidate, had also written a series of books and advocated the same principles as Browne, except Schiff concentrated on the income tax, which he claimed was not mandatory and there is no law requiring its payment. He had joined the Libertarian Party 20 years before and tried to get it to expose how the government was collecting taxes illegally. Because he tested out his theory with the IRS, Schiff ended up in jail for tax evasion.

He divulged to Gregg, "I was a political prisoner. What the federal judges have been doing is illegally putting people in jail for violating crimes that do not exist in order to intimidate the American public and to pay a tax that no law requires them to pay." He conducted a series of seminars in Manchester where he taught audiences, "How to stand up to the Internal Revenue Service and win." On primary day Schiff received 317 fewer votes than Browne.

It should be noted that in 1992, the only other year when the

Libertarian Party appeared on the New Hampshire presidential primary ballot, its candidate for president, Andre Marrou, received 3,219 votes. In Dixville, he beat both of the Republican candidates, George Bush and Pat Buchanan, along with Democratic candidate Bill Clinton. In 1996, Libertarian candidates Browne and Shiffe received no votes in Dixville.

Though they have not been on the ballot for the New Hampshire presidential primary, many other well-known parties such as Dr. John Hagelin's Natural Law Party and Ross Perot's Reform Party have secured sufficient petitions for their candidates to be listed on the state's ballot in the following November general elections. It takes 3,000 signatures in New Hampshire for a minor party candidate to secure name placement on the ballot for the general presidential election, whereas Tennessee requires only 25. Texas requires 56,000 and California 128,000.

As reported by Amanda Milkovits of *Foster's Sunday Citizen:*

> "About 300 to 400 people run for president every four years," said Ian Stirton, spokesman for the Federal Elections Commission. "Some join the two major parties, while others hook up with third parties which suit their views or start their own. At least 30 political parties are listed by Project Vote Smart, a nonprofit, bipartisan organization."

In 1992 there was the abortive situation of Lenora B. Fulani, Ph.D who was the head of the New Alliance Party. It was not recognized in New Hampshire, so she signed up and ran as a Democrat in the primary. "I'm an Afro-American woman in support of some things some people would call Marxist and some would call Communist and some would call Democrat."

Her Alliance Party described itself as a "black-led, multiracial (and) pro-gay" political organization which "creates the environment for people to say the unsayable about violence, racism, the Democratic Party, blacks and Jews, sex and crime, presidential politics, U.S. policy in Africa and the Caribbean and more."

> *Fun along the Campaign Trail*
>
> **Article 10 of the state constitution still preserves the people's Right of Revolution, saying "The doctrine of nonresistance against arbitrary power and oppression is absurd, slavish, and destructive of the good and happiness of mankind." Fortunately, they haven't yet made use of this right, but frequently somebody says it might be a good idea.**

Previously she had run for president, governor and lieutenant governor of New York and mayor of New York City. She knew she had no chance of winning—yet she received substantially more in federal matching funds than almost any of the other candidates in the race.

Fulani opened a Manchester headquarters and ran full-page newspaper ads directed to undecided Democratic and Independent voters against the "Big Five": Clinton, Tsongas, Kerry, Harkin and Brown. At the same time, she charged "Big Shots" in Washington for keeping her out of the debates with the "Big Five." She said the "Big Five" were not real leaders, "they're just the puppets for the Big Guys who are running the show." On primary day she came in eighth with 402 votes.

In 1992, Ralph Nader received 3,258 write-in votes in the Republican presidential primary and 3,054 write-ins on the Democratic ballot. He returned for a one-stop appearance in 1996 when running elsewhere as a candidate of the Green Party, but he did not file here. He advocated putting a "none of the above box" on every ballot everywhere and require new elections when it got more checkmarks than the total of the other candidates.

Nader asked voters in 1996 to write-in his name on the Republican or Democratic ballot, which he considered the same as voting for "none of the above." Ninety-four Republicans and 187 Democrats answered his call, along with 12 Libertarians, a bonus he hadn't counted on.

It's interesting that in the 2000 general election he received 22,198 votes as the Green Party candidate, when Bush's margin over Gore was only 7,211. He may have cost Gore the national election, as it was New Hampshire's four Bush electoral votes which assured Bush the presidency in that tight race.

A consumer advocate, Nader attacked candidates in both of the major parties, saying their claim to eliminate federal red tape is meaningless; "big business is dismantling so much of our democracy." Nader's objective was not to become president, rather to ask hard questions of other candidates.

An ambitious New Hampshire couple from Jackson, Jeff and Cici Peters, in 1995 began building their own version of what the country needs, entitled the "We The People Party." Alleged to be a summa cum laude graduate of Harvard with a master's degree in government and member of the Democratic Leadership Council, Mr. Peters said, "I feel it is my destiny to encourage my fellow citizens to take back our country."

The party's mission was to increase voter turnout, by addressing finance, education, environmental and other reforms with national referendums to determine the priority of the peoples' interests. Traveling countrywide in their RV, augmented by their website and the Internet, they planned to reach every state, to offer all party members the opportunity to vote on the issues with a two-thirds majority required for passage. The results would be given to Congress for action.

Peters hoped they could draft one of the potential "drop out" candidates from the 2000 presidential primary to become the nominee of the We The People Party in the general election. He said, "the people would decide who the messenger would be." If they didn't get Bradley or McCain, they'd be honored to have Warren Beatty or, as a backup option, they'd take Peters himself.

Peters claimed that he and Cici had registered the People Party in every state as either a political party, a nonprofit organization or a political action committee. While not expecting to win, he filed as a Democrat in the 2000 New Hampshire primary and received 156 votes. Thereafter he positioned himself as the alternative to Pat Buchanan for the presidential nomination of the Reform Party.

In 1999 it didn't stop another New Hampshire resident, The Lobsterman, from forming the Crustacean Party. With his trademark fancy boots, red cape and lobster-claw mittens he announced as a write-in candidate: "Besides being a professional wrestler and dressing like a lobster on weekends, I'm a normal guy." So normal, in fact, that Jeff Costa received a commendation from Governor Shaheen for his work in professional wrestling.

Da Vid, another write-in candidate identified as a naturopathic doctor from San Francisco, founded the Human Ecology Party, later renamed the Light Party, which would solve the country's ill health with holistic solutions. In 1992, interested voters were invited to his evening of "a moving musical dance experience featuring fabulous music artistically integrated with beautiful computer graphic special effects." In 1996 he alleged, "I hold the position that I already claimed the presidency."

Nor should we overlook Mike's Party which included Mike Strauss and his running mate, the dog Husker.

Independents and Undeclared Voters

Today it's difficult to understand the passionate dedication which voters held for the electoral process during the period from 1853 to 1878. In 1853 our native son, Franklin Pierce, was the president, and our elections were held annually in March. In 1877, elections were shifted to November. In those days everybody voted. Apparently it was a once-a-year requisite ritual for all men (women were not allowed to vote).

As historian James O. Lyford wrote, "The voter who was not willing to make his vocation or business subsidiary to politics was regarded as unpatriotic. Men gave freely of their time and money to carry elections. Absent voters were brought home." Fortunately, though watered down by the exigencies of modern life,

New Hampshire's own Jeff "The Lobsterman" Costa won fame when he ran for president in 2000 dressed as a lobster, and formed the Crustacean Party. He is also planning a run in 2004.

this tradition of voter turnout in New Hampshire remains relatively strong today.

Of even greater contrast with today's electorate was the omnipotence of the party system in the days of Franklin Pierce. Lyford continues, "Men had strong allegiances to political parties. The Mugwump did not flourish on New Hampshire soil. Party followers were taught that their own party was radically right and the other party radically wrong." Lyford relates how "men might not like their leaders, but they obeyed their orders."

Oh, how things have changed! Never mind the Green Party, the Libertarian Party, the Natural Law Party, the Reform Party or dozens of other lesser-known political affiliations, there's that great swing block of 328,556 registered voters (38.4 percent) in the Granite State who prided themselves as being Independents in 2000. They won't partake in any regimented political philosophy. While many of them have sentiments which jell with one of the two national parties, they still don't want to be so identified. They withhold their judgments in each election cycle, to analyze the views of the candidates presented.

Further, as is obvious in New Hampshire, more and more of today's voters vote for the man or woman who makes the best impression from personal contact. Is the candidate someone who is akin, likable, trustworthy, of sound judgment, good health and appropriate experience? The candidate's political sentiments, unless totally nonconformist, are of secondary importance. These Independents are not political activists who vote for the Republican or Democrat candidate because of the candidate's party platform—or maybe just because their grandfather was a member of the same party.

Fun along the Campaign Trail

Although he finished last in 1976, Vice President Hubert Humphrey was realistic about his poor showing: "I never thought my speeches were too long. I enjoyed them."

This trend is now leading to an increasingly significant role for Independents and a decreasing core of party "activists." Not that in the foreseeable future there could ever be enough damage done to destroy the prominence of the nation's two-party system. Even the potential threat of third parties has never seriously effected the underlying clout of the two major parties.

But this development does give rise to challenges for those concerned with solidifying party strength. Until the early 1970s, once a New Hampshire voter had participated in a party's primary, he or she could never return to an Independent or undeclared status except by re-registering in a new place, and a person's party affiliation was posted on the checklist for all to see. Many people didn't want to be committed to a particular party, so they retained their undeclared Independent registration and didn't vote in primaries.

While New Hampshire does not permit crossover voting between registered members of the two major parties, there is now a right for any unregistered voter to show up for the first time on primary election day and, upon proper proof of residency, take either a Republican or Democratic ballot. That new voter has the option thereafter, on the same day, to revert to his or her Independent or undeclared status after having been, transiently, and for a few minutes, a Republican or a Democrat. The same applies for those registered voters who have not declared a party affiliation. On primary day, they can take a ballot for either party and revert back to undeclared status upon leaving.

On the plus side, these "voter friendly" ground rules do create greater voter participation in both primary and general elections. Yet this convenience is anathema to many dedicated party loyalists, as these temporary members may be in sufficient number to swing an election among primary candidates. For example: if two Republicans are running against each other with one being the favorite, an Independent voter with leanings toward a strong Democratic candidate might cast his ballot for the underdog Republican candidate in the hope of a win for him. In the general election to follow, the weaker Republican would be more vulnerable to the Democrat.

In 2000, some believe it was the Independent vote which gave McCain the Republican victory over Bush, though, considering the different strategy in the way the two campaigns were run, this is certainly a very debatable conclusion.

Also in that year, for the first time in history, this more liberal opportunity for Independents resulted in the Independents' proportion of total registered voters to be 38 percent versus 35 percent for Republicans and 26 percent for Democrats. Previously, since the introduction of the presidential preference primary, more Republicans had been registered than either Independents or Democrats. As between Democrats and Republicans, New Hampshire has always been a Republican state.

Still the potential for Independents to alter primary elections in New Hampshire raises two divergent questions: should the state require Independents to identify as a member of a national party for a period prior to the election day, thereby supporting the position of loyal party "activists," or should Independents continue to be permitted the freedom of the current system which encourages larger turnouts? Answer: the first-in-the-nation presidential primary is proud that anyone can be a player.

❈

Chapter 8

Leaving the Party Early
Buchanan and Smith in 2000

I N 2000, PAT BUCHANAN AND BOB SMITH quit the Republican
Party. Although Pat Buchanan and Bob Smith initially campaigned as Republican candidates in the 2000 New Hampshire presidential primary race, they had disavowed the party
before the formal filing period.

Republican Patrick Buchanan

In 1996, Buchanan had won the primary in a close upset victory
over favored Bob Dole by 56,874 to 54,738. In 1992 he had finished second against President George Bush in the New Hampshire presidential primary when he captured 35 percent of the
total vote.

In mid-April of 1998, he reappeared for a commercial signing
in Bedford of his book, *The Great Betrayal*. He expressed an interest
in making a third try in 2000, with a probable announcement of
his decision after November. Also he noted: "One of the two parties has got to represent populist conservatism, economic nation-
alism and America first, because it is a majority view at the grassroots level even though it is not the elite view in either party."

In Washington on March 2, 1999, he formed an exploratory
committee for 2000, and the next day returned to Manchester for
an enthusiastic welcome by about 300 supporters to the familiar
chant of "Go Pat, Go." His theme was: "It is time to clean up all
that pollutes our culture, to call down the curtain on the sorry

Former Nixon speechwriter, TV commentator and columnist Pat Buchanan answers questions from listeners on a WGIR radio talk show in Manchester.

soap opera in the White House and restore dignity to our national stage."

As Liz Anderson wrote in the *Eagle Tribune*, "he promised to outlaw abortion, create a new tax code, put American products above imports, build up the military, cut foreign peacemaking efforts, hold the line on immigration, and eliminate affirmative action."

Several days later he appointed Shelly Uscinski, on a leave of absence as director of the New Hampshire Christian Coalition, as his state chairman. At a meeting in Concord, Pat told a small group of followers that in his previous campaigns the Republican establishment had not supported him and that they'd not do so this time because they didn't accept his views which "challenge vested interests tied together in Washington."

In mid-May he opened a campaign office in Manchester having assured his workers that "this time we're going to go all the way." When it was announced that the General Electric plant in Somersworth was planning layoffs, Pat showed up at the premises to blame NAFTA for causing manufacturing businesses to leave the USA due to regulations and taxes.

In June, he was down to single digits in the Republican polls and had distributed a fund-raising letter. He said he wasn't concerned about other better-financed competitors like Bush because they were not paying attention to saving American jobs or lowering the trade deficit. At the same time, he was aware that Ross Perot's Reform Party might accept him as their candidate, thus making available to him $12.6 million of federal campaign funds.

In July, he received 58 percent of the straw votes cast in a meeting of conservatives at the Hopkinton Fair Grounds. The next day as he and his wife, Shelley, rode on the Winnipesaukee Scenic Railroad he commented, "this is going to be a battle by February, just as it was the last time." In August, he finished fifth in the Iowa straw poll.

By September, his sister, Bay, a campaign advisor, admitted they were considering joining the Reform Party. On a WMUR-

TV talk show in Manchester Pat said he thought he could become the president by becoming the nominee of that party's ticket. He stressed his dissatisfaction with the Republican Party which he considered to be under the control of The New World Order crowd and stated, "I know the look of a stacked deck when I see one." He added that 90 percent of those who supported him in his previous two campaigns were encouraging him to leave the GOP.

On October 25th, Buchanan left the Republicans to join the Reformers, but the Reform Party was not recognized by New Hampshire's election law and thus shut him out of a place on the ballot for the 2000 primary election. There was a further local complication for Buchanan in New Hampshire because the national Reform Party was in dispute over voting rights with a breakaway group calling themselves the Granite State Reform Party, chaired by Shelly Uscinski, a Buchanan leader. The two local groups went their separate ways.

Shelly Uscinski said her breakaway group had been treated "like second-class citizens." The Reform party loyalists wanted to encourage other Reform candidates to get into the race for the presidential nomination, whereas the Buchananites were loyal only to him. Subsequently, the Federal Elections Commission held that Buchanan was the legitimate nominee of the Reform Party and entitled to the $12.6 million of federal matching funds.

When Pat returned to the state in mid-January of 2000 during his Reform Party campaign, he scorned both the Republican and Democratic Parties as "virtual Xerox copies. We have one-party government masquerading as a two-party system."

Buchanan lucked out by avoiding the 2000 New Hampshire

Fun along the Campaign Trail

In 1993, when the Republicans were boasting about their Big Tent, it was Pat Buchanan who advised, "When you stretch the tent too far the tent poles collapse."

primary; he received more money elsewhere. He built his case on the fact that neither the Republican nor Democratic Party any longer represented his principles.

Perhaps Pat did give up his lifelong identification as a Republican and obvious political strength in New Hampshire because he'd lost faith in them; or maybe it was because he received substantial funding from the Reform Party. It's a personal judgment call as to the real reason.

New Hampshire Republican Senator Robert "Bob" C. Smith

After two failed House campaigns, thereafter serving four terms in Congress and one term in the U.S. Senate, Senator Smith was reelected to a second Senate term ending in 2002, all as a Republican. Although it had been rumored, and Smith had previously told Washington columnist Bob Novak, it wasn't until August 25, 1997 at a Republican fundraiser in Manchester that Smith surprised the political community by saying he was considering a run for the presidency in 2000.

Two days later, in a conference call with New Hampshire journalists, Senator Smith said he planned to form an exploratory committee to consider being a candidate who would provide "inspirational leadership" in the Oval Office. He believed the country wanted someone with "integrity, character, values and principles they stick with."

It had been forgotten that in late December of 1993, Senator Smith had a similar thought when he announced he was prepared to run for the Oval Office in 1996. "If there is a sincere interest in me being a candidate for president, I would consider it. If things fell into place, it would be a great honor." He said then he'd received hundreds of letters "from almost every state in the union" over the previous two or three years asking if he'd consider undertaking such a campaign and "it is a thing that has some momentum."

Because there was much concern that his name on the primary ballot in 2000 might cause other potential candidates to skip the

New Hampshire primary, he was quick to say he would not run as a "favorite son. If I'm not a serious national candidate in a year or so, then I won't run, because then it would mess up the primary." Curiously enough, he had said precisely the same thing in 1993 about participating in the 1996 primary. There was also the prediction it would be "a grassroots campaign" as he was promising for 2000.

If he ran as a favorite son, it would be the first time the state ever had one on the Republican ticket. Even the *Manchester Union Leader,* which had twice endorsed him for the Senate in his previous campaigns, editorialized, "Wise old carpenters advise to measure twice, cut once. Senator Smith should think again, measure twice in effect before he commences to sawing on the presidential timber." From the tone of other local negative editorials which followed his making his plans known, the senator probably wouldn't have been a 'favorite' son anyway. Also, unlike Senator Bob Dole, he said he would not resign his Senate seat before campaigning for president.

By late September he had made visits to the caucus states of Louisiana, (where he had previously helped Phil Gramm) and Iowa. Smith had established his Live Free or Die PAC and raised $20,000. By November, the hometown papers remained unforgiving in their criticism. Mike Pride, editor of the *Concord Monitor* wrote: "There are plenty of candidates out there with views akin to yours and the ability to express them in a more politic and polished way. If you quit now, you'll be in a good position to influence your party's choice for the 2000 ticket." In a Manchester WMUR-TV poll he had placed sixth.

By the end of 1998, he said his PAC had raised close to $300,000, to "provide financial support to men and women across the country who will bring a high standard of personal character and conservative leadership back to public office." He also reported he'd canvassed Iowa for 45 days, more than any other candidate, and visited a total of 20 states.

The senator's stump speech contained the lines, "I'm a red-blooded American, I'm a country music Republican, not a country club Republican." He said there was a trending split between the traditional conservative GOPers and its social conservatives. He wanted to bring them together.

Previously having filed with the FEC, he announced, by a letter dated January 21, 1999, that he was running for president in 2000 with a unique fundraising approach. Smith offered stock certificates to "Invest in America" at a value of $20 each with a goal of selling one million shares. The *Concord Monitor* commented: "We'll give Smith's nascent candidacy this much: At $20 a share, he has priced his stock right. But even in a bull market, Smith for president is a bad investment."

David Yepsen of the *Des Moines Register* wrote, "Smith has a good message and put a lot of time into it. I'm not sure it's translating into a groundswell of conservative support for him."

In mid-February, Smith returned to the Kingswood Regional High School in Wolfeboro, where he had taught American History before becoming a politician, and gave a rousing speech to supporters and students while officially announcing his candidacy in friendly territory. Immediately after being elected, he promised he'd "send Congress a bill defining life as beginning at fertilization." The next day he was off again for another two-day tour of Iowa in his "Chart The Right Course for America" bus with emphasis on the Right. As the AP reported, he was unafraid to take a stand even if everyone else remained seated.

The senator also introduced the idea of a "Space Force" as perhaps a fifth military branch and to be controlled by friendly countries to challenge the existing earth-based paradigm. He admitted being criticized at a Republican meeting in California when he predicted the GOP would "fall into the ash bin of history" if it didn't make outlawing abortions its top priority.

By early May he had qualified for federal matching funds. He claimed to have raised $1 million in contributions and pledges, with his treasury growing at an average rate of $25,000 per day. He picked Judy Thayer, former state School Board Chairman, as

New Hampshire Senator Bob Smith with his wife and children announces his candidacy for president at Wolfeboro High School February 18, 1999.

his senior national policy adviser and New Hampshire chairman. Barbara Hagan, past president of the local Right to Life Committee, was in charge of office operations.

In mid-May the senator told the *Washington Times* that conservatives were considering leaving the Republican Party because it was not taking strong enough positions on such issues as abortion and the right to own guns. He viewed the GOP as a "charade." Further, he indicated that if a new party was formed, he would consider leading it. "If it happens, I'm not leaving my party—my party is leaving me. If you take the pro-life, pro-gun and Christian conservative people out of the Republican Party, well, you don't have a Republican Party."

On June 2nd, John DiStaso of the *Manchester Union Leader* reported that while Smith was not advocating a third party he had thought about starting one in front of Independence Hall in Philadelphia on July 4th. Meanwhile he had been approached by the Reform Party and was considering the nomination of the Libertarian or U.S. Taxpayer's parties because the GOP "has become the party of globalism and big money and elitists and special interests." He told DiStaso, "This is either history in the making or a career-ender. I'm not interested in a career. I've had my career. I'm interested in doing what's right for America."

Michael Powell, *Washington Post* staff writer, reported Smith was running about two percent in the national polls, but the CNN/ Gallup poll reported he had only one percent of Republican support.

At the New Hampshire Taxpayer's picnic in Hopkinton on the fourth of July the senator drew loud applause with the lines, "If you like me as senator, you're going to love me as president. I'm going to raise hell." The next day at Hesky Park in Meredith he said, "I've been a Republican all my life and I'm proud of it. I'm not proud to say we've walked away from certain issues."

Later in the week, he told some of his insiders that he would leave the Republican Party. It was rumored he'd join the U.S. Taxpayer's Party which had been founded by Howard Phillips and was considering a name change to the American Constitutional Party. Phillips was quoted, "Smith's willingness to burn his bridges in the Republican Party is a great testament to his commitment to principle."

After the news got around of the senator's possible abandonment of the Republican Party, New Hampshire's state GOP chairman, Steve Duprey, threatened it would be the end of Smith's Republican career if he later tried to be reelected to the Senate as a Republican. Republican National Committee Chairman, Jim Nicholson wrote Smith, "This would not be a case of the party leaving you, Bob, but rather of you leaving our party. I hope you do not confuse the success of our shared message with your own failure as its messenger."

On July 13th, he formally announced in a farewell speech on the floor of the Senate his withdrawal from the Republican Party to seek the presidency as an Independent, because the Republican Party had abandoned the conservative principles outlined in its platform. The Senate leadership had assured him retention of his chairmanship on the Ethics Committee and seniority on other Senate committees for the balance of his term even though he no longer belonged to the GOP.

While Smith did not indicate what party he would join to gain the presidency, he did say, "The Taxpayer's Party is much closer to me than any other party." On August 10th he confirmed he would seek that party's blessing and be a candidate for the nomination at its convention in St. Louis on September 4th.

Fun along the Campaign Trail

When Secretary of Labor Lynn Martin toured the state as a surrogate for George H.W. Bush, her handlers presented the local volunteer driver with a sheaf of instructions, including one which read: "The secretary is to be seated in the back seat opposite the driver. In transit, the radio must remain off and the policy on speaking is to speak when spoken to."

Meanwhile, Steve Duprey called the senator a mutineer "because Bob has abandoned our party, he is not to be invited to address any Republican event put on by a town, city, ward, county or state committee." The senator replied, "I had a 99.9 percent voting record of support for Republican leadership. It might be interesting to ask Duprey who the real traitors are." Smith closed his New Hampshire GOP presidential campaign office, dismissed its three employees and, although banned from continued participation in the Iowa Republican straw poll at Ames, nonetheless finished last with eight votes.

On August 18th at a "Politics and Eggs" breakfast speech in Bedford, Smith shifted gears again by disclosing he was not going to join the Taxpayer's Party after all, "I owe allegiance to the Constitution, not to any political party. I am an Independent." He said his wife, Mary Jo, had been hospitalized and possibly he'd give up presidential campaigning altogether.

On September 2nd, Karen Hickey, Smith's campaign press secretary, said Mary Jo had recovered and her boss was continuing his presidential campaign as an Independent. "He wants to give the American people a viable third choice." Smith also told the AP that if he lost, he'd consider running in 2002 for a third term in the Senate as an Independent.

On October 24th, Republican Senator John Chafee of Rhode Island, Chairman of the powerful Environment and Public Works Committee, died. As a nine-year member of the committee, Smith was next in line as its successor chairman, a position he could not fulfill as a registered Independent. Outside the Capitol Building in Washington four days later, after having reinvigorated his Independent campaign for nearly two months, Smith announced he was giving up all presidential aspirations for the year 2000.

In the interim, both Senate and New Hampshire Republican leaders had been soliciting his return to the GOP. He admitted his Independent campaign was running low, with only about $250,000 remaining, which might eventually be used on another run for president or for reelection to the Senate in 2002.

A week after Senator Chafee's death and the pending committee chairmanship, Smith announced, "I owe it to every conservative in America, and especially the people of New Hampshire, to
empower them in the United States Senate and it would be irre-
sponsible for me to delay this announcement" that he was renewing his membership in the Republican Party.

The next day, on the advice of GOP Majority Leader Trent
Lott, the members of the Environment and Public Works Committee elected him chairman. It was the first Senate major
chairmanship granted to a New Hampshire senator since Styles
Bridges was chairman of Appropriations in 1953. Ironically, he
had been able to retain his chairmanship of the Ethics Committee even while being an Independent, as it is not a major committee and its membership is traditionally divided evenly between the
two major parties.

Smith had gone full circle from his July resignation speech in
the Senate when he alleged, "The party platform is not worth the
paper it is written on." He now felt Republicans had been "wonderful" in welcoming him back and confirmed his intention to
run in 2002 for his third term in the Senate, but the media did not
review kindly his political escapades.

David Nyhan, writing in the *Boston Globe,* said of him, "You
pretend to be an oak-hearted solon in the mold of Daniel Webster.
Let us hope as well. But off your recent record, when push comes
to shove, yours is a heart of oaf." After Smith had apologized for
leaving the party and hoped they'd forgive him by the time of the
next election, the *Lawrence Eagle Tribune* predicted, "unfortunately
for him, that hasn't yet proved to be the case."

Back in New Hampshire, campaigning to keep his Senate seat

Fun along the Campaign Trail

**Mike Barnicle, columnist for the *Boston Globe,* commenting on
the presidential primary, wrote, "Some who live here (in New
Hampshire) take hours to watch *Sixty Minutes* on television."**

for another term beginning in 2002, 'Born-again Republican' Smith consistently repented, "I made a mistake and I admit it. I thought the best way to fight for conservative principles was to leave the party. I was wrong. It was a bad mistake."

Bob reactivated his previously effective fundraising vehicle, the "250 Club," and brought Bob Goodman, a longtime Republican political activist, on board as his Finance Director, and set sail for the year 2002. But he was defeated for that third-term Senate seat in the New Hampshire Republican primary by Congressman John E. Sununu. Smith still professed loyalty to President Bush, the probable Republican flag-bearer for 2004, but turned down the president's invitation to join with him at a Sununu Republican Party dinner after the primary.

Probably Senator Smith's flirtation with the vision of being president was more motivated by vanity than reality, thus an impossible quest. While it could not have happened without a lot of money, it wouldn't have happened even with it. This offbeat experience was a curious flight of fantasy which defies categorization.

For whatever reason, in mid-May of 2003, following eight months of political silence, he returned to Manchester for a well-attended dinner of enthusiastic supporters honoring his 18 years of elective Congressional office. Although he did not indicate any future political plans, he did reflect on "people who you thought were your friends who aren't your friends and who stabbed you in the back."

On the same occasion, Smith announced he was establishing The American Patriot Foundation to benefit families with lost or injured members resulting from war. It would provide such services as scholarships, health insurance, job training and other needs which they might have. Shortly thereafter Smith affirmed he had a new job as a real estate specialist selling expensive homes in Sarasota, Florida.

❋

Chapter 9

The Hare and the Tortoise I
Ten Candidates Who Did Not Finish the 2000 Race

A S IN LAMAR ALEXANDER'S CASE (see chapter 5), there is no question the need to raise funds is a substantial challenge for anyone who does not have the financial wherewithal. Consequently, it's assumed every potential aspirant is aware of that compulsion before planning an exploratory tour at the home of the nation's first primary. Although not mentioned, when a candidate withdraws from a race, there are usually other reasons motivating the decision. Lack of funds can sometimes serve as a convenient excuse.

Tennessee Republican Governor Lamar Alexander

One might even question Alexander's concern about funding as the real reason for his not filing in the 2000 campaign if you take into consideration he had previously suffered the calamitous experience of running the course in 1996. Nonetheless he still returned to spark another effort by a three-day visit in the fall of 1997. It included a hiking tour of the Presidential Range with John Harrigan, publisher of the *Colebrook Sentinel* and dinner with his North Country supporters. He said at the time, "I may be a candidate but it's too early to make those decisions."

Alexander, however, did return in 1999 and with Tom Rath again as his chairman, began a campaign for the 2000 primary. But he did not go the distance, and withdrew in advance of the filing period. At that time he said the effort required for fundraising

Former Tennessee Governor Lamar Alexander answers New Hampshire Statehouse reporters' questions.

made it impractical for him to continue. Rath subsequently signed on as a spokesman for the George Bush campaign.

Missouri Republican Senator John Ashcroft

Senator John Ashcroft and his wife first showed up in New Hampshire on an early August weekend of 1997 to address the New Hampshire Auto Dealers Association, yet he used the occasion to hold a closed-door session with GOP conservative activists. He returned to address a fundraiser for the Conservative Political Victory Fund in mid-February of 1998, when he was quoted as saying he was "still seriously considering" running for president in 2000.

Previously, he had been raising funds for his PAC, "Spirit of America," by sending fundraising solicitations to small donors and attending major fundraising dinners around the country. He had seized upon the Clinton/Lewinsky relationship as a good campaign issue.

In August, the Ashcrofts took a four-day tour of the Granite State and released a proposed Economic Proposal, "A New Beginning," which included conclusions from conversations with people nationwide including "the hardhats and supervisors at the Anheuser-Busch Brewery in Merrimack, New Hampshire."

While on the campaign trail he addressed the state's GOP Convention and distributed pro-family videos. Perhaps, more importantly, he had formally endorsed several candidates in the state's local primary including Jay Lucas, one of five Republican candidates for governor. Kevin Landrigan, a reporter for the *Nashua Telegraph*, had commented, the "risk may be worth it if Lucas wins." He did!

The *Manchester Union Leader* was somewhat stronger about the Lucas endorsement saying, "We don't know that we have ever seen a presidential primary hopeful so clueless as to meddle in a state primary election. A U.S. senator from far away who presumes to know enough to choose among many hopefuls is extremely arrogant or just fishing for payback votes or both. In any case, it is a dumb thing to do." The paper had endorsed a Lucas opponent.

In September, Ashcroft's American Values PAC began spending $90,000 for TV advertising on WMUR and cable to plug his Economic Plan. As California was in the process of moving its date up in March, he reacted, "A good bit of what propels people in California is their performance (the candidates) in New Hampshire. So I think . . . New Hampshire will be even more important because they will launch the momentum in California." In October, Ashcroft appointed Dean Dexter, a former New Hampshire legislator and congressional candidate, as the New Hampshire Director of the American Values PAC.

On January 5, 1999, after more than a year of shaking hands here, he formally announced he would not run for president in 2000. Instead he would concentrate on being reelected to the U.S. Senate for a second term. He was to have been opposed for his Senate seat by the then Democratic Missouri Governor Mel Carnahan who was considered to be moderate in comparison to the conservative stance of Republican Ashcroft. Subsequently, Carnahan was killed in a plane crash. Carnahan's wife defeated Ashcroft for the Senate seat and Ashcroft was appointed by President Bush to be U.S. Attorney General.

After Ashcroft's departure from the New Hampshire race, pollster Dick Bennett of the American Research Group said, "For someone who spent a significant amount on television advertising, he didn't benefit from that very much." Dean Dexter, Ashcroft's paid consultant, remarked, "He (Ashcroft) wasn't making much headway at all. He wasn't up here much and he really wasn't doing anything."

It's anybody's guess. Was it worry about a poorly run presidential campaign or a revival of interest in keeping his Senate seat that caused Ashcroft to withdraw from seeking the Oval Office? It was fortuitous circumstance that he eventually ended up as the nation's top law enforcement officer.

Missouri Democratic Congressman Dick Gephardt

Gephardt had run in the 1988 New Hampshire primary and ended up second after Michael Dukakis. As Minority Leader in the U.S. House of Representatives, he returned in March of 1997. He told the press he was "looking at what we are doing right now. The future will take care of itself. No decisions right now." He said he was a recruiter for candidates to challenge the state's two Republican office holders in the House, Congressmen Sununu and Bass. He congratulated Democrats Joe Keefe and Arnie Arnesen, who had failed in "very difficult" congressional state primary races the previous year.

The congressman returned a second time in May, and said he still had not made a decision on running for president in 2000. On a third visit, at a meeting in Goffstown in late September, he told a class at St. Anselm College, "My mother once told me . . . when I would be asking things about the future, 'Dick, only cross one bridge at a time and deal with what is in front of you.' The bridge we are on is '98." On a third visit, in March of 1998, he again gave no firm indication that he'd file in 2000.

On several subsequent return trips to the state, the congressman once more tirelessly promoted his party and its local candidates for the 1998 mid-term New Hampshire state and congressional elections without predicting his own personal agenda. His Democratic Congressional Campaign Committee contributed more than $80,000 to the local Democratic cause. Because he was simultaneously traveling the country on the same mission, it was assumed his motivation had been to bolster stronger support for the Democrats and possible control of the House.

The evidence appears to prove that Gephardt never seriously intended to undertake a presidential campaign in 2000. Having by-passed the 2000 primary, it was assumed Gephardt might try again in 2004.

In June and December of 2001 and March of 2002, Gephardt returned to the state to rally support for both local and national

Missouri Representative Richard Gephardt speaks to a crowd of neighbors in front of the home of long-time state and local office-holder and current state senator, Lou D'Allesandro, in Manchester during a campaign house party.

Democratic candidates in their forthcoming elections. Specifically, he endorsed Governor Shaheen for the U.S. Senate, Katrina Swett and Martha Fuller Clark for the U.S. House and John Kacavas for the Executive Council.

On visits after the state's 2002 primary he added state Senate nominees Joe Foster, Maggie Wood Hassan and George Disnard to his list of beneficiaries. At the same time he supported the president's action in seeking U.N. approval before attacking Iraq, and took positions in favor of tax credits for college tuition, reimbursing prescription drug costs and against privatizing Social Security.

On each visit he made clear his "focus now is winning the House back in the year 2002. I have been focused on that and working on that for about five years now." If he was successful in that mission it was assumed he might become majority leader or even the speaker of the House. In light of this possibility, he would probably wait until after the general election that year before making any decision about seeking the presidency in 2004. Nine days before the November general election he returned again to lead the troops, and accused the Republicans of deregulating American business by allowing "the crooks to virtually take $5 trillion of investment that people had in this country and steal it."

After the national sweep by the Republicans in the 2002 general election, the congressman announced he was stepping down as House Democratic Leader saying, "We need to evaluate what we've been doing and what our vision is and what our ideas are and what our thinking is." Roger Simon, political correspondent of *U.S. News & World Report* had previously written, "Just about everyone in Democratic politics knows that Gephardt is going to run for president next year."

On January 6, 2003, the congressman filed a presidential exploratory committee, stating he offered "a different direction for our domestic, economic and national security polices." He noted that since 1985, "I've been coming back in every election since then trying to help people run for the House and Senate and other offices." In mid-February, he formally announced his candidacy, saying the United States should be less dependent on Middle East oil and in opposition to free-trade initiatives. Even though Gephardt had originally backed legislation giving the president power to attack Iraq if necessary, the congressman said it was too early to commit that he'd support the president if he decided to attack Iraq without United Nations approval. At the same time, he ridiculed Bush's "cowboy talk." At the close of the Iraq invasion he admitted the planning strategy had been good but that there was no plan to back it up. He called it "phony macho business" for Bush to taunt the discontents of the aftermath to "bring 'em on."

He said health care was his top priority and favored universal health insurance. His plan would give employers a 60 percent tax credit for the health insurance they buy for their employees, which would be financed by abolishing the tax cuts the Bush administration had granted to high income individuals and corporations. If an employer provided no health coverage, the credit would go directly to the employee. He said the state of New Hampshire would be eligible for similar grants. The congressman's son, Matt, who himself was a childhood cancer survivor, visited the state in support of his father's health plan.

At the same time, the government would pay off student loans for those who would work in targeted districts. "This is an opportunity to spread universal democratic values across the entire world." The congressman also attacked Bush's 'No Child Left Behind' law with a statement, "It's been a great slogan but a failed policy. There's nothing behind the slogan."

The congressman took pride in saying, "I'm the one who led the fight against NAFTA and my own president." In return for his lifelong support of labor he received several labor union endorsements, including Jimmy Hoffa and the Teamsters Union. He also advocated an international minimum wage with an end to slave labor.

At the close of the Iraq War, the congressman faulted Bush, saying the president "was handed the best economy we've had in

50 years. He came in and squandered the surplus." By contrast, Gephardt promised to stand for fiscal responsibility. "It's time to throw the money-changers out of the temple and have a president who will do the right things for the environment and for this country." He also disagreed with Bush's support for oil drilling in Alaska and the president's rejection of the Kyoto treaty on global warming. The president was criticized for "trying to blame intelligence problems on the CIA."

Nebraska Democratic Senator Robert Kerrey

Senator Bob Kerrey visited New Hampshire at the end of October in 1997. In 1992, he had run here and finished a poor third behind Tsongas and Clinton, but gave no indication he would try again in 2000. He came again in January of 1998 in tribute to Portsmouth's former Mayor Eileen Foley and in March to help raise money for local Democrats. Also, as head of the Democratic Senatorial Campaign Committee, he talked with Democrat George Condodemetraky who was planning to run against incumbent Republican Senator Judd Gregg.

Steve Jarding, his national political director, said, "Here we are two years out and Bob's been here three times (since October) and he'll be back many more times." As for himself, Kerrey told the press that "people who finish third have no chance of winning the nomination" and that the New Hampshire primary was the most important one. "Back in '91 or '92 I made an impulsive decision with an insufficient amount of preparation and it showed. It showed here and it showed elsewhere."

By his sixth trip in August, Kerrey said he'd make up his mind on running for president in December or January. Jarding observed that Kerrey had tried to visit the state once a month in contrast to 1992 when he got into the race just four months before New Hampshire's primary. Jeff Woodburn, the state's Democratic Chairman, noted, "He's been working it hard, been back a lot." By October, Kerrey had set up a Manchester office for his political action committee.

Congressional Medal of Honor recipient and Nebraska senator, Bob Kerrey speaks to reporters just after filing his declaration of candidacy papers at the Statehouse.

It was on December 13, 1998 in Omaha that Kerrey formally announced he would not seek the White House in 2000. Steve Bouchard who was the state director of Kerrey's PAC, Building America's Conscience, had attended the closure session and reported that while many supporters didn't want him to quit the presidential race, others were concerned with his no longer serving as their senator, particularly the Nebraska farmers.

As was the case with Congressman Gephardt, it probably wasn't a lack of funding which discouraged Kerrey; rather it was perhaps rethinking the mistakes of his 1992 venture in New Hampshire which kept him from filing again in 2000.

It should be noted that Kerrey also announced in April of 2001 that he did not intend to run for president in 2004.

Massachusetts Democratic Senator John Kerry

Gerald F. Seib, *Wall Street Journal* political columnist, wrote in late 1997 that Senator Kerry was "thinking of running for president in 2000." He pointed out that Kerry's wife, Teresa Heinz, had "an enormous personal fortune that just might help finance a run." He did not make note of an approximately $500,000 deficit from Kerry's 1996 reelection campaign against Massachusetts Governor William F. Weld.

The senator was highly decorated for service in Vietnam, earning three Purple Hearts and the Silver Star. After returning home, he later participated in demonstrations against the war.

In March of 1998, Kerry got off to a bad start in New Hampshire when, allegedly, he tentatively agreed to attend a St. Patrick's Day breakfast and a flag day event, both by invitation from the Manchester Democratic City Chairman, Ray Buckley. Apparently due to a misunderstanding, Kerry did not show upon either occasion. In October, the *Boston Globe* announced Kerry was planning a trip to the state to promote local Democrats, but Kerry had not so advised Buckley. Buckley's comment: "If this is the way he is kicking off his presidential campaign, I don't think the others have much to worry about."

Kerry made several trips north of the border in 1998 and admitted they were for the purpose of testing the water of his neighboring state for a possible Oval Office run in 2000. At a meeting in November he said he'd make a final decision in January or February of 1999 and, "I don't find doors slamming shut." Finally in late February of 1999 he bowed out.

One of the reasons the senator gave for withdrawing was the extraordinary demands of fundraising and the need to raise between fifteen and twenty million dollars by year-end. He apparently didn't know how Gary Hart did it. He also mentioned that defeating Al Gore in the race would pose some problems.

Considering his wife's wealth and her contacts, it's unlikely money was the principal reason that kept Kerry out of the 2000 presidential race. More likely the challenge of beating Gore was a much greater frustration. After Gore's nomination Kerry led a delegation of Massachusetts mayors for house-to-house canvassing for Gore in Nashua. Having by-passed the 2000 primary, it was assumed Kerry, like Gephardt, might try again in 2004.

While saying he was focusing on his own 2002 reelection campaign, the Massachusetts senator made several political appearances in New Hampshire during 2001. He raised money for and endorsed local democratic candidates, made a symbolic stop at a firehouse and addressed an AFL–CIO convention. In July, Ray Buckley, then the New Hampshire House Deputy leader, said, "Right now the frontrunner (for 2004) is clearly John Kerry." Kerry returned in March of 2002 to address the Democratic "100" Club dinner and attacked Republican leaders. He came again in July to assist congressional candidates Martha Fuller Clark and Katrina Swett, saying he was "looking at" 2004. In September, he returned to support state Senate candidate Dennis Kalob.

On an October visit, as a three-time Purple Heart recipient from the Vietnam War, he plugged veterans issues, saying, "We need to keep faith in our veterans in this country." Later in the month he was advocating prescription drug benefits from Medi-

Massachusetts Senator John Kerry conducting a person-to-person campaign with voters at the Peterborough library, the nations's oldest public library.

care and opposing privatization of Social Security. He also said, "If we really want to bring Saddam to his knees, we should send over the Bush economic team." After winning his fourth term as a Massachusetts senator by 81 percent of the vote, Kerry returned in November to address veterans in Nashua.

It should also be noted that Melissa Robinson of the Associated Press reported in January of 2002 that, "Kerry is aggressively preparing for a possible run for the 2004 Democratic presidential nomination, raising millions of dollars, hiring staffers and consultants with national experience, traveling and launching a new website."

She also wrote that the senator and his wife had decided in 2000 that it would then have been inappropriate to use their own money for a presidential campaign. It was later disclosed that his wife's (formerly Teresa Heinz) estimated fortune of $550 million or more could not be tapped directly for his campaign anyway under Federal Elections Commission rules, except for her personal donation of $2,000.

Finally, in early December of 2002, the senator filed with the Federal Elections Committee to organize a national campaign. He said, "I believe my war record and the time I've spent in the military give me an insight to some of the choices we face that is different from some of my colleagues." He disagreed with Bush's policies on taxation, education, Iraq and North Korea, saying the president should work more closely with our allies, China, Japan and South Korea. Later, at an address in Hanover, Kerry endorsed universal health care and renewable energy as primary issues.

He opposed drilling for oil in the Arctic National Wildlife Refuge. Rather, he would promote the development of alternative fuels to reduce dependency on foreign oil. "We spend $1.8 billion in subsidies for oil and gas . . . and only $24 million for alternative and renewable energy." Kerry believed finding new sources of energy would create millions of new jobs. "I'm here to make a pledge to replace the 2.7 million jobs this president (Bush) has lost. I will replace those jobs in the first 500 days of my administration." His plan would include federal work programs in school and road construction.

Following prostate surgery in early 2003, Kerry was back on the campaign trail attacking Bush on a wide range of issues, from the lagging stock market, rising crime rates and dwindling budget surplus to increasing health care costs and inadequate prescription drug coverage. His health care plan included having the federal government pay 75 percent of the cost for laid off workers and costs for catastrophic health care above $5,000 a year. He would fully fund special education, introduce school breakfasts and reestablish the arts in public schools. Asked about those people worried about his not having a prostate, he replied, "The problem is we've had too many Republican presidents without a heart."

Satirically he commented, "Just because the Supreme Court made the wrong choice for president doesn't mean that America has to live with it for another six years." Saying Bush was "frozen in the ice of indifference," Kerry called upon him to release oil from the Northeast Home Heating Reserve to counter increasing oil prices in New England.

The senator described Bush's budget as "the most disgraceful example of reverse Robin Hood I've ever seen." Also, just as the Iraq War was getting underway, he said, "It will take years to repair the needless damage done by this administration, damage to our international standing and moral leadership, to traditional and time-tested alliances, to our relations with the Arab world, ultimately to ourselves. The nation with the strongest military on earth should not have the weakest diplomacy in history." He received loud Republican protest for suggesting that in Iraq a "regime change" was needed for Saddam Hussein, but one was also needed in the United States.

Kerry was against vouchers and building charter schools, preferring instead that the money be used to fix public schools. He also took a broad stand against special interests because in his four senatorial elections he "never took a dime of PAC or soft money." At the same time he claimed the Bush administration was damaging the environment. Kerry said he would create a new enforcement office within the Environmental Protection Agency and propose "Environmental Empowerment Zones" to assist minority communities to fight pollution.

The senator attacked Bush's proposed tax cuts as a "cheap political trick" which would primarily benefit the wealthy. He claimed, "The bottom 60 percent of taxpayers get less than one percent of the benefits. He would repeal all tax cuts except those applying to the middle class, "the working people of America who deserve to have money put in their pocket so we can start the economy moving again." The top 20 percent get 94 percent of the benefits and the top one percent get 54 percent of the benefits." At the same time he did not favor the administration's plan of lowering taxes on dividends or capital gains. Nor did he agree that any of the president's proposed tax reforms would create new jobs. He supported legislation to provide 100,000 new jobs for firefighters.

Addressing a labor convention in North Conway, Kerry charged the Bush administration as being "out to stop organized labor." He presented his "payroll tax holiday," whereby no Social Security or Medicare tax would be levied on the first $10,000 of a worker's income for one year, and which could be extended.

Before veterans' posts and students at his alma mater, St. Paul's School in Concord, he spelled out extensive proposals for student community service, including a federally-funded plan whereby all public high school students, to qualify for a diploma, would first be obliged to take a locally created civics course. Also suggested was a four-year federal college tuition grant for students who would volunteer for two years of community service. The Peace Corps would be expanded and government aid would not be given to colleges which prohibited ROTC programs.

The senator also faulted the president for cutting back on AmeriCorps, saying, "He (Bush) is choosing to give the wealthiest Americans a tax cut at the expense of service." The senator said there were not enough U.S. troops in Iraq to rehabilitate the country. He would ask NATO and the U.N. to provide more military support for that purpose.

Following the lead of rival former Governor Dean, Kerry used the Internet for collecting petitions. The senator opposed what he claimed was Bush's "sneak attack on basic worker rights" by promoting a change in overtime standards. He said even firemen and policemen might not be able to collect time-and-a-half pay when they work over 40 hours.

Minnesota Democratic Senator Paul Wellstone

Senator Wellstone first staked out the 2000 New Hampshire possibility in early November 1997 with his friendly conception that "New Hampshire . . . has a healthy skepticism of anything too big, big government, big corporations, big everything." He said he was serious about running and otherwise wouldn't have come. "You don't want to take up a lot of people's time."

In late April of the following year, he came again, promoting his familiar theme of representing "the Democratic wing of the Democratic Party" and adding, "I will say I'm optimistic and determined." He was back again in June and December. Democratic State Chairmen Jeff Woodburn viewed all his effort: "He's comfortable being an underdog, and he relishes the fight."

On January 9, 1999, Wellstone gave up his bid for the White House, writing his constituents, "I could not become a candidate due mainly to chronic back problems and to a growing realization that I could not represent the people of my state in the Senate as vigorously as I felt I must while running for president." He had undergone successful surgery a year earlier for a ruptured disk from college wrestling days. Nonetheless Wellstone subsequently did revisit two more times to speak on behalf of Senator Bradley in the campaign against Vice President Gore.

It was obvious that the senator never really had sufficient motivation or the physical stamina to repeat again in New Hampshire the arduous campaign exercise which had worked for him in

Minnesota. Unfortunately he died while seeking his third term as a U.S. senator.

Republican Elizabeth Dole

By way of background it should be noted that Elizabeth Dole's husband, former Senator Robert Dole, had been a contestant in the New Hampshire presidential primaries in 1980, 1988 and 1996. She had frequently appeared with him during those earlier campaigns. When asked if his wife would participate on her own in 2000, her husband said he could not speak for her. On October 21, 1998, she came to New Hampshire by herself to endorse Jay Lucas, a candidate for governor.

In November of that year, the Doles sent Thanksgiving greeting cards to New Hampshire political activists. By year-end, a group from Elizabeth Dole's native state of North Carolina had begun a draft to entice her into the 2000 presidential race. It included former North Carolina Governor Jim Holshouser and Earl Cox, who was already scouting for her in New Hampshire.

In early January of 1999, Dole announced she was leaving her position as head of the American Red Cross to consider a run for the White House. On February 8th she was the featured speaker at the nonpartisan annual dinner of the Manchester Chamber of Commerce. Her topic was supposed to have been 'volunteerism.' She had been invited to attend in October, thus well before her retirement from the Red Cross.

Sarah Koenig, reporting for the *Concord Monitor*, wrote "It would have taken a detective to follow the volunteerism theme woven throughout her references to North Korea, taxes, cocaine cartels, military spending and the now tarnished presidency." Mark Hamilton, vice president of the Chamber, summarized it as being "a little more political than most people thought it was going to be. Maybe I was naive." Dole admitted she was assessing and exploring, but she did not announce her candidacy.

The following morning at an "invitation only" breakfast at the Bedford Inn, Dole was the beneficiary of "sign-up cards" on the

Elizabeth Dole campaigns at the popular New Hampshire International Speedway, prior to withdrawing her candidacy for the New Hampshire primary.

tables. Speaking to the audience, she said, "If you're ready to sign up to be on the team, I would love to know that and to have your phone number so I could call you."

In March, at a professionally scripted appearance and speech to potential supporters at C.R. Sparks restaurant, she allowed, "I'm not a politician . . . and that may be a plus these days." A 30-minute TV commercial had also been running, yet she had still not declared herself a formal candidate.

On April 20, she mailed a widely distributed letter to Republicans soliciting funds for her exploratory committee which read, "if I run." At the same time she picked Jesse Devitte, Chairman of the New Hampshire Software Association, to head her local organization along with an impressive leadership team, and planned to open offices in Manchester and Concord. When she spoke with student groups in May, she was enthusiastically welcomed, but adults did not warm up to her suggested restrictions on firearms.

The *Keene Sentinel* editorialized, "Elizabeth Dole is not yet a declared candidate for president, and she may not become one. The stir she has already caused by taking a few perfectly reasonable positions is casting a cold light on the Republican nomination process."

In early June, another letter went out which read, "I'm leaning strongly toward becoming an official candidate for president and your advice and support will help me decide." Needless to say it included a return envelope with a gentle reminder that "I need to raise approximately $20 million in the next ten months." There had also been an appeal for funds from husband, Bob. Unfortunately Bob had upset some people with his concurrent TV advertising for Viagra.

In mid-June, speaking before the Seacoast Board of Realtors in Portsmouth, still undecided about entering the fray, Dole said, "Why would I want to undertake this arduous process of running for president? I think America is ready for a woman leader, and I believe I can bring something to the table with my experience."

By July, the media began bugging her at every stop about her New Hampshire polling results, which showed that Bush had achieved a 36 point lead over her as opposed to the deadlock which separated them at the beginning of the year. Also, she had raised only $3.5 million through the first six months of 1999 versus Bush's $40 million. Not discouraged, she felt it was so early that less than five percent of the voters were then focused on the primary and she was not distracted by polling or dollar figures.

In August, after a third-place finish in an Iowa straw poll behind the better funded Bush and Forbes, Dole's New Hampshire campaign was energized. She told the press, "I'll demonstrate that the candidate with the most experience is more qualified than the candidates with the most money." It also generated another fund-raising letter which read, "As I prepare to make my formal official announcement as a candidate for president...."

Her's was a stepped-up campaign schedule in the fall, yet still with no declaration of candidacy. A letter dated October 16, paid for by the Elizabeth Dole Exploratory Committee, was individually addressed to potential Dole supporters asking for the customary assistance of volunteers at headquarters, phone callers, sign placements, use of bumper stickers and hosts for home receptions.

Suddenly and totally unanticipated, just four days later in Washington, Elizabeth Dole announced she was withdrawing from the race—a race she had never formally entered! Jackie Calmes reported in the *Wall Street Journal* that Dole had "scheduled a formal announcement of her candidacy for November 7th."

On January 4, 2000, Dole endorsed Bush and actively joined his campaign. Even though she had not filed as a candidate for the February 1st primary, she received 231 Republican write-in votes and 9,547 write-ins for vice president.

Why the change of plans only three months before the votes would have been cast? Was it a lack of funds? Maybe. Was it the polls? Perhaps. Or, was it a strategy for the possibility of being chosen as vice president by George Bush? If it was, it didn't work.

Ohio Republican Congressman John R. Kasich

As early as March of 1997, Eric Pianin, reporting in the *Washington Post*, wrote that party officials were speculating that Kasich would run in 2000 and that he "won't deny his presidential ambitions, but he does little to discourage speculation." In April he showed up as the guest speaker at a Lincoln Day Dinner in Milford.

Beginning in February of the following year, he became a frequent visitor who would spend several days at a time in the state and was much in demand to address Republican events. At that time he said the only restraints on his decision concerned his job as chairman of the House Budget Committee and money.

The congressman created the Pioneer PAC which mailed solicitation letters to raise funds, not for him but rather to help elect "candidates who understand the need for government to help lead the way with a strong economic agenda." It contributed $10,000 to New Hampshire Republican Senate candidates. On June 29, 1998 he was the first candidate to sign the Iowa/New Hampshire pledge that he would not enter the Delaware primary. In December, in an interview with *Manchester Union Leader* reporter John Toole, Kasich said he was increasingly optimistic about running and that he had received a great response from potential New Hampshire supporters.

In February of 1999, he filed with the Federal Elections Commission for an Exploratory Committee, and noted he'd need about $18.5 million to finance a national campaign. Talking with Kevin Landrigan of the *Nashua Telegraph,* the congressman told it like it was: "I'm not a famous kid. I'm not a millionaire's son. I think we'll get the money. It's like this. If Jimmy Carter and Bill Clinton never had tried to beat the odds like I am now, they would never have been elected." He told Jim Abrams of the AP, "The beauty of this system is that you can go to Iowa and New Hamp-

Ohio Representative John Kasich takes time off from his campaign schedule to get a haircut in Milford at a popular barbershop for politicians.

shire, and that's where people smell you, they poke you, they look you in the eye."

Kasich continued getting a good press with his grassroots rounds of the Granite State, sampling everything from sled dog racing in the winter to tapping the maples in the spring and fly-fishing in the summer. In mid-April, at a neighborhood meeting in the home of Bob and Howie Coffey at Newmarket, while the congressman was still an undeclared candidate, his press secretary, Todd Harris, commented: "If you elect your president by television commercials, you never know the measure of that individual. But if you elect him on the basis of meeting him in your living room, you have a better chance of knowing the man who will lead you."

Linda Kaiser's 13-year-old Shetland sheepdog, Magic, was killed when she ran over him as she hurriedly backed from her driveway to get last minute supplies for a coffee reception in her Amherst home to introduce the congressman. Time was pressing; she was hysterical. She covered the dog's body, and placed him in the barn. When Kasich arrived and learned of the tragedy, he suggested canceling the coffee. Linda, despite her tears, said, "No." When the guests had left, Kasich stayed. "I'm not leaving here without burying this dog," and he did. Days later Linda was quoted in the press, "I don't know if I would see the other candidates doing that. When you watch them on television, they always seem so busy. He wasn't too busy."

On the campaign trail Kasich almost never talked about his funding base, but in May he did tell the Associated Press, "I believe that raising money for me, and staying alive in this campaign will be hand-to-mouth." He added that he was trying to conserve his money to spend on TV and mass media for use closer to the 2000 primary election day in February. By July, in sounding his familiar theme of needing "to run the country from the bottom up, from our families and communities to the top, rather than people from a faraway place giving us orders," Kasich had spent more days in the state than the combined visits of all of his major potential competitors.

It was July 14th when the Congressman finally threw in the towel, making him the first of 12 potential major aspirants in the Republican Party to quit the race. Simultaneously he announced he would be working for George W. Bush and would not run again for his seat in the House. Ironically, New Hampshire Congressman Charles Bass, a member of Kasich's House Budget Committee, had been an initial supporter of competitor Governor Bush, which had been a disappointment to fellow Congressman Kasich.

Because Kasich said he would travel the country for Bush and no longer be in the Congress, some pundits predicted he would end up in the White House if there were a Bush win. Alan Keyes, a competitive candidate for the presidency, maybe believed Kasich's campaign had been planned as sort of a stalking horse for Bush from its inception when Keyes made the remark, "Plants are things that don't grow only on trees."

Kasich had been low in the polls and believed the lesson learned from New Hampshire voters to be, "We love you, but it's not your time." He had raised $1.7 million, much of it contributed in his last Congressional race. New Hampshire Republican Party Chairman Steve Duprey commented, "Money and polls have never cast a single vote. I think it's way too early for anyone to decide to opt out."

Duprey might have also noted that during the past century no sitting House member has ever made it to the presidency. Those who have tried include: Jack Kemp, Richard Gephardt, Phil Crane, Morris Udall, Paul McCloskey, John Ashbrook and Wilbur Mills.

As with the case of Elizabeth Dole, what was the real reason Kasich withdrew his bid for the White House? Money, low polls or a chance for a better job than being a congressman?

It should be noted that after Bush became president, Kasich

did not serve in the White House; rather he became a successful lobbyist in Washington.

Former Republican Vice President James Danforth Quayle

After President Bush's defeat in 1992, Quayle considered running for president in 1996, but cited family reasons for not doing it. In January 1997, at a seacoast Chamber of Commerce dinner, former Vice President Dan Quayle told the press he would make no announcement before 1999 as to whether he would seek the presidency in 2000.

Later at a Manchester GOP dinner in October, he appeared to be warming up when he issued a challenge to Vice President Al Gore to "come to New Hampshire and let us debate the issue of family values. I very well may run in 2000." He distributed a fund solicitation letter, dated December 3, 1997, on behalf of the National Right to Work Legal Defense Foundation with an attack on Big Labor.

Both Quayle and his wife Marilyn made frequent appearances in the state during 1998 and 1999. Sometimes she went solo. The Quayles used some tours to endorse or fundraise for local candidates such as Jay Lucas for governor, Tom Colantuono for Executive Council, Mary Brown and David Wheeler for the Senate and Tim McGough for state representative. The Bush/Quayle Alumni Association with its Alumni Directory was a novel approach to raise money and enlist old friends from the Bush presidency.

The former vice president also established a PAC, Campaign America, and chose Attorney Ovide Lamontagne, ex-chairman of the New Hampshire Board of Education, as head of the New Hampshire chapter and campaign manager. Often he was accompanied by former Governor John Sununu, his national cochairman, whom he credited as "an adviser, a friend, a confidant ever since we worked together in the White House." A campaign office was operating in Manchester.

On February 11, 1999, Quayle announced the forming of a

Former Vice President Dan Quayle greets onlookers at a Milford parade. Such parades are important campaign stops for presidential hopefuls.

presidential exploratory committee, "I've been working my heart out for the Republicans and the Republican Party, and now it's my turn." He admitted he was not well prepared to be vice president under Bush but that he was now up to the top job. "When John Sununu and I were there, we were fighting for ordinary Americans and for the rank and file. He can tell you and I will tell you the battles we had within that administration. We were fighting for those outside even though we were on the inside."

Quayle took a position in a local tax controversy which raged around a decision of the New Hampshire Supreme Court regarding education. In July he assisted the New Hampshire Republican State Committee by authorizing a fundraising solicitation letter on its behalf. By August a New Hampshire poll had him at two percent.

Although finishing eighth in the Iowa straw polls, he continued to be confident, saying, "It's not a make or break for me," and he'd stay in the race "all the way to New Hampshire." Often references were made to Governor Bush's remarkable ability to raise money, but Quayle seldom alluded to his own less successful fundraising prowess and never used it as an excuse for the apparent popularity gap between them. Instead he stuck to his issues.

On September 5th at the Hopkinton Fair, the former vice president told the media, "New Hampshire is number one. We're going to make an extraordinary effort here." Four days later, Adam Nagourney writing in the *New York Times* said, "Some of Mr. Quayle's aides have quit for other campaigns, his old friends from the White House privately describe his presidential ambitions as hopeless."

In Dover shortly thereafter, Quayle was quoted, "I haven't been here as much as I'm going to be," and advised he had enough money for the New Hampshire primary in February with the further hope that more would come thereafter for an effort in the March California primary.

In Phoenix on September 27th, Quayle announced his withdrawal from the race. The media reported that the decision was based on his not being able to raise enough money to continue beyond New Hampshire even if he won the state, because front-runner Bush had already collected over fifty million.

In the Iowa polls he had finished next to last of the nine contestants participating. Considering the weakness of this campaign effort in both states, one might wonder, even if he had spent as much money as Bush, would he have had any chance of doing well here?

Utah Republican Senator Orrin Hatch

In June of 1999 there were rumblings that Senator Hatch would join the presidential race, when he assigned Ken Egan and Patrick Hynes, GOP State Committee staffers, to head up a New Hampshire exploratory team for a contest in which there were already ten Republican entrants. Hatch said if he did well enough in Iowa and New Hampshire there would be enough cash to carry him forward thereafter.

Lyn Nofziger, who was a confidant of President Reagan along with Hatch, commented, "I think Orrin Hatch is a tool of George W. Bush" who would split the Mormon vote which otherwise goes to Buchanan or Bauer.

On July 13, 1999, Senator Hatch made his first venture into the Granite State for his potential quest of the presidency in 2000 and was the last of the major contenders to join actively. He claimed having previous commitments of $700,000 but said, "I'm going to need $12 million to $15 million to make this a race." He returned in August and vowed to raise $36 million "from the people" and added "wouldn't that be a wonderful thing to have a president who is elected by the people instead of big money. We're going after the skinny cats, rather than the fat cats." By the end of September, he had opened a campaign headquarters in Concord under the chairmanship of Bryan Gould.

On November 8th, Hatch filed with the secretary of state for the 2000 race, announcing, "I have the most experience of

U.S. senator from Utah, Orrin Hatch, greets a group of young New Hampshire students during a summer campaign visit to Concord.

anyone running in either party. I have a better record of accomplishment than any of them and people know that." He told the *Nashua Telegraph* editorial board that he had raised close to $2 million from small contributors. He advised others "all I need is one million people to write checks for $36 or more and I'll win the election. I wouldn't want to be elected any other way." In January the senator bought local TV time to attack the Clinton/Gore administration, saying it, "may be remembered as the most deceitful and corrupt in our nation's history."

Two days following a last-place finish in the Iowa caucuses, where he received one percent of the Republican votes, Hatch dropped out of the 2000 race. It was a week before the New Hampshire primary, where he actually received 163 votes. He said perhaps his long-shot campaign should have been undertaken earlier. At the same time he endorsed George W. Bush.

True enough, he should not have waited so long to get in the game, yet chances are he got out when he recognized his chickens in New Hampshire weren't Hatching.

※

Chapter 10

The Hare and the Tortoise II
Seven Who Made It to the Finish Line in 2000

THE 2000 NEW HAMPSHIRE PRESIDENTIAL primary set record voter turnouts as the media concentrated on the Republican contest between Governor Bush and Senator McCain and on the Democratic race between Vice President Al Gore and former Senator Bill Bradley. On the Republican side there were three other candidates: Dr. Alan Keyes, Gary Bauer and Steve Forbes.

Republican Ambassador Dr. Alan L. Keyes

In 1996 and 2000, Keyes was the only major black candidate in the presidential races from either the Republican or Democratic parties. In his position as the unpaid volunteer chairman of Black America's PAC (BAMPAC), Keyes made a mailing to New Hampshire voters which included a photograph of J. C. Watts, the sole black Republican Congressman.

It was not a solicitation for Keyes presidential campaign, rather it was to raise money for BAMPAC's mission of recruiting black voters for conservatism. It stated: "The liberal politicians think they "own" the black vote, and take black voters for granted. And the liberal media would have us believe that if you are a black American, then you must be a liberal Democrat and let Jesse Jackson do all the talking." It described Congressman Watts as a powerful conservative role model.

In mid-December of 1996, after having finished sixth with

149

5,572 votes in the New Hampshire presidential primary, Alan Keyes sent his manager, George Uribe, back to the state to announce that Keyes was interested in 2000. A year later, Keyes showed up at a Gun Owners of New Hampshire forum in Manchester where he favored the right to have guns, reclaiming control of schools, renewing respect for God and was against abortion and the income tax.

He returned in early February of 1999, and in March began a series of well advertised statewide "free admission" public rallies. Although he said he hadn't made up his mind to run, buttons, bumper stickers and lawn signs were available, reading, "Alan Keyes 2000." Dan Godzick, one of his campaign consultants, said the campaign was better funded than in 1996.

His rallies were well attended with audiences varying from 200 to 400. A colorful orator, Keyes charged Clinton with being "the most shameless, lying, conscienceless, corrupt man we have ever had in the White House. He has been a nuclear holocaust in moral terms all by himself." By midyear Keyes said he'd raised at least $1.3 million which he said came mostly from people who could give only $20, nor would he ever knowingly take money from anyone who was pro-abortion. The money bosses "won't buy and sell me; I don't want the millions in the bank to be an emblem to the bondage of betraying America."

Constantly campaigning in New Hampshire, the ambassador was not discouraged with his seventh-place finish in the August Iowa straw poll. Finally on September 21st at C.R. Sparks Convention Center in Bedford, though still running in the single digits, he formally declared his candidacy saying, "The grassroots Republicans in this state deserve a real conservative choice and I am determined that they will have one." In November, he was the first major candidate to put up the $1,000 filing fee for the February 1, 2000 primary.

When fellow conservative competitor, Senator Bob Smith, left the Republican Party, Keyes commented, "I see Smith leading some people off into the wilderness."

Ambassador Alan Keyes declares his candidacy at C.R. Sparks Convention Center in Bedford.

At Plymouth State, Keyes lectured, "I burn with no ambition to be president of the United States. And if I burned with that ambition, I would, I believe, be disqualified for the office of president. . . . We've actually allowed this phony media to convince us that hunger for the office is a qualification for the office. . . . The hunger for office is corrupting ambition."

Dean Spiliotes, a Dartmouth faculty member at the time, thought Keyes' impact on the polls was out of proportion with his speaking ability to impress audiences. "The main reaction I've seen to him from hearing him speak is, 'Wow, he's a really fantastic speaker, but I still don't think I'll vote for him.'"

Keyes did well in the Iowa caucus, finishing a strong third behind Bush and Forbes. A week before the New Hampshire primary he addressed its Legislature, where he compared the abolition of slavery to the outlawing of abortion. In addition to extensive newspaper advertising, not undertaken by his adversaries, the Keyes campaign produced an expensive, attention-getting twelve inch by eight inch four-page mailer which included a bumper sticker and a return address donation envelope. As a special bonus for those who sent in $25 or more the donor could receive an airfare discount coupon worth up to $100 on "all 7 airlines."

Although he had anticipated at least a strong third-place finish behind Forbes, on election day he received only half as many votes as Forbes and ended up in fourth place. Yet he remained upbeat, pledging to continue his campaign elsewhere with "unswerving commitment. We have found here in New Hampshire good hearts and good spirits who are willing to go out and work against the odds in order to raise the standard of moral integrity in our party."

Why did he stay in so long? Probably because he had nothing to lose. The other "so-called" stalwart conservatives, except Bauer, had dropped out. Keyes knew he would never be elected president, but he had a focused message he wanted to deliver. Apparently money was no problem; there was also the possibility he might have come in third after the media concentrated its attention on the McCain/Bush race. If he had beaten Forbes, then his voice would have resounded loudly in those primaries which followed.

Republican Gary Bauer

In early April of 1998, conservative Christian lobbyist Gary Bauer, president of the Family Research Council, told Joan Lowy of Scripps Howard News Service he was considering running for president in 2000 because other Republican candidates did not have family values as the basic platform of their campaigns. He said he wanted to see someone "willing to pick up the Reagan mantle of lower taxes, smaller government, family values and pro-life. I don't see somebody really presenting those four things as a coherent program for the presidency."

In August, as Chairman of the Campaign for Working Families, the nation's second largest political action committee (CWF), Bauer opened a Manchester office to raise money for the election of conservative, pro-family, pro-life, pro-free-enterprise candidates for public office. "We are going to elect candidates who agree with us and do our best to defeat those who don't," he said. Michael Biundo, who had worked for Pat Buchanan in the 1996 campaign, was the New Hampshire political advisor.

His PAC contributed $50,000 of radio and TV time in support of Jay Lucas, the New Hampshire Republican gubernatorial candidate who was defeated in November, but Bauer did assist in the election of three new state senators. After several 1998 New Hampshire visits, in late January of 1999 he resigned as chairman of CWF and thereafter became an active campaigner for president, admitting he had little chance of gaining the nomination.

Bauer took positions in local affairs such as tax issues and also said, "I think here in New Hampshire the problem is you have an unelected Supreme Court, setting itself up not only as a legislature but as the school board." In the first seven weeks of his candidacy he reported raising $1.4 million.

The candidate's stump speech emphasized lower taxes, smaller government, strong national defense, pro-family and pro-life values, while he tried to portray himself as the heir of Ronald Reagan for whom he had worked. In late July, although never rising above single digits in the polls, he acquired former *Manchester Union Leader* editorial writer, Richard Lessner, as a senior political adviser who proclaimed, "Gary Bauer will not appoint stealth liberals like David Souter."

In August he won a surprise fourth place in the Iowa August straw poll behind Bush, Forbes and Dole, but ahead of fellow conservatives Quayle, Buchanan and Keyes. "I think I surprised even myself," commented Bauer. Sometimes traveling by bus, "Asphalt One," Bauer with his wife, Carol, and children, toured the Granite State in the traditional grassroots fashion. He introduced new issues, from delaying transfer of the Panama Canal, agreeing that Microsoft was a monopoly, taking a tough stance on China, to demanding an end of discrimination against Catholics and other Christians. In October, he said by adding the federal matching grants due him, he'd have about eight million of available campaign funds.

When Bauer filed in November, he said he was not bothered by his single-digit poll numbers because there had been fourteen others either in the race or thinking about it. By then it was down to six. "I intend to be the last guy standing."

After traveling with the candidate one day, John Harwood of the *Wall Street Journal* wrote "he doesn't look like a president, no motorcade, no security detail, no politician's perpetual tan—it's just short, pale-faced Gary Bauer and a few aides in a green Chevrolet Suburban pulling into Shannon McGinley's driveway for a breakfast reception. In the 2000 presidential race, Mr. Bauer is still small fry on the Republican playground. His poll numbers are minimal, and his campaign resources are dwarfed" by Bush, Forbes and McCain.

Gary Bauer, president of the Family Research Council, speaks to supporters at his Manchester headquarters while campaigning for the Republican presidential nomination in New Hampshire.

When Bauer again finished fourth in the January Iowa caucus, it was not like the summer straw poll. It was a disappointment, as Keyes was in third place. He complimented Keyes, saying he was a "great guy" and "I would be happy to appoint him to the Supreme Court." Bauer said he'd raised $11.5 million and had no intention of dropping out. "I've got to win some primaries along the way . . . I'd like that to begin in New Hampshire." Unfortunately, he received only 1,640 votes on primary day, to finish fifth behind McCain, Bush, Forbes and Keyes. Shortly thereafter, he withdrew from the national contest.

Lack of financial backing was not the reason Bauer quit the race, rather it was his poor showing in New Hampshire which terminated his aspiration to gain the White House. He'd worked hard, but his hard-core conservative message never caught fire, perhaps because he did not have the rhetorical eloquence of competitor Alan Keyes who appealed to the same audience.

Republican Malcolm S. "Steve" Forbes

Following his fourth place finish in the 1996 New Hampshire primary, in the spring of 1997, Forbes established a New Hampshire chapter of Hope, Growth and Opportunity (AHGO). It was a not-for-profit corporation, with Steve Forbes as honorary chairman and with a mission to champion a pro-family, pro-growth, pro-freedom vision and to launch innovative strategies to shrink the size of government. Wallace E. Stickney and Patricia G. Humphrey were the local co-chairs.

As reported by Paul West of the *Baltimore Sun*, AGHO had been running ads in Iowa promoting the flat tax, term limits, Social Security reform, parental control of education, and restrictions on late-term abortions. The same ads began appearing in New Hampshire after Forbes reappeared here.

In May 1997, Forbes addressed the Lilac Luncheon of the New Hampshire Federation of Republican Women at Windham, where he said he would make up his mind in 1998 about the possibility of again being a presidential candidate in 2000. He returned in September to speak at a University of New Hampshire forum in Durham and a political group in Manchester.

In November, at a Rivier College lecture series in Nashua, he said "I made it clear two years ago, and if I run again, I'll do it again, and that is I'm going to take my message to as many voters as possible." Translated that meant he'd again campaign actively in Delaware, something the other major candidates (except Alexander) had pledged not to do and it would again be an affront to the New Hampshire primary.

Meanwhile, solicitation letters for AHGO charter memberships at $100 and basic memberships at $5, along with more expensive opportunities to support AHGO's 17 percent Flat Tax Lobby, were sent throughout the state. Subsequently, in 1998, memberships were offered in the Chairman's Council of the AHGO for $1,000 and the National Executive Committee of the AHGO for $5,000.

Forbes also sent out a survey form and request for funds to support his flat tax for the Citizens for a Sound Economy Foundation. He did a similar thing for Children's Educational Opportunity Foundation (CEO America) which provided tuition scholarships to low-income children to attend the schools of their parents' choice, also for the Heritage Foundation, a conservative think tank, and for the Media Research Center, a conservative media watchdog group.

In January of 1998, Forbes said a New Hampshire Constitutional Amendment was needed to preserve its local control of schools. AHGO sponsored radio ads and a full page print ad in favor of the idea, while Stickney and Humphrey, on behalf of AHGO, requested voters to send pledge cards to legislators "to restore the peoples' right to raise taxes for and to regulate schools." Forbes had no compunction against taking strong stands on local issues.

In April, Forbes did the same thing for AHGO with a full page ad signed by many New Hampshire citizens, and a TV call-in show to plead for abolition of the Federal Tax Code, saying, "The only thing you can do is to kill it and drive a stake through it's heart so that it never rises again to terrorize the American people."

In the summer of 1998, Forbes made two trips to the Granite State which drew good crowds, and in the fall he returned to support Republican candidates for local offices. During this period both his national and New Hampshire chapter of AHGO kept the post office busy with frequent mailings, though he had not formally declared his candidacy for president.

On March 16, 1999, using the Internet as a unique venue, Forbes made an announcement of his presidential candidacy. "This is going to be a new, information-age campaign about great ideas and enduring values. I'm going to run the first full scale presidential campaign on the Internet because I want you to be involved in every step of the way."

As opposed to largely financing his campaign from his own funds as he did in 1996, he said he'd also be raising funds the traditional way, would not be taking federal matching funds and that he was the only Republican candidate, "not beholden to the Washington culture of special interest lawyers, lobbyists and lifetime politicians." Survey/fund letter solicitations were then sent out to seek contributions for "Forbes, 2000, Inc." It was later reported in the media that this effort for third-party contributors to his New Hampshire campaign only netted about $5,000.

As an addendum to his previously proposed flat tax plan, Forbes offered the taxpayer the alternative choice of continuing to use the existing tax code. In April of 1999 he ran a full page ad for 'Tax Code Termination Day' as he had done in 1997, only this time it was signed by many more people and "Paid for by Forbes, 2000, Inc." In May, he ran another full page flat tax ad as part of a $10,000 short-term national campaign. Al Col, his campaign manager, said that ads would run on local TV with "high frequency."

Full-page ads followed on other issues, bolstered by frequent radio and TV commercials, outspending all of the other candidates. Nonetheless, his poll numbers remained in mid-single digits. Not discouraged, Forbes told the press, "My whole life has been spent beating expectations."

In June, Forbes and his wife, Sabina, opened a Manchester office. Paul Young, a senior political adviser, said, "new and different people are signing on, people who are highly energetic and enthused by his campaign." Forbes advocated that all Americans should be free to purchase affordable, portable private health care, while being free to chose their own doctors and he advocated freedom for parents to choose schools for their children.

Forbes favored private investment of Social Security retirement accounts, saying, "If you put a pot of honey in the forest, the bears are going to come. If you put a pot of money in Washington, the politicians are going to put their paws on it. They can't help it, so why tempt them?"

When Forbes finished second in the August Iowa straw poll, the *Wall Street Journal* said it gave him "the claim to be the conservative standard bearer." In September he published a book, *A New Birth of Freedom*, and began to spend more time here door-knocking and in the streets to meet people one-on-one. He frequently used signed copies of his book as a "give away" promotional piece.

Later, at the Mt. Washington Hotel, where the Bretton Woods Monetary Conference had been held in 1944, he told an audience that he would abolish the International Monetary Fund, which he characterized as the "Typhoid Mary of Modern Economics." Normally his stump speech revolved around seeking more control and options for health care, education, social security, taxes, the military, appointment of judges and right to life.

Just before Forbes formally filed with the secretary of state on November 17th, a flap developed when the Republican Leadership Council (RLC), an independent advocacy group with most of its top members being Bush supporters, ran TV ads warning Forbes not to run attack ads against his rivals as had been alleged to have been done in the 1996 primary.

Forbes replied by calling it a phony front organization using

Publisher Steve Forbes denounces the federal tax code, by burying it,
at a campaign rally in historic downtown Portsmouth on April 15th.

soft money for the Bush campaign and filed a complaint with the Federal Elections Commission. Both Steve Duprey, New Hampshire Republican Chairman, and Senator McCain immediately supported Forbes in claiming the ads were unjustified.

In early December, Forbes received the backing of the *Manchester Union Leader* with a Joseph McQuaid editorial: "Steve Forbes is not charismatic. (Some would say he looks like a geek.) But he's also not a phony. Ask him a question, you'll get a thoughtful answer, not a sound bite." Forbes reacted, "It's an enormous boost to the campaign because the *Union Leader* has a reputation for backing candidates based on conservative principles and not bending with the conventional winds." It perhaps should also be noted that McQuaid said of George W. Bush, "He is a nice guy but an empty suit with no philosophical underpinning."

In late December, Forbes was still running 20 percentage points behind Bush and McCain, yet he remained confident of a favorable outcome, blaming the media for "pretending I don't exist" and promoting the two frontrunners, Bush and McCain.

On January 24th, Forbes, with 30 percent of the vote, was second after Bush in the Iowa caucus. Over 50 percent of the total vote was split between him and the other two "so called" conservatives, Keyes and Bauer (McCain did not participate). In Iowa he had promoted his anti-abortion position and relied on the Christian Right. "The establishment has been put on notice. It has met its match," said Forbes of the Iowa result.

The Republican Leadership Council again attacked Forbes in the final weeks of the campaign over an issue of Bush's tax record as governor and Forbes' 1996 treatment of Dole, and it endorsed Bush. Jack Kemp, who had been close to Forbes, came to New Hampshire on behalf of Bush, causing Forbes to react, alleging Kemp, "is part of the establishment, so it's no surprise the establishment rally around their own."

In the closing days of the campaign, Forbes hit heavily with overwhelming TV, radio, full-page print advertising in the *Manchester*

Union Leader, abetted by a constant stream of direct mail, including expensive brochures tailored for specific issues. Even his daughter, Moira, was used as a telemarketing presenter on the telephone.

When the New Hampshire votes were counted he came in third after McCain and Bush, yet he found solace that McCain had defeated Bush because the "attempt at a coronation by the establishment" had been defeated and McCain "had decked them." Shortly thereafter he withdrew from continuing the race in other states.

Many have said the Forbes experience demonstrates that no matter what amount a candidate spends or how well-known a celebrity he may be, he'll never make the presidency unless he has first held some major elective office or military command. Certainly it's been true since the days of our founding fathers and military presidents that such experience has been requisite for White House residency, but that probably is not why Forbes failed.

Forbes had four things which brought him down in the 2000 primary. First: His race in 1996 had left a lingering bad impression, when he attempted to "buy" the election with extensive use of paid advertising as opposed to the traditional New Hampshire eyeball-to-eyeball approach. Many New Hampshire voters remembered that history.

Second: His reinvention of himself from a 1996 candidate primarily concerned with economic issues to one dedicated to social issues in 2000, particularly the overworking of his pro-life position after Iowa, worked against him.

Third: By attempting to be a full-fledged conservative candidate in 2000, he misjudged the state's Republicans, the majority of whom were probably not of that persuasion.

Fourth: His decision to return to Delaware for the second time in 2000, an action which all of the other major candidates disavowed, hurt him.

Fifth: He failed to equate with the majority of New Hampshire voters by taking hardened stands on local issues.

Texas Republican Governor George W. Bush

It is said that George W. Bush's father, former President Bush, resulting from his frequent appearances here beginning in 1978, as a presidential candidate, vice president and president, greets more people in New Hampshire by their first name than most politicians, including our own. He is widely respected by a legion of admirers cultivated over more than two decades.

The senior Bushes spend their summers at a home just over the Maine border in Kennebunkport, which has served as a base for family visits within our state. However, Texas Governor George W. Bush did not participate in New Hampshire during any of his father's campaigns and was personally unknown here prior to the 2000 primary campaign.

On the son's first official visit as a candidate to New Castle in June of 1999, he was welcomed by a horde of curious media and enthusiastic potential supporters. At that time, with his national name identification and substantial financial backing, he was clearly the presumptive nominee of the Republican Party regardless of competition. As late as August, a poll predicted his margin over McCain would be 45 percent to 11 percent.

He spent a total of 36 days here, which initially were carefully structured events designated as "firehouse" chats before large audiences. As the campaign developed, his approach to the voters became more personal, with his participating in many traditional stratagems of the trade such as flipping hamburgers, marching in parades, reading to children, meeting local newspaper editorial boards, accepting numerous celebrity endorsements and attending a baseball dinner with Ted Williams. All of these activities were supported by a very heavy dose of political brochures, television advertising, telephone contacts and direct mail.

In October, he was criticized for skipping the first of two all-candidate debates at Dartmouth and the University of New Hampshire. The depth of his "compassionate conservative" message was questioned and his stand on issues was disparaged for

Texas Governor George W. Bush, just days before the 2000 New Hampshire primary, drives a snowmobile at the Hooksett Kawasaki Polaris dealership owned by New Hampshire House Deputy Speaker Mike Whalley and his wife Purr Whalley, campaign supporters.

not being clearly defined. He continued to draw large crowds. His chairman, Senator Judd Gregg, described him as the most engaging and energetic candidate Judd had ever known—a cross between Teddy Roosevelt and Ronald Reagan. In November, Bush himself said he believed he had "the best organization ever put together by anyone running for president."

In early January of 2000, his brother, Governor Jeb Bush of Florida, joined the fray for a quick visit which was followed by their mother, father and other family members arriving the week prior to election day. At that time most of the polls had substantially changed and indicated a close race with Senator McCain. Yet no one predicted the 19 point loss which Bush received in his second-place finish. Not discouraged, the defeat was absorbed by the Bush team as only a "bump in the road."

It was an interesting aside that on the Friday before the Tuesday primary, former New Hampshire Governor John H. Sununu, who had served for a while as Chief of Staff in the previous Bush administration and who earlier in the new campaign had been working for Dan Quayle, endorsed the younger Bush for the presidency, saying, "I want to make sure that the negative numbers in the polls turn into positive numbers on Tuesday. I don't want anyone ever to be elected president without winning the New Hampshire primary."

Many theories have been advanced for Bush's defeat. Bush advisers were critical that the governor had not spent more time in New Hampshire. They realized his was a national campaign and he'd still given the state more days than he campaigned elsewhere. There was also concern that, as has happened in so many New Hampshire primaries, much too much direction was invoked from Austin rather than by the locals more familiar with the Granite State's political folkways. Many of his workers were upset with competitor Steve Forbes, whom they felt had made unwarranted attacks relating to Bush's positions on issues.

After becoming the presidential nominee of the Republican

Party, Bush returned to the state in late July for a GOP fundraiser in support of the party ticket. Thereafter, in the general election, New Hampshire was the only northeastern state to give him a victory. Its four electoral votes were enough to put him in the White House. The former governor had turned his earlier loss into a critical victory and praised Joel Maiola, Gregg's chief of staff, as one of the "smartest political consultants in the country."

In January of 2002, at a stop on a bipartisan 1,600 mile national tour, President Bush visited the University of New Hampshire. He was accompanied by Republican Senator Judd Gregg and Democratic Senator Ted Kennedy to celebrate the signing of an education reform law, known as The No Child Left Behind Act, in which effort they were the key players in the Senate. Thirty-five hundred people turned out for the event, honoring the legislation that provided $26 billion of federal money to improve the country's educational system.

The closeness of the New Hampshire Senate race between Democratic Governor Jeanne Shaheen and Republican Congressman John E. Sununu in 2002 made New Hampshire one of the key states in the GOP effort to regain control of the Senate. In the closing days of that race, the president made two visits to the state and mustered the voters to vote for Sununu. The First Lady also made a solo appearance on the weekend before the voting. The president drew large and fervent crowds, resulting in a Sununu win which also carried the other major Republican candidates to victory.

Though it is anticipated the president will have no substantial opponent in the Republican Party to his expected run for reelection in 2004, these three visits substantially weakened the drive of the local Democrats, reinvigorated the existing Bush activists and created a deep resource of support from Independents. Assuming no personal, governmental or political catastrophe occurs prior to 2004, the president achieved a position with the New Hampshire electorate which will be difficult to challenge by a candidate from either party in the 2004 election.

Arizona Republican Senator John McCain

Senator McCain addressed a New Hampshire party fundraiser in 1997, and came again in the spring, a year later, to meet privately with key Republican leaders as the guest of his close friend, former New Hampshire Senator Warren Rudman. It was not until June of 1998 when McCain was the keynote speaker at the annual Lilac Luncheon of the New Hampshire Federation of Republican Women, that voters began to become aware of his serious interest in joining the 2000 presidential race. Under the aegis of an exploratory committee he was in full steam by early 1999.

His campaign here was formally launched in April, led by manager Mike Dennehy, who had served previously as executive director for the state Republican Party, and had helped convince all of the major Republican candidates to boycott Deleware in support of the New Hampshire pledge. The campaign produced an effective video cassette of McCain's personal background entitled, "The Character To Do What's Right—The Courage To Fight For It," which was mailed to 50,000 homes, of people who had voted in the previous two presidential primaries. The theme emphasized a man of character and one to be trusted.

In the summer, he skipped the Iowa straw poll, nor did he participate in its January 2000 caucus campaigns. These were political calls which he described as being the "wisest non-investment of time and energy that I've made in my political career." Meanwhile in New Hampshire, he was constantly articulating his major themes of support for the military and campaign finance reform. While not a "compassionate conservative," he was certainly passionate, particularly in promotion of youth voting and solicitation of veterans' votes though he did favor military base closures.

In late summer, the campaign inaugurated a unique version of the state's one-on-one approach to the voter. It was dubbed "The Straight Talk Express," a bus which eventually carried him to 114 so-called "Town Hall Meetings" throughout the state. It included a grassroots itinerary, generating support in the smaller towns where he faced sizable crowds of citizens to whom he

Arizona senator and former Vietnam P.O.W. John McCain, speaks to a gathering of voters in the town of Haverhill in New Hampshire's North Country. Haverhill Representative Douglass Teschner (front row right) helped organize the McCain effort. McCain's grassroots campaign held 114 town meeting events throughout the state.

normally responded without political equivocation or simplistic sound bite platitudes. It also picked up substantial numbers of Independent voters who otherwise probably would not have attended a party rally. It was the ultimate retail approach to campaigning.

During the fall, the senator enthusiastically attended book signing opportunities to promote his then newly published family memoir, *Faith of My Fathers*. It related how his life was influenced by his father and grandfather (both four-star admirals), his captivity during the Vietnam War, his temper, fast-living past and domestic problems. By November, it was obvious his polls were rapidly increasing.

On primary day, it was estimated McCain had picked up 60 percent of the Independent vote, which accounted in large part for his surprising first-place victory of 115,606 votes to 73,330 over Bush, followed by 30,166 for Steve Forbes.

Although he had been outspent approximately six to one and did not receive as many high profile endorsements, McCain had more than made up that deficit by the additional time he'd spent in the state and the closer contact he'd developed with its citizens. His relationship with them was considerably more unscripted than that of George Bush.

The senator also kept in close touch with the media. Anne E. Kornblut wrote in the *Boston Globe* that McCain was "always approachable, has been so accessible that journalists have occasionally asked him to go away."

In October, Senator McCain returned to the state for a visit where he spoke on behalf of Congressman Charles Bass and the election of George Bush as president.

Former New Jersey Democratic Senator Bill Bradley

Senator Bill Bradley had talked about running for president when he was serving as a three-term member of the Senate in both 1988 and 1992, but left the Senate in 1997 without doing so. In September 1998, he came to New Hampshire to support Mary Rauh in her campaign for the 2nd District U.S. House seat and other Democrats running for local offices. By early December, he had formed an Exploratory Committee and was effectively on the campaign trail against Vice President Al Gore.

Many of his disciplines were unusual for a political candidate. In addition to having played as a Hall-of-Fame forward on the New York Knicks professional basketball team for over a decade, Princeton graduate Bradley had also been a Rhodes Scholar at Oxford. He explained: "My mother wanted me to be a success, my father wanted me to be a gentleman. Neither wanted me to be a politician."

After leaving the Senate he had written four books, earned approximately $2.7 million in lecture fees and nearly $1 million as a consultant, which occupations were criticized by the Gore forces as aligning him with special interest groups.

His speaking style was restrained, professorial and low key, yet it was dedicated to the varied issues he espoused. Principal among them were reducing the number of children in poverty, health care for all Americans, fundamental campaign finance reform, registration of all handguns, public financing of Congressional campaigns, interracial unity, helping working families cope with a changing American society and a higher level of integrity in government, though proposed without a direct attack on President Clinton.

Bradley campaigned in the traditional "talk to everyone" without a large staff entourage. He visited businesses, spoke before service clubs, met people on the street but appeared to enjoy most the meetings in private homes with small neighborhood gatherings. He did not accept funds from PACs nor would he take more than $1,000 from any individual.

His performance was, overall, positive until perhaps near the end, when he roughed it up with Gore over their respective health care proposals, planted seeds that perhaps Gore was not trustworthy and maybe had been inside the Beltway too long. By contrast, Bradley claimed, "I had a life before I got into the Senate; I had a life after I got out of the Senate." At a Claremont event, he shook hands with Republican candidate McCain when the two agreed neither would take "soft money" if they became nominees of their respective parties.

In the final weeks, volunteers poured in from everywhere to assist his efforts. One week the count was estimated at 500 from 14 states. At the beginning, the polls rated Gore a two-to-one leader, but Bradley's momentum grew in the months before primary day. Unfortunately, when some of them were beginning to view him as the possible winner, he lost the Iowa caucus two-to-one. Nonetheless, Bradley recouped well in the New Hampshire primary, with a close vote of 70,502 for second place behind Gore's 76,897 victory total.

In November, Bradley had said, "The more politicians talk about change, the more things stay the same. The system works to help those who are in power to keep that power, so why should they want to rock the boat?" *Wall Street Journalist* Gerald F. Seib found Bradley "too complex to pigeonhole easily."

The Gore/Bradley contest had been pretty much a difference in presentation between two men who in many ways were very much alike. Neither one was exciting, inspirational or forceful. Their views on similar issues were not substantially different and sometimes very difficult to articulate. Bradley addressed substantially fewer subjects than Gore. Gore had a distinct advantage with the trappings of the vice presidency. At the same time, he had the burden of carrying the shortcomings of the Clinton administration. Bradley was untried in the White House.

The result was a classic case of the New Hampshire voter sizing up the candidates on a personal basis, not so much on the issues, and determining by a close call that Gore was the safer candidate to go with. It could only happen here.

The former senator returned to the state in May of 2002 to endorse Mark Fernald, a Democrat running for governor, along with the candidate's pro-income tax platform.

*Former U.S. senator from New Jersey and NBA basketball star Bill
Bradley and Vice President Al Gore greet each other at a Democratic
debate on the campus of the University of New Hampshire in Durham.*

Democratic Vice President Al Gore

Vice President Al Gore has been a familiar figure in New Hampshire from innumerable appearances here dating back to his own presidential campaign of 1988. In 1996, he was suspected of setting up for another try for the top office in 2000 when both he and President Clinton were in the state on behalf of the Democratic ticket. By mid-1998, he had made 12 trips here as vice president, frequently for the purpose of announcing federal grants for a variety of purposes, or giving talks on health care, the environment and high technology.

At that time, New Hampshire Democratic State Chairman Jeff Woodburn observed that Vice President Al Gore should not assume he'd be the flag-bearer as the Democratic presidential nominee in 2000 because "New Hampshire is an ornery, independent state that makes up its own mind."

In January 1999, the vice president filed the Gore 2000 Committee with the Federal Elections Commission. Shortly thereafter, his wife Tipper, who often was at his side, made one of many solo visits, giving credit to the media for the way in which they had protected the privacy of Chelsea, Clinton's daughter. In reference to Clinton himself, she said, "I think we also understand that what the president did was wrong."

In March, the vice president announced that Bill Shaheen, Governor Shaheen's husband, would serve as Gore's New Hampshire chairman. Simultaneously, there was talk of Governor Shaheen being chosen the running mate for Gore. Later she was reported to be one of six on his short list for the job, though she said, if offered, she would decline. Meanwhile most of the recognized leaders of the state's Democratic Party were joining the Gore team.

Upon his official entry to the race in June of 1999, Gore was welcomed to the state and the 2000 primary by the Republican National Committee with a full page ad in the *Manchester Union Leader* asking him to level with the American people. His response noted the country had gone from the biggest budget deficit to the biggest budget surplus, nineteen million new jobs had been created and the country was in a period of good economic prosperity under its administration at that time. Gore said it's "a positive change that makes a difference for working families."

Early on, Gore's speeches were glib and polished. They pounded heavily on environmental protection and the need to right the environmental wrongs of the past, focusing on the dangers of global warming, the importance of high-tech jobs and New Hampshire's leadership in making them available. He was against proposed GOP tax cuts, believing the money could be used for other purposes, such as shoring up Social Security and Medicare and creating more work opportunities by empowering the disabled.

He dealt with a myriad of issues, including worldwide free trade, better health care for the elderly, universal access to education with smaller class sizes and teacher ratios from 1 to 20 and attacked important health care decisions made "by HMO bureaucrats who don't have a license to practice medicine and who don't have a right to play God."

His campaign style was to practice retail politics, with few big structured rallies: jogging with supporters, living room gabfests, public street-strolling without rope lines and with minimum security, considering the necessary Secret Service and VP media coverage. In September, when the polls began to report his being overtaken by Bradley, he claimed himself to be the underdog and recognized his demeanor was too stiff and stoic.

Adjusting to this personal problem, he moved his headquarters from Washington to Tennessee and reinvented himself. He recognized the dilemma of campaigning under the auspices of the White House as opposed to being a free agent. In November, Kevin Landrigan of the *Nashua Telegraph* noticed the transformation in reporting the difference "between the obedient vice president he has been for the past seven years and a more fun-loving, spontaneous candidate he's been on the stump for more than a month." Gore worried less about being a team player, was more casually dressed, no longer "wooden" and, as a supporter commented, "not the same guy I'd seen on TV."

In the closing days, Bradley's rival health care plan became the major issue. Gore trashed Bradley's idea of replacing Medicaid for the poor and disabled with federal subsidies for low income needy to obtain private insurance as being too costly, saying it would eat up the surplus. Gore was disturbed to learn that New Hampshire elderly residents were being bussed to Canada to buy less expensive drug prescriptions. His solution was to preserve Medicaid and Medicare while making them more affordable and providing coverage for lower cost generic drugs. Despite testy exchanges, Gore allowed, "Senator Bradley is a fine man with a bad plan."

When the Gore/Bradley fracas was over, there must have been jubilation in the Shaheen household because for the second time their candidate had won the New Hampshire Democratic primary. In 1984 it was Gary Hart. This time Al Gore. Jeanne was Hart's chairman and her husband, Bill, was Gore's chairman—the masterminds behind both candidates. For 2004, Bill is Kerry's chairman, but Jeannie is uncommitted as of the date of this publication.

In late October of 2001, the former vice president returned to address the Democratic Jefferson-Jackson Dinner. Sporting a light beard and as a private citizen without fanfare, he spent a couple of days traveling throughout the state visiting old friends, but gave no indication that he'd try here again in 2004. Slightly prior to the 2002 general election Gore contributed $50,000 to assist New Hampshire Democrats.

It's an interesting footnote to this chapter that of the fifteen candidates highlighted who ran in the last primary, only three will probably try again for the brass ring in 2004. They are: Republican President George Bush who ran the whole course along with Democrats, Senator John Kerry and Congressman Dick Gephardt who were winnowed before the filing date last time.

Observations
on the Primary
Some Good, Some Bad

Oklahoma Governor Frank Keating, former member
of Republican National Committee:

**"In every conversation I've had, the principals agree
that New Hampshire's role should
not be touched."**

Hendrik Hertzberg—The *New Yorker* magazine:

**"If you had to pick one of the fifty states and confer
upon its citizens vastly more influence in the choice
of president than those of any other, you probably
wouldn't pick this one. New Hampshire is small,
provincial, and atypical."**

Newsweek—What will survive the 21st century?:

"New Hampshire Primary"

Claremont (New Hampshire) *Eagle Times:*

**"Protecting the primary because of the dollars it
means to the state is perfectly legitimate. But those
who are fighting the battle should admit that their
motives come down to money, instead of dishing out
hogwash about New Hampshire's unique and proud
tradition of Democracy and voter participation. Any
state can make the same claim."**

The Boston Herald:

"Every candidate for the presidency of the United States is a better contender and eventually a better president for having been tested by the fires of this primary season and the chill winds that blow out of New Hampshire."

William Safire, Columnist, *New York Times:*

"The New Hampshire primary has generated into a media-saturated joke. The state's citizens are overexposed, over-polled, over-campaigned upon. Busloads of snowblind itinerant pundits descend on a rural state unrepresentative of the nation's population, skewing the process of selecting a candidate."

Edward Anderson—*Providence Journal*:

"The primary does smoke candidates out of their holes, exposing their flaws and strengths. The Granite State keeps telling us things we need to know about those who would be president."

Jim Shea—*The Hartford Courant:*

"The truth is, everybody in this part of the country thinks New Hampshire is weird."

The Boston Globe:

"The state speaks well because it listens well. New Hampshire deserves to be first."

Kate O'Beirne—*National Review:*

"The disproportionate attention paid to New Hampshire voters demonstrated by the tiresome quadrennial jokes about locals being undecided because they had only met a certain candidate five times has made them too obnoxiously self-aware to provide a valid test of candidates."

Fortune Magazine:

"It is not easy to accept the notion that the leaders of New Hampshire know what they're doing. The Granite State's politics have long had a flavor of fruitcake. It's hard to escape the aura of nuttiness— but also hard to escape the sense that they're doing something right."

Dale McFeatters, columnist for
Scripps Howard News Service:

"It's time our 42nd largest state, with four-tenths of one percent of the U.S. population, to give it a rest and let some other state get a little attention. The grotesque amount of political resources poured into New Hampshire Is distorting the political process."

Vice President Al Gore:

"I support New Hampshire's role and will protect it. I will make certain the Democratic Party always has New Hampshire go first."

Halton Adler Mann, political consultant writing in the
San Francisco Examiner:

**"New Hampshire's quadrennial charade is a colossal,
collective delusion of democracy, a fraudulent
and failed experiment that has put many worthy
candidates asunder."**

Jay Ambrose—*Scripps Howard News Service:*

**"In a place like New Hampshire, with all its town
meetings and all the press conferences and debates,
it's hard to hide out on issues."**

Richard Brookhiser—*The Wall Street Journal:*

**"As for . . . New Hampshire, you've had your day.
Time has come to focus on . . . skiing."**

Jules Witcover—author, *No Way
to Pick a President:*

**"The New Hampshire primary continues to be
extremely important in the winnowing-
out process"**

Tip O'Neill—Speaker of the House:

"New Hampshire is an odd-ball state"

David Broder—*Washington Post* columnist speaking
in New Hampshire:

**"I firmly believe that the New Hampshire primary
will be where it always has been, first in the nation,"
then he joked, there was probably a passage in the
Bible that said, "And New Hampshire shall lead
them."** (Amy Diaz, *Manchester Union Leader*)

Mike Roko—*Chicago Sun:*

**"New Hampshire should get the choice of moving its
primary back "into the pack where it will receive the
attention it deserves—which is none—or be thrown
out of the United States."**

California Governor Pete Wilson writing to Basil
Battaglia, chairman of Delaware's Republican
Committee, April 1995:

**"California too boasts of many firsts—the telegraph,
computer microchips and motion pictures, to name
just a few. For any other state to attempt to take that
away would simply be unacceptable. For this reason,
we must work together to protect the historical role
New Hampshire citizens play every four years in
the primary selection of candidates for
the presidency."**

Phil Rosenthal—*Chicago Sun Times:*

**"That's the beauty of coming to the New
Hampshire primary. It's politics as
performing art."**

Lisa Rogak—*The Christian Science Monitor:*

"The next time another state wants the primary, most of us would agree. You can have it. We just have to find another excuse to get together on a blustery winter day every four years."

Jeff Rapsis—*Milford* (NH) *Cabinet:*

"The candidates for leading a nation of nearly 290 million people are chosen in large part by the same few hundred thousand voters every four years. However this whittling-down process came to exist it's unrepresentative, unfair and just plain strange."

President Bill Clinton in February 7, 1995
WMUR-TV interview:

"I always believed in the New Hampshire primary process as an observer. But after I went through it, I felt more strongly about it, because I don't think you could go there and be with those folks without being profoundly moved by the human dimension of public life . . . the truth is that the people there are intensely public-minded and know a phenomenal amount about the issues, and they're fair-minded."

Former New Hampshire Democratic
Chairman Chris Spirou:

"Our state's primary will be on the Fourth of July, four years before the next election, if we have to. That's it. The Statue of Liberty is located in New York. The first-in-the-nation primary is in New Hampshire. When they move the Statue of Liberty, we'll move our primary."

Dayton Duncan and Peter Goelz on March 21, 1985—*Boston Globe Magazine:*

"Almost since its inception, the New Hampshire primary has walked a fine line between being a serious political event and an act of vaudeville, between enhancing the state's image and dragging it into gross caricature, between taking legitimate advantage of its unique role in the national spotlight and abusing its privilege."

Patrick Caddell, pollster to politicians:

"You won't find any place better [to start the primary season]. The electorate's very attuned to politics. They take it *very* seriously."

Historian Theodore H. White wrote in 1980:

"What makes the nation take this state's voting seriously is not only that it comes first, but that New Hampshire voters and politicians are among the most sophisticated in the nation."

Bob Nardini, *Concord Monitor,* reviewing Charles Brereton's book, *First in the Nation:*

"Whether this New Hampshire attraction proves as enduring as the Old Man or goes the way of Benson's Animal Park, a legacy is now on record."

Excerpts from a conversation on May 28, 2003 between former president Bill Clinton and presidential historian Michael J. Beschloss at the John F. Kennedy Library and Museum, as recorded and transcribed by *Boston Globe* staff writer Michael S. Rosenwald (not an official transcript):

"I know you can say this is my bias because I'm from a small state . . . One of the things that bothers me about the whole presidential nominating process is that the more you front-load it and put it into big primaries, the more you consign these candidates to spend all their time raising money . . . But the presidential campaigning is supposed to be for the candidate as well as the voters. It was good for John Kennedy to have to go to West Virginia to see all those white poor people—all those Protestants living in the hills and hollows. Good for him to have to go in to the inner city. Good to have the time and obligation to go and listen to the stories of people who were different from you. That's the thing I loved about New Hampshire. For its quirkiness, it's a beautiful place, because they had a sense that they owed the country something. They owed the country a good decision and they were determined to give everybody a listen."

Chapter 11

The 2004 Primary
The Democrats Who Are Now in the Starting Gate

O THER THAN THE MECHANICAL AND constitutional requirements of qualifying for future presidential primaries, there's the practical question of the specific individuals who might find it a worthwhile endeavor. Unfortunately,
this book will be published before all of them can be positively
identified. That date will not occur until November 21, 2003, the
final filing date to register for the 2004 New Hampshire presidential primary.

Among them, we'd hope for a generous assortment of the so-
called "lesser-known" candidates who perhaps run solely for the
exercise, the certificate of participation, to entertain or to passion-
ately promote a personal agenda. In a few cases all that's wanted
is a certificate to hang on the wall. Their number has been decreasing slightly over the last two primaries, however indications
are that the 2004 primary will reverse that trend. In addition to
offering almost any citizen the opportunity to run for president or
vice president as is inherent in the American dream, they add a
colorful zest to the event.

The U.S. Supreme Court has ruled that anyone who so desires
may spend as much of their own money as they wish under the
Constitutional protection of free speech. There are those multi-
millionaire celebrities who might take the challenge of entering
the contest, such as Donald Trump and Warren Beatty, both of

Fun along the Campaign Trail

Some aspirants are ferociously up to the challenge, like Patrick J. Buchanan: "Mount up and ride to the sound of the guns."

Or, New Hampshire's Senator Bob Smith, who temporally left the Republicans to run as an Independent: "The roadside is littered with the remains of those who have underestimated Bob Smith."

More realistic than Smith was his fellow Representative Robert K. Dornan who preached, "I am fearless but not foolhardy."

---

whom indicated some interest in the past. Steve Forbes first used that approach in 1996. It didn't work for him.

Then there will be the multitude of current or former well-known governors, U.S. congressmen and major city mayors readily available, maybe even a Cabinet member or former First Lady. Some, as did President George W. Bush, would be able to raise enough money from private sources to wage a winning national campaign. Others will have to depend on federal matching funds to sustain the whole route of a national campaign.

Elsewhere in this book we hope that the myth that being a serious contender requires twenty million dollars in hand before entering the New Hampshire primary has been dispelled. Obviously, no such fiction applied to Estes Kefauver, Henry Cabot Lodge, Gary Hart, Jimmy Carter or Pat Buchanan. Disputants will point out that those campaigns were conducted in the dark ages, not the cyber age, back when costs of Internet exposure, media promotion, campaign strategists and professional marketing services were minimal or didn't exist. Perhaps they never checked Governor Bush's record in 2000, who learned the lesson that his computer-based and flushly-funded effort here did not stifle the competition.

Certainly, if this assumption were correct, that before coming up here there has to be multi bucks in the bank, then future presidential Granite State primaries would likely be so limited as to be dull and unexciting. Worse yet, New Hampshire would no longer serve its purpose. Those players who had the dough would risk it on the gambling tables of the more expensive political casinos and the "lesser-knowns" could forget any chance of participating in the game.

Conversely, our position is that the old fashioned way still applies. Any creditable candidate who is really willing to take the time and make the effort to sit in the voter's kitchen, visit his place of business, talk to his service club, greet him spontaneously in the street and enjoy such interaction, will still win here. It doesn't cost millions of dollars, rather it takes shoe leather, sweat, tolerance and a smile.

Computerized graphic capability allows for promotional pieces and newsletters to be generated in-house. It does require a few dedicated and compensated, native loyalists who have previously been around the track and possess the expertise of setting up a volunteer organization throughout the state. An effective structure also requires a dedicated non-staffer chairman in every precinct. As has been said before, the New Hampshire primary is a traditional home industry with a trained labor force, and is free for the asking.

These grunt workers are easy to find and don't get paid. Remember we take our elections seriously and often, thus they become an avocation for party activists who are constantly "on call" for some political purpose. These volunteers consider their services as contributions to their community, much as their personal time given to charitable causes. They want their candidate to win no matter what the challenge.

Just as long as the candidate's out-of-state's advisers don't repeat the frequently made mistake of mandating operating procedures which perhaps worked well in other jurisdictions, our home-grown experienced workers will do the job. Granite Staters are stubborn about how politics should be played here. They've played by their rules many times before. It's still a small homogeneous place where people personally relate through friends, business or wide social relationships.

If the sparsely funded candidate operates within these New Hampshire guidelines and wins, immediately he becomes a factor in the national race thereafter. It's then when the twenty million falls into the campaign chest. In other words, after New Hampshire, not before. It turns on his ignition for the money and media notoriety which automatically elevates him to a recognized competitor status in the countrywide race which follows. Again, this is why New Hampshire has such prestige in the entire elective process. It is the only place where an underfunded self-starter has that opportunity.

Even in Senator McCain's situation, where he may have already had the twenty million before coming to New Hampshire in 2000, there was a question as to whether it would be enough to offset Bush's sixty million. McCain, to play it safe, used the time-tested one-on-one routine of "lets fuse with the voter" which brought not only victory but a huge bundle of additional cash thereafter. His victory here impelled voters elsewhere to loosen their purse strings in support of a previously considered dark horse.

By our theory, there is no reason to anticipate our first-in-the-nation game won't continue to be the leadoff to the championship for the duration of the current primary system. In those years, when an elected president is running for a second term, as may be the case for George W. Bush in 2004, it's probable the thrill won't be as great, with perhaps a contest only on one side of the ballot. Nonetheless all of the foregoing applies to the major party out-of-office, plus any Reform, Libertarian or other parties which gain ballot status.

So, as we move into the new millennium, the state will continue to provide a springboard for anybody who wants to be president—be they fringes, multimillionaires or identifiable rich or poor, financially or otherwise, politicians. Many have already visited to express their interest for inclusion in campaign 2004.

DEMOCRATS (9) Candidate	Office	Home State	Born (Age)	Religion	Military Service	Education	Occupation
Howard Dean	Ex-Governor	Vermont	11/17/48 (54)	Congregationalist	-	Yale, B.A.; Albert Einstein College of Medicine, M.D.	Physician
John Edwards	Senator	North Carolina	6/10/53 (50)	Methodist	-	No. Carolina State, B.S.; U. of No. Carolina, J.D.	Lawyer
Richard A. Gephardt	Representative	Missouri	1/31/41 (63)	Baptist	Air National Guard	Northwestern, B.S.; U. of Michigan, J.D.	Lawyer
Bob Graham	Senator	Florida	11/9/36 (66)	United Church of Christ	-	U. of Florida, B.A.; Harvard, LL. B.	Real estate developer; cattle rancher
John Kerry	Senator	Massachusetts	12/11/43 (59)	Roman Catholic	Navy (Vietnam veteran)	Yale, B.A.; Boston College, J.D.	Lawyer
Dennis J. Kucinich	Representative	Ohio	10/8/46 (57)	Roman Catholic		Case Western Reserve, B.A.; Case Western Reserve, M.A.	Video producer; public power consultant
Joseph I. Lieberman	Senator	Connecticut	2/24/42 (62)	Jewish	-	Yale, B.A.; Yale, LL. B.	Lawyer
Carol Moseley Braun	Ex-Senator	Illinois	8/16/47 (56)	Roman Catholic	-	U. of Ill., Chicago Circle, B.A.; U. of Chicago, J.D.	Lawyer
Al Sharpton	-	New York	10/3/54 (49)	Pentecostal	-	Attended Brooklyn College (no degree)	Minister

Source: Politics in America (CQ Press), The Almanac of American Politics (National Journal)

For 2004, There Are Now Nine Democrats in the Starting Gate

It is unlikely there will be any major opposition in 2004 on the Republican side to the reelection of President George W. Bush. The primary action in New Hampshire will probably be all on the Democratic ballot among six candidates: Senators John Edwards, John Kerry, Joe Lieberman, Bob Graham, Congressman Dick Gephardt and former Governor Howard Dean. Our experiences with Kerry and Gephardt have been outlined previously in this book (see chapter 9). We offer here a snapshot into the beginning of the race, realizing that much will have changed by the time this book appears.

Congressman Dennis Kucinich, Reverend Al Sharpton and former Senator Carol Moseley Braun, all Democrats, will perhaps also be in the race. Of these nine major potential candidates, two are African-Americans (Sharpton and Moseley Braun), while two of the three senators (Kerry and Lieberman) and the governor (Dean) are from New England. Prior to the last day of filing on November 21, 2003, it's likely some of the nine will withdraw as occurred in 2000.

The *Rhodes Cook Letter* further identifies these potential nine candidates as seen in the chart on the opposite page.

The statements attributed, information provided and quotes taken from the following candidates were made in New Hampshire or in local media conference calls emanating from outside the state during their presidential travels. We have intentionally not attempted to report their activities or remarks made elsewhere.

Former Democratic Vermont Governor Howard Dean

As early as 1996, Democratic Governor Dean of neighboring Vermont was recognized in New Hampshire as a potential candidate for president in 2000, when he appeared in Keene at the opening of the Cheshire County Democratic headquarters. As Chairman of the National Governors' Association and Democratic Governors Association, plus being a medical doctor, he had received considerable national notice. Although he did not run in 2000, it looked as though he would in 2004. He has been a constant visitor in New Hampshire, appearing to some as though he was spending more time here than in his own state. Maybe it's just because he crosses the Connecticut River to do his shopping here where there is no sales tax.

Dean prides himself on being a novel kind of politician, saying, "Physicians are trained differently than lawyers. We make decisions quickly. We gather as much information as we can. We make the decision and move on. You don't have time to fool around when there is a serious problem." During the past several years he has consistently received warm receptions at all kinds of Democratic events in New Hampshire and has endorsed Democratic candidates at all levels in our state elections. Among others, he appeared on behalf of state Senate candidates Beth Arsenault, Jerry Sorlucco and Dennis Kalob, along with House candidate Ned Densmore.

The governor signed Vermont's first-in-the-nation civil unions law supporting rights of the gay and lesbian communities. He said, "I think they're (the people) going to be amazed to find out there's a candidate who dared to sign a bill people didn't like, because he thought it was the right thing to do," and he believed it would help his candidacy. In the fall of 2001, he formed a political action committee, Fund For a Healthy America, to finance his national travel.

Dean charged that the No Child Left Behind law, which was cosponsored by Democrat Senator Ted Kennedy and Republican Senator Judd Gregg, was an "unfunded mandate" which would terminate local control of schools. He referred to it as the "No School Board Left Standing" bill, which requires programs that have to be paid whether or not the federal government funds them and results in higher local property taxes to pay for education. He also took a different stand on abortion, saying, "It's none of the government's business."

Former Vermont Governor Howard Dean, a medical doctor, speaks at a health care forum at the Kimball-Jenkins estate in Concord. He has spent considerable time campaigning in the state and some believe he is using the Jimmy Carter model.

The governor's record is one of a fiscal conservative with liberal positions on social issues. He says, "you can't have health care for kids, environmental protections, and equal opportunity in education without a balanced budget." Dean also proposed universal health care, including a prescription benefit. It would be accomplished by expanding existing federal programs to make affordable insurance for everyone and an expanded Medicaid program to provide insurance for low-income adults under 25 making less than $50,000.

He believes all of President Bush's tax cuts should be repealed and half the tax cut used for medical insurance with the other half to eliminate deficits, fund Social Security and pay down the national debt. "If you got rid of Bush's tax cut for those who make more than $300,000 per year, you could easily help every man, woman and child get health insurance." Most important is a balanced budget which he says the Republicans haven't done in 34 years. "Money is coming out of the Social Security Trust Fund in order to give tax cuts to people who don't need them."

He later said cutting taxes would not stimulate the economy. Dean charged that between the president's tax cuts and foreign policy, 2.3 million jobs had been lost in the past two years. Instead he would raise taxes to subsidize the infrastructure, such as schools and renewable energy. While in the state he gave strong endorsement to New Hampshire Democratic Governor Shaheen in her bid for the U.S. Senate in 2002, but would make no decision on his running for president until after his fifth Vermont gubernatorial term ran out in January of 2003.

After 19 visits to the state in the year before the 2002 general election, Dean announced he had hired two outstanding Massachusetts fundraisers for a mission of collecting $10 million before the 2004 New Hampshire primary. One of them said, "He knows to be viable, he's got to beat the other northeast candidate in New Hampshire, that being Kerry." Meanwhile Dean was charging that his Democratic opponents were identifying themselves as "Bush-lite" by noting that Gephardt, Kerry, Edwards and Lieberman had voted Bush the authority to invade Iraq. Dean did not endorse a preemptive attack against Iraq.

On his 27th visit here, the governor asked, "What are we doing supporting unilateral intervention in a country that is not an immediate threat to the United States? This is the wrong war at the wrong time. Iraq does not have a nuclear program." He blamed Bush for a "bullying" foreign policy that allows the United States to attack anyone we disagree with. It was his belief that Iran, Syria, Saudi Arabia and Libya were the primary countries sponsoring world-wide terrorism.

He felt it was more important to fight the war with Al Qaeda and stop North Korea from being a nuclear threat. He faulted Vice President Cheney's former company, Halliburton, for its post-Iraq war contract to manage the country's oil supply as a cozy relationship with the Bush White House, "an emblem of an administration that has sold this country down the river."

The former governor was critical of the Bush administration for not establishing a homeland security grant for Portsmouth, saying, "improving security at the Port of Portsmouth is essential to protecting New Hampshire's citizens. We must not neglect small ports, which form a crucial part of our nation's infrastructure."

College students at the University of New Hampshire and elsewhere were rallying to the Vermonter's peace talk, somewhat similarly to the situation which occurred in 1968 when Senator Gene McCarthy opposed President Johnson's support of the Vietnam War. The principal difference between the two political generations was that many of today's students were Democrats protesting against a Republican president. Dean supported AmeriCorps, saying downsizing was "wrong and, like so many of the president's policies, short-sighted."

Dean pounded hard on his guarantee of health coverage, particularly to labor groups. Also he proposed raising the minimum wage and more money for local law enforcement agencies as the first line of defense against terrorism. He supported the death penalty in some cases and opposed national gun control, believing each state should control its own laws. By February of 2003, he'd been in New Hampshire at least 26 times. The governor was talking conservation and development of alternative energy sources like wind and solar power for less dependence on foreign oil. "I'd like to see 10 percent ethanol in every gas tank." He proposed "livable communities" supported by renewable energies, with 20 percent of the country's electricity coming from such sources.

Subsequently, his health plan was detailed to cover prescription drugs for people over 65, and make grant subsidies to small businesses to cover eligible workers for their health care. The former governor would also require all citizens covered under his health plan to sign a living will or a substitute document. As a doctor, and campaign ploy, he initiated the idea of "house calls" to spur his one-on-one Granite State effort. At campaign events his supporters occasionally wore lab coats and distributed tongue depressors stamped with the name of Dean's website.

Further, he promised to change pension regulations to protect employees against corporate raids of money earned. He also complained that New Hampshire teachers' salaries were below the national average, and said, "It's an inexcusable failure when qualified and motivated teachers are forced into other professions to make a living."

The former governor attributed Bush's success to the president's clear outline of his positions, whereas "the reason the Democrats are weak is that we appear to be willing to say whatever it takes to win." In late June he was the first potential candidate to run ads in Iowa.

Finally, seven years after what was presumed to be the beginning of his presidential quest in New Hampshire and innumerable visits in the interim, on June 23, 2003, Dean officially announced he would be a candidate for the job in its 2004 primary. At the end of the month he had raised more money in New Hampshire than any of his competitors, with over 1000 contributions from

883 supporters which totalled $103,461, and he collected a total of over five million via the Internet.

Democratic North Carolina Senator John Edwards

Democratic North Carolina Senator John Edwards made his first political trip to New Hampshire in February of 2002. Following a successful career as a plaintiff lawyer suing major corporations, he was serving his first elective office as a first-term U.S. senator. The senator would not discuss any interest he might have in running for president. He said he did not take money from political action committees, instead he raised funds from individuals. It was his view that the average person has no lobbyist in Washington, a position he strove to fill. Ordinary Americans who "play by the rules get taken advantage of by wealthy, well-connected people at the top."

The senator returned in June when he outlined his stance on many issues. He is pro-choice on abortion, wants full funding for special education, more fuel-efficient automobiles, better qualified and paid teachers in smaller schools, expanding after-school programs, a patient's bill of rights, campaign finance reform and cheaper prescription drugs. He was critical of the president's position on tax-cuts, health care and homeland security. While in the state at Democratic fundraisers he endorsed Shaheen for the Senate, Fernald for governor and Katrina Swett for Congress, whom he referred to as "Christina." In October, as its featured speaker, Edwards again rallied the troops at the Jefferson-Jackson Dinner.

Despite his three trips to New Hampshire, Edwards was not making the same effort to identify himself here as he had done in other early voting states. The AP reported national polls were showing his name ID to be below potential rivals, including Al Sharpton. In Iowa he directed 800,000 mailings in support of local candidates and in South Carolina he spent $200,000 on the radio to encourage voting, In February of 2003, the senator hired Colin Van Ostern who had served as New Hampshire Demo-

North Carolina Senator John Edwards makes a point to workers at a shirt-manufacturing plant in Derry during one of many visits to the Granite State.

cratic Party Communications Director and had said Edwards was the only Democrat that "worried" both President Bush and his advisor Karl Rove. By March of 2003, he had raised more money nationally than any of his announced competitors, yet he ran well behind them in New Hampshire popularity polls.

On a fourth trip in February of 2003, accompanied by his wife who campaigned at a Dover rest home, the senator accused Bush of being out of touch with "regular Americans. He doesn't see the effect this economy is having, loss of jobs, people's loss of their pensions." He also said, "It's a small group of insiders who are running this country. They run it for insiders and the American people are paying for it." He compared an average worker's pay as increasing by only 10 percent in thirty years whereas corporate executive officers' compensation had gone up by 3,000 percent. "I'll be a champion for regular Americans who are being left behind every day." In his opinion Bush values wealth, where wealth is inherited, not earned, and cannot relate to an average person, whereas the senator values hard work and understands the working man.

Edwards would repeal the administration's tax cuts for the most wealthy one percent of taxpayers while continuing tax relief for the middle class. "We need to keep jobs here and keep the tax code so that companies keep jobs here." He believed the government should award $500 per family as a refundable tax credit to alleviate increased energy costs and disagreed with President Bush on education, judicial appointments, environmental issues, and affirmative action. He would support about $200 million for the state's homeland security and would fund additional fiscal aid to the states by shrinking the federal bureaucracy. The senator also proposed subsidizing the first $2,000 of private child care aid for qualified reservists and guardsmen while they were on active duty.

When in the state's "North Country" the senator said, "I don't think President Bush is paying attention to the rural community."

This was an area with which he identified from his own background. As reported in the *Conway Sun*, he proposed a $1 billion plan to create rural development zones, boost small-town businesses and bring such areas high-speed Internet access.

He attacked the "Clear Skies Initiative" of the Bush administration with the charge it would adversely affect the state's economy and health of its citizens. At the same time he said he would fund special education and the No Child Left Behind bill. Edwards offered a "College for Everyone" plan which, among other benefits, would give free first-year tuition to students attending state or community colleges if they worked at least ten hours per week to help pay for their education. Additionally, by a 10 percent cut in the federal bureaucracy, he proposed $50 billion to assist the states with their budgets.

Before election to the Senate, Edwards had made millions as a trial attorney trying cases which included medical malpractice cases. As part of his health care plan he proposed a "three-strikes-and-you're-out" program to curb frivolous malpractice lawsuits against doctors and insurance companies. Lawyers who consistently filed such cases would be subject to discipline. Colin Van Ostern said this program was a better way of benefitting health care than limiting jury awards. "It's a recognition that medical malpractice insurance increases are a problem for doctors."

In July of 2003, Americans for Job Security, founded by the American Insurance Association, headed by Dave Carney, a New Hampshire political professional, placed posters in the Manchester airport assaulting the senator. Carney accused Edwards of being, "the epitome of the smooth-talking, slick lawyer in terms of perpetrating a tort system that allows someone to sue Nabisco . . . over the fact that Oreo cookies make you fat."

To energize his New Hampshire campaign, Edwards promised a series of town hall meetings as he had conducted in North Carolina when running for the Senate. He would make child health care insurance mandatory by providing refundable tax credits to parents to cover the cost. Among a number of reforms for corporate accountability he said that stock options should be treated as expenses, commenting, "The abuse of stock options that are hidden from balance sheets have been central to the corporate scandals." In Nashua, he was critical of the FBI and suggested a new agency to fight terrorism should be established within the Department of Homeland Security.

Democratic Florida Senator Bob Graham

Senator Graham, who had undergone heart surgery, was unable to make his first visit to the state until mid-April of 2003. As a former Florida governor, he considered himself a political centrist who could beat George Bush in that state. Previously his only campaign trip here had been in 1984 when he came to support former Florida Governor Ruben Askew in his quest for the presidency.

Graham explained that his electioneering style included brief substitutions in the everyday jobs of average voters to get a better feel for their occupations. He said the tactic helped him "not only to learn how people earn their livings, but also how they live their lives." The senator's first undertaking was as a history teacher at Oyster River High School. He also spent time playing checkers at Robie's Store, a traditional campaign stop for presidential candidates. There was also a promise that before his campaign was over he'd "be a total pest in New Hampshire." Subsequently he served as a conductor on the 11-mile run of the Conway Scenic Railroad which primarily serves out-of-state summer tourists.

As a former chairman of the Senate Intelligence Committee, he charged that the nation's international credibility would be substantially impaired if weapons of mass destruction were not found in Iraq. Although he had voted against military action in Iraq, Graham suggested possible missile strikes against Syrian terrorist training camps. "This is the first time we've gone to war without being attacked or being seriously under the threat of at-

Florida Senator Bob Graham plays checkers at Robie's Store in Hooksett, the site of numerous presidential candidate visits throughout the history of the presidential primary.

tack." He charged that the administration's programs for homeland security were restricting civil liberties and rights of privacy.

He accused the White House of shading and manipulating information to sell its policies to the American people and our allies around the world. "I believe he (Bush) is being deceptive."

Graham predicted our troops would be in Iraq for five years or longer at a cost of $25 to $50 billion per year. The senator also took exception to President Bush's "bring 'em on" remark, concerning post-invasion attacks on U.S. peacekeeping soldiers by Iraqis, feeling it could cause even greater risk to our men and women stationed there. "This Las Vegas boxing ring comment is not going to be a very comforting statement for the families of the 175,000 troops in Iraq," he said.

Graham explained he voted against tax cuts because, "I didn't think it was a good idea to pass a trillion dollars worth of debt onto the next generation." Nor did he believe that the wealthy who benefitted from the cuts would reinvest the money to improve the country's economy. Further, he blamed the president for losing three million jobs, saying, "we now have the highest rate of unemployment in nine years."

The senator proposed a plan for economic renewal which would hike taxes on the wealthy but cut them for others. It would cost over $300 billion over five years and balance the budget by 2010, after building schools, highways, parks, and water resources and strengthening homeland security.

He also criticized the No Child Left Behind Act as not properly funding the obligations placed on the states to enforce it. The senator proposed increasing Medicaid for those who qualified and expanding Medicare to assist early retirees. His health plan called for stages of increased insurance during his first term, which would cover two-thirds of those currently uninsured; "then in my second term, we'll deal with the other one-third."

By mid-2003, the senator had made five trips to New Hampshire and had identified his main concerns as the environment, social security, health care, education and the economy.

Ohio Congressman and former mayor of Cleveland, Dennis Kucinich, greets students at Manchester Central High School, the oldest public high school in New Hampshire, while visiting the state's largest city during a campaign tour.

Democratic Ohio Congressman Dennis Kucinich

Antiwar protester Kucinich believes "the peace movement is changing the world and it will change American politics. I'm offering for the people of New Hampshire an opportunity for a fundamental change, a real shift in our priorities and a return of government to the people." He claims to run well on a sloppy track and will stand out as a candidate. On his first trip to the state in late March of 2003, staking out a strong position for education and against the Iraq War, he asked, "Why do we have money to ruin the health of Iraqi children and not repair the health of our own?"

On his second visit he advocated a Department of Peace which could be at Cabinet level with a mission of preventing violence everywhere and designed to make war "archaic." At the same time, he slammed the Patriot Act as undermining basic American freedoms and he would rescind the North Atlantic Free Trade Agreement (NAFTA) which he felt abridged workers' rights and led to cheap labor from Mexico. He would cut the military budget to support such domestic programs as free education for every child from "kindergarten all the way through college."

The congressman told reporter Daniel Barrick of the *Concord Monitor* that he identifies himself as a member of the "progressive wing of the Democratic Party," advocating federal work programs, free education, universal health care and higher taxes on the wealthy.

He said he would decide in June whether to remain in the race, admitting he was "the most unlikely candidate in this race. I'm used to winning elections people say are unwinnable." On a third visit in early August, he opened a Manchester headquarters, saying he was "the progressive and liberal alternative" for the Democrats.

Democratic Connecticut Senator Joe Lieberman

In November of 2001, Senator Lieberman returned to New Hampshire on a "thank you" tour for the support he received in his vice presidential quest when running with Al Gore in the 2000 presidential election. He had formed a political action committee to raise money for Democrats.

The senator admitted he was exploring the possibility of being a presidential candidate in 2004, providing Al Gore did not again seek the office. He was supportive of President Bush's conduct of the war on terrorism, favored shoring up volunteer defense programs, supported ROTC, civil defense, and believed Homeland Security should have Cabinet status. Yet he disagreed with the president on tax cuts which he felt had benefitted only the rich and drained money from worthwhile programs such as education.

On a return trip in March of 2002, he endorsed Democratic candidates and participated in a Democratic St. Patrick's Day dinner. In an August visit he again was supportive of Bush, saying, "every day that Saddam remains in power with weapons of mass destruction is a day of danger for the U.S." At the same time, he was critical of the president for going too slow in reacting to corporate fraud. On another two-day tour in October, while endorsing Democratic Congressional candidates and State Senator Disnard, he attacked Bush on economic issues but allowed, "we've got a president today who's given us some leadership in the war on terrorism. But that's about all."

The senator criticized Republicans who "talk a moderate talk, but don't walk a moderate walk. Their values aren't representative of mainstream America." The senator believed he'd have the word from Gore by year's end on the former vice president's political plans. In mid-December 2002, Gore announced he would not again seek the presidency and a month later Lieberman made his campaign official. Meanwhile his PAC had donated $98,000 to New Hampshire Democratic candidates in the 2002 election and to the Democratic State Committee.

Lieberman's wife, Hadassah, had made a Concord appearance in support of Congressional candidate Katrina Swett.

United States senator from Connecticut, and 2000 Democratic vice-presidential candidate Joe Lieberman at a "Politics and Eggs" breakfast at C.R. Sparks in Bedford. During their campaigns, most candidates speak at this event held for members of the business community.

Thereafter in midyear of 2003, she began solo appearances for her husband with her special interest of health care and assisting single parents. His mother, Marcia, also campaigned to stir up petitions at senior centers on behalf of low-income children, pointing out that Lieberman had said they were being left out by Bush's tax cuts.

The senator said, "This administration (Bush's) refuses to acknowledge that everything its supposedly done to get the economy going again has failed." He was also critical of federal programs reducing environmental regulations, alleging, "They've shown disrespect for some of our great open spaces and wildlife areas. They've been willing to allow development or misuse of them." While opposed to a military draft, he did believe young Americans might be involved in some sort of mandatory national service, not necessarily in the armed services. On a visit to Portsmouth in late January of 2003, he said Bush "has got to do a better job of making the case for why we need to go into Iraq and had no real economic recovery plan."

Lieberman set himself apart from most of his Democratic competitors by pledging to support Bush in whatever action the president might take against Iraq, but he also added, "When more people around the world see the American president as a greater threat to peace than Saddam Hussein, then you know something is really wrong with our foreign policy. We are saddled with an administration that has forgotten that family responsibility and faith matter more than power, partisanship and privilege." He was also suspicious of Bush's awarding a no-bid contract for extinguishing Iraqi oil fires to Halliburton, the same corporation which his vice president, Dick Cheney, had previously supervised.

At the same time, he was concerned that the Bush administration had not put an Iraqi in charge of its oil wells, because "They'll (the Iraqis) think we started the war not to overthrow Saddam Hussein, but to grab the oil industry." He was proud of being the only one of the nine major competitors who supported both the 1991 Gulf War and the attack against Saddam. The senator also thought the best way to fight terrorism is to give Muslim countries economic assistance.

Sometimes there's a wrong time or place for a candidate to be campaigning, such as at the New Hampshire Democrats Annual dinner when the speaker was honoring a local longtime and much respected party activist, Joe Millimet, with an exhortation to the excited crowd of "Let's hear it for Joe!" At that point guess who inadvertently made a parade entrance with his retinue? Of course he later redeemed himself when he said, "I believe New Hampshire has been, should be and will be the first-in-the-nation primary."

The senator considered himself as more pro-business than any of his Democratic competitors and further alleged "President Bush may be the first president with a Master of Business Administration degree, but he has compiled the worst business record in 50 years." The candidate proposed tax credits for businesses that create new jobs or invest in new information technology and the elimination of capital gain taxes for those who, under certain conditions, risk investment in start-up businesses. His concern centered on the loss of manufacturing jobs, particularly those going to China.

"America has lost 3.1 million jobs under the Bush administration, and 2.4 of them have been in manufacturing," said Lieberman. To emphasize the severity of the problem he introduced his "Jobs Tour," to talk with employees at manufacturing plants as he travelled the state, because "finding a good job is what it's all about."

He believed Bush had not concentrated enough on alternative energy sources. The senator would promote more energy-efficient hybrid cars and offer tax credits to their purchasers. His plan for "Declaration of Energy Independence" included a program for producing fuel from coal. New jobs would be created by stabilizing gas prices and home heating costs along with encouraging consumer purchasing of U.S. made products. The senator would give tax credits to qualified companies which keep manufacturing jobs in this country.

Former Illinois Democratic Senator Carol Moseley Braun

Senator Moseley Braun was the second African-American and first woman to express an interest in running for president in 2004 by her New Hampshire visit on February 16, 2003. "I am here to say we want them (men) to take the 'men-only' off the White House door. I hope to inspire this generation to put a woman in our nation's highest office." She said while being a budget deficit hawk, she was a peace dove. Her appearance was sponsored by the American Women Presidents, a political action committee. This was the only appearance she made prior to the publication of this book.

Democrat Reverend Al Sharpton

In mid-February 2002, Reverend Al Sharpton, an African-American, spoke to students at Keene State and Dartmouth along with an appearance at a church in Pelham to test the waters for a possible presidential run in 2004. He said, "someone who has the whitest state in America can hear someone from another experience of America."

Previously, he had been a candidate for mayor of New York city, twice ran for the U.S. Senate and spent time in prison for trespassing on a U.S. Naval Base and was known as a street activist, "The Rev." He was critical of the Democratic Party for being too much like Republicans, saying, "I think its time to move the party back from reactionary behavior . . . There's nothing more humorous than to see an elephant dressed like a donkey." He also accused the Bush administration of taking advantage of terrorist threats to undermine civil rights and civil liberties.

A few days before formally announcing his candidacy for the 2004 presidential primary, he returned in mid-January of 2003 to address an audience at St. Anselm College. He claimed to be the only Democratic candidate opposed to war with Iraq, was against selective service, the death penalty, welfare reforms that humiliate people and tax cuts which he said only benefit the rich.

Former U.S. senator from Illinois and United States ambassador to New Zealand, Carol Moseley Braun, speaks to voters in Manchester at an event during President's Day weekend.

Reverend Al Sharpton of New York leaves a Concord restaurant following a luncheon speech during a campaign swing through the state.

He would raise the minimum wage by $2 and favored federal enforcement of the rights of workers to organize. The Reverend also viewed war as a policy which supported the wealthy and was critical of corporate America. "We cannot have an America where we tell young men and women that it is an honor for them to go and risk their lives in Iraq, but it's a burden for the wealthy to pay their taxes at home in America."

Sharpton was sharply critical of Bush's opposition to affirmative action saying, "This president (Bush) is the recipient of more preference than anyone in American history."

By curious coincidence, as Sharpton's campaign was warming up, a group identified as Democracy First was advocating that the District of Columbia should replace New Hampshire in conducting the first presidential primary.

Potential "Late Starter" Candidate: Retired General Wesley Clark

Although not saying he was a Democrat or a member of any political party, the former NATO commander and Rhodes scholar from Arkansas admitted in February of 2003 that he'd been considering a White House run as a Democrat in 2004. Later, during a May visit to New Hampshire, the general continued to say he was not a candidate. Meanwhile he had been presented with petitions urging him to join the race. By early July, Susan Putney of Dover announced that a draft committee had been established for his support and was opening an office to start his campaign. She told the press, "We're running a campaign without a candidate. We are prepared to make this a write-in if we have to."

A Procedural Change for the 2004 Primary

In previous New Hampshire presidential primaries all of the registered candidates' names were listed on the ballot by last name in alternate rotation "so that each name shall appear thereon as nearly as may be an equal number of times at the top, at the bottom, and in each intermediate place." This required the state to print an excessive number of ballots to conform with the law.

Consequently, our frugal legislature saved $32,000 of printing expense by providing that the names will be listed alphabetically on the ballot, beginning in 2004.

Some believe that name placement on the ballot can effect election outcomes. Others, including our Deputy Secretary of State David Scanlan, a former majority leader in the New Hampshire House, disagree that the listing sequence makes a difference. The primary ballot only lists the candidates for president and vice president. When there is a long list of names, it is actually easier to find your choice if the names are alphabetical. Very few voters walk into the voting booth undecided.

In any event, if there is such an advantage, it's likely that Governor Dean will have that privilege unless General Clark or an ABC fringe candidate decides to file.

❋

Chapter 12

Are Retail Politics Being Threatened?

As John Harwood pointed out in the *Wall Street Journal,* there has been tremendous development in the primary system in just a generation. In 1968 only 14 states and the District of Columbia conducted presidential primaries and only New Hampshire held its primary before the end of March.

Rhodes Cook, former Senior Political Writer for the *Congressional Quarterly,* reported that in 2000, 42 states, plus the District of Columbia held Republican primaries and 39 states plus the District of Columbia held Democratic primaries. Most of them were over by the end of March.

In 1996, Republican Washington Senator Slade Gorton and Democratic Connecticut Senator Joseph Lieberman, concerned with the ever increasing number of primaries and the interfacing of their schedules, designed the "Presidential Primary Act of 1996." It provided for regional primaries—but it never went anywhere.

During 1998 there was a great rush of states to move up their primary dates for the year 2000, hoping to be more competitive in the election process. Some were considering regional primaries, such as a proposed "Big Sky Primary" of western states to be held on Saturday, March 11 and before the original "Super Tuesday" of the southern states. Governor Mike Leavitt of Utah, a principal sponsor of the plan, said it was not their intent to usurp the tradition and prestige of the early New Hampshire primary. In the Midwest there was talk of a "Prairie Primary."

New Hampshire's neighbors were considering what would effectively be a "Yankee Day Primary" somewhat reminiscent of what occurred in 1975, except this time the other New England states were planning for March 7, well behind what had already been determined would be New Hampshire's leadoff date in 2000.

Still New Hampshire didn't seriously worry about national front-loading until California decided to move up from March 26 to March 7, followed by updating of the other big states of New York and Ohio. California accounted for 17 percent of the delegates elected to the Republican National Convention and 20 percent of the delegates elected to the Democratic National Convention.

California also had a "winner take all" prize for the Republican candidate who secured the most votes, as contrasted to most states, where delegates are awarded on the basis of the proportional votes received by each candidate. California is thus the big gorilla in the Republican zoo.

Even though New Hampshire's 2000 primary would precede March 7 by over a month, this dramatic front-loading trend was already concerning the state's political activists about what might happen in 2004. If these larger states or a consortium of smaller ones should move to within one week of New Hampshire, its longtime prestige and value to the country would be lost. Further, it would limit the playing field only to wealthy candidates.

In his 1992 campaign, when Delaware was attempting to upstage New Hampshire, Bill Clinton at Dartmouth opposed Delaware's interference, saying it would cause "the dam to break" and other states would also encroach on New Hampshire "and then nobody would learn anything about the candidate " except from TV sound bites and airport receptions."

In most states it is the secretary of state who is responsible for the administration of election laws. He or she exerts considerable influence in designing statutes and procedures for their respective legislatures. In some states, such as Connecticut, Idaho, Mary-

Fun along the Campaign Trail

During George Bush's campaign against Ronald Reagan in 1979, an airport reception had been arranged in Lebanon to greet the plane on its landing from Keene. A crowd of enthusiastic supporters and a generous dose of media were on hand. But the weather became so bad that everyone was moved into a hangar, hoping the rain, thunder and lighting would run out. It didn't. Meanwhile the candidate was secretively driven by car to the airport, put unnoticed into a parked plane at the remote end of the runway and taxied into the hangar.

Of course, as his handlers pointed out, nothing less would have been expected of the country's youngest pilot in World War II, who had been shot down in the Pacific. Nor was anyone any the wiser as they saluted the war hero all over again for undertaking the brave flight in the fierce storm. Probably the ruse would never have worked if he had not also served as director of the CIA!

land, Massachusetts, Mississippi and Washington, their authority extends to determining whose names are actually placed on presidential primary ballots.

In New Hampshire the secretary has the unique exclusive authority, within statutory limits, to determine the date of the primary. Because New Hampshire is a small state, it is possible for him to implement a quicker turn-around for a new date than could be accomplished by most potential successor states. For example, ballots can be printed here rather quickly.

As well stated in the Lebanon *Valley News,* "So important is the 'first-in-the-nation' primary to New Hampshire that it changes the date every four years to make sure that no other state can cut in line and diminish the significance of the event."

New Hampshire Secretary of State Bill Gardner has served as President of the National Association of Secretaries of State (NASS) the oldest organization of elected officials in the country and is the senior member. In 1996 he served along with Ron Thornburgh, secretary of state of Kansas, to co-chair a bipartisan subcommittee of NASS to study the primary and caucus systems in use by all the states.

At a secretaries meeting in Washington in May of 1996, the 17 secretaries who attended unanimously approved a resolution: "The presidential nominating process should start in a few small states to allow retail politics. Early small states serve an important purpose in narrowing the field of candidates, yet give any candidate an equal opportunity to participate in the process. New Hampshire and Iowa currently serve this purpose."

Subsequently the secretaries appointed a Committee on Presidential Primaries, co-chaired by Democrat William F. Galvin, secretary of state of Massachusetts, and Republican Bill Jones, then secretary of state of California. Both men had always been supportive of New Hampshire's first-in-the-nation position. They presented a plan for rotating primaries beginning in 2004 which was adopted by NASS in February, 1999. It was supported by the Council of State Governments and exempted New Hampshire and Iowa from the rotation.

Jones explained, "In an attempt to prevent states from engaging in presidential leap-frog, the political party rules have come dangerously close to creating a de facto national primary election day. To reform this process, all 50 states must work together to develop a system of regional primaries that rotates every four years to allow

---

Fun along the Campaign Trail

When George Bush was sailing around Lake Winnipesaukee on the excursion boat *The Mount*, the vessel was followed by a fleet of speedboats, cabin cruisers and anything else that could float, with loyal partisans aboard yelling their hearts out. Suddenly a motorized sea dragon appeared with its green hind end decorated with a "Bush for President" banner. "Hey, you guys," yelled Bush from the deck of the ship, "you've got the flag on the wrong end."

each state's voters to have a say in the selection of presidential nominees. In doing this, we must ensure that several small states like New Hampshire and Iowa remain at the front of the process to require candidates to engage in one-on-one retail politics."

The plan called for four regional elections: eastern, southern, midwestern and western. Each region would follow an election calendar cycle on the first Tuesday of March, April, May and June. The regions would then rotate every four years to allow each region an equal opportunity in the presidential nominating process. The Iowa caucus and the New Hampshire primary were specifically exempted, both being permitted their traditionally earlier dates in all rotations. To take effect this idea would require endorsement by the legislatures of the 50 states and the two national political parties.

The *New York Times,* after commenting editorially on the confusion from the front-loading fiasco, wrote, "The National Association of Secretaries of State, whose members oversee the state primaries had been perhaps the only group taking the problem as seriously as it deserves. It is working on a proposal that would create five regional presidential primaries, held a month apart, with the order rotating from one election year to the next. New Hampshire and Iowa would keep their traditional role as the season openers in February."

The NASS solution to the primary problem sparked a number of other plans. The original "Delaware Plan," designed for the GOP by Delaware's Republican Chairman Basil Battaglia, also called for a rotating system of monthly elections except the smallest states would hold their primaries first, followed by two groups of successively larger states and the largest states would be the last to vote. It was a fixed rotation which did not change with each four-year election cycle. Obviously it didn't get the blessing of the big states for being the permanent caboose, but it did exempt New Hampshire. An amended version, approved by a national GOP committee which tossed New Hampshire in with the first group, never made it to the 2000 national GOP Convention.

Another approach, The Ohio Plan, sponsored by Republican State Chairman Bob Bennett, was somewhat similar to the Delaware Plan except the constituency of the regional "pods" was different. It only dictated the starting point for a primary; any state could "opt-out" to hold its election during the period of a later pod or it could be held at any time after May 1. Again New Hampshire would be first, but only by four days.

Martin Dunleavy, political affairs director of the American Federation of Government Employees, offered a scheme with "rotating sectional primaries" where the country would be divided into four regions and then further divided into three sections per region. After Iowa and New Hampshire voted, one of the western sections and one of the southern sections would vote first, followed three weeks later by a section from the midwest and one from the east.

Former New Hampshire Senator Bob Smith also devised a "Fairness in Primaries" plan. Clearly it was New Hampshire born and bred, because New Hampshire was the first state in the nation to introduce a lottery and his plan was based on one. It allowed both small and large states within four regions to draw for their positions and it would eliminate the "winner take all" prize, at that time offered in some states, such as California. Quite appropriately it allowed his home state to continue to set the pace.

Carol Casey, Treasurer of Americans for Democratic Action, would entice the national parties back to caucuses by allowing only those states which used them to hold their elections in the first month of the election cycle. Her objective would be to deliberately reduce the number of primaries and regress to a caucus system which she felt is not as dependent on money and the media. We assume she was frightened by the state of "Live Free or Die."

Haley Barbour, former National GOP Chairman, agreed that the system should be changed, "but New Hampshire's and Iowa's first-in-the-nation status should be retained because it offers not only the voters of those two states, but those throughout the nation, insights into the candidates that will be unavailable if that status is lost."

The *Boston Sunday Globe* editorialized, "Iowa and New Hampshire have proved themselves. No meddling should be allowed—for the sake, not of the states, but of democracy."

It's unlikely that any of these plans, or other proposals not mentioned here, would take effect before the 2008 primary anyway, due to GOP rules which do not permit such changes except at its national conventions. The 2004 convention would be the first time any of these new ideas could be acted upon; this pretty much assures the New Hampshire primary will continue its current position at least until 2008. The Democrats had no other pervasive plans on the table in 2000.

While this "on hold" situation works well for New Hampshire, it reflects adversely on the process of choosing the president in 2004. If the 1999–2000 "rush to frontload" is repeated or, worse yet, exacerbated in 2003–2004, as a practical matter the winning candidates will have been determined before mid March in 2004 and probably even earlier.

Further, the choices will have been predetermined before some states will have had the opportunity of having any input into the selection. There will be a minimum duration of nine months of campaigning until the general election in November. The campaigns will become tedious, dull and exorbitantly expensive.

Both the Republican and Democratic parties are concerned about this dilemma yet they have been unable to resolve the problem. A solution may be for a non-partisan commission to be established, funded by a nationally respected private foundation, to study the subject, with a mission of producing a plan which could

Fun along the Campaign Trail

Dick Bosa, two-time New Hampshire candidate for the presidency and former mayor of Berlin, cautioned his followers not to spell his name backwards.

gain consensus from both the political parties and the states. The members of the commission would be eminent citizens representative of government and the political system, perhaps appointed by the president as was done in setting up the Grace Commission to cut costs of the federal government.

In August of 2000, Gregg appealed without success to the Public Policy section of the Pew Charitable Trusts to undertake the foregoing proposal. Since then, Wyoming Republicans moved the date of their county conventions for the selection of delegates to the GOP 2004 national convention to February 3, 2004, the earliest date permitted under rules of the National Republican Committee. "Wyoming can be the New Hampshire of the West as far as the Republican Party is concerned," said Wyoming Republican State Party Chairman Becky Costantino. They thereby gave leadership by initiating a front-loading trend for 2004!

If Wyoming is serious about upstaging New Hampshire on its primary date, there would be several factors which perhaps it hasn't considered. First, if it's only their Republican Party that plans to move up, their county conventions would not be "similar" to our primary, which includes the Democrats. Our law would not require we move ahead of Wyoming by a week. Secondly, Wyoming has always been a caucus state, not a primary state. If it's planning a caucus, it would not disturb New Hampshire anyway. Third, Wyoming as the fifth largest state (96,989 square miles) is more than ten times the geographic size of New Hampshire which is only 44th in land area (8,993 square miles). The impediments of covering such an enormous area would be an overwhelming disadvantage and cost to the candidates. Fourth, New Hampshire, having twice the population of the western state, gives it a substantially wider base upon which to make projections. And finally, New Hampshire has its eighty years of experience in being first, without criticism of how elections were conducted.

Meanwhile if the front-loading trend gets any stronger, the situation could look very much like a national primary. And there's always the highly improbable possibility that Congress might step

> *Fun along the Campaign Trail*
>
> **Mike Levinson from Buffalo, a self-confident regular among the lesser-knowns, was once a write-in candidate and was quoted as saying, "If you can't be bothered to write my name on the ballot, then you don't deserve to have me."**

in and establish one. Just the thought of such a debacle strikes fear in all the states, because each one wants its own proprietary share of the pie. Only the wealthy and well-known would need apply as potential candidates. Obviously it would be the death of grass-roots campaigning.

It is an amusing note to this discussion that in the opinion of former Illinois Senator Paul Simon, who ran in the 1988 New Hampshire primary, regional primaries "would be a great mistake." He wrote in his *Autobiography* that campaigning in a small state like New Hampshire is of a great advantage to a candidate of limited resources and if he'd done things differently in Iowa and New Hampshire, he would have been the nominee! That's a sound conclusion—made by many others, though perhaps for different reasons.

※

This cartoon appeared in the book New Hampshire the Primary State, *published in 2001 by Gregg-Resources NH, courtesy of David Tirrell-Wysocki, Mel Bolden and Charles Russell.*

Bill Gardner makes an entrance as Paul Revere in a 1994 cartoon by Bob Dix in the Manchester Union Leader. *"Secretary of State William Gardner wants to keep the date flexible and quiet and quickly hold the election before other states can match us" reads the scroll.*

Chapter 13

Back off!

U NTIL 2000, THE REPUBLICAN PARTY had let the states determine most of the rules for delegate selection to the national convention. Until 1980, all New Hampshire delegates were chosen by the voters on the primary ballot. In 1979, the New Hampshire General Court had decided to remove delegates from the ballot, who instead would be selected by the presidential candidates and made known to the voters just before the primary. Although the number of delegates for each state is determined by the national party, New Hampshire law says delegates will be apportioned based on the outcome of the primary. Any candidate getting ten percent of the vote would receive delegates proportional to the vote. Those receiving less than ten percent would not get delegates and that pool would be added to the winner of the primary.

Unlike the Republicans, the Democratic Party has not followed state law for delegate selection since 1980 when the delegate names were removed from the ballot. The actual date of the primary is determined by state law and that has been followed by both national parties.

The Republican National Committee had a rule in 2000 which precluded New Hampshire or other states from holding Republican primaries before the first Monday of February. This date fell on Monday, February 7 in the year 2000. It also provided for waivers when its rule required a state to break its own laws.

The Republican rule was in sharp contrast with the Democratic National Committee's rule at that time, which permitted no

223

primaries earlier than the first Tuesday of March, although New Hampshire and Iowa were specifically exempted.

In some states, the Republican and Democratic primaries are not held on the same day. The two parties do not necessarily *have* to hold their primaries on the same day. The parties themselves can set the dates for their respective primaries. In New Hampshire, the date is determined by the state statute previously quoted. Even here, however, there is nothing to prevent the parties from selecting and running their primaries on a different date.

Unquestionably the greatest deterrent to a satisfactory scheduling of primaries, whether it be by the parties or the state legislatures, is the fact that the two parties do not look out the same "windows," and/or exemptions therefrom, when setting primary calendars. Speaking for New Hampshire as its Democratic National Committeeman, Joe Keefe said, "The core of this will be an expression of desire to work with the Republicans to convince them to adopt the same window as the Democrats." Because Republicans have a different view, from their window, the parties are, unfortunately, not getting a similar perspective on the elective process.

The Democrats required delegate selections or primaries to be reported by the states to the National Committee by May 1, in order to give the party time to print its election calendar. The Republicans required their selections to be submitted by July 1.

Inasmuch as the New Hampshire Legislature is the authenticating body for determining the date of the state's primary, neither the Republican nor the Democratic National Committees have any say in when the state fixes its date. Yet both national parties could punish delegates elected to their respective national conventions by not seating them if they were elected outside of the windows allowed by national committee rules, unless a special exemption was granted for such a circumstance.

Actually the question of whether or not state laws override federal jurisdiction on the question of who has the final say as between the rights of the political parties and the state legislatures in presidential primary elections has not been fully tested. The U.S. Supreme Court did rule in favor of political parties versus state law when it overturned California's "open" ballot law.

Tom Cole, Chief of Staff at the GOP National Headquarters said, "It's a murky area. We have party rules, but we also recognize that the state of New Hampshire has a law and the state is not a political party." The answer of a well-trained pol trained not to answer!

Professor William Mayer of Northeastern University notes that since 1975 "the Supreme Court has granted political parties and party procedures an increasing measure of freedom from both state and federal legislation," but he goes on to say, "the only club the national parties hold over states that decline to go along with a new calendar would be to refuse to seat those states at the convention."

New Hampshire's primary laws have not been tested in court. In view of this circumstance, at a national convention delegates from a state unhappy with New Hampshire delegates, who were elected outside of the window provided by party rules, might successfully challenge the seating of the Granite Staters. As a practical matter, that is unlikely to happen, because the national party would want the New Hampshire vote in the following general election regardless of when its delegates were elected in the primary.

Or, as Mark Siegel wrote, "It remains to be seen if a national party will ever have the will (even if it had the legal authority) to enforce party rules by denying accreditation to state delegations selected outside the parameters of party rules."

Fun along the Campaign Trail

Caroline Killeen, running against the first George Bush, coined a slogan, "America needs trees, not Bushes."

Setting the Primary Date

When State Representative Stephen Bullock's bill passed the General Court and became law in 1913 the New Hampshire presidential primary was brought to life. It called for a May primary but was changed two years later to have it coincide with town meeting day, which for over two centuries was the second Tuesday in March. State Representative John Glessner, who sponsored the bill in 1915 changing the date, thought it would save the towns money if the primary was held on town meeting day rather than at a separate time.

When the first New Hampshire presidential primary was held in 1916, it was not first in the nation. It took place on the same day as Minnesota's and one week after Indiana's. It became first in the nation four years later in 1920 when Minnesota decided to discontinue its primary and return to a caucus, and Indiana moved its primary from March to May. For fifty-seven years following Glessner's amendment the first-in-the-nation primary remained on the traditional town meeting day and there were no changes affecting the date until the primary of 1972.

Florida had traditionally conducted its presidential primary in May, but in 1971, with a notion to muscle in and move to the front, changed its date to be the same day in March as New Hampshire. Florida legislators at the time rhetorically asked "Where do you think presidential candidates would rather be in December, January and February?" The belief in the Sunshine State was that by holding the primary the same day as New Hampshire they would steal the limelight from a small cold-climate state. It didn't work. The Granite State met the challenge by moving its primary date and town meeting day to the first Tuesday in March, a week ahead of the traditional town meeting day—and thus had the primary one week before Florida.

New Hampshire House Speaker Marshall Cobleigh, a Republican from Nashua, and Minority Leader Robert Raiche, a Democrat from Manchester, among others, introduced House Bill 1012

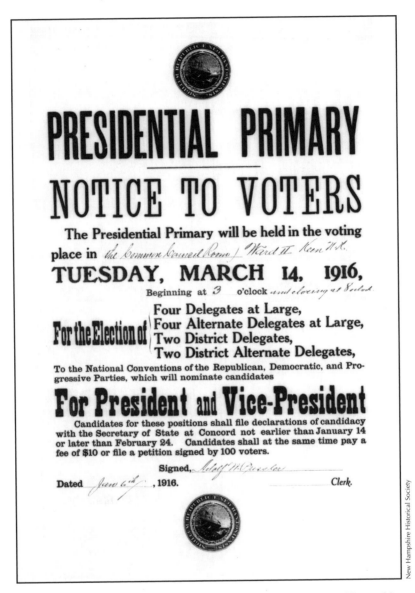

This official notice was posted in a public place in every New Hampshire city and town prior to the first presidential primary in 1916.

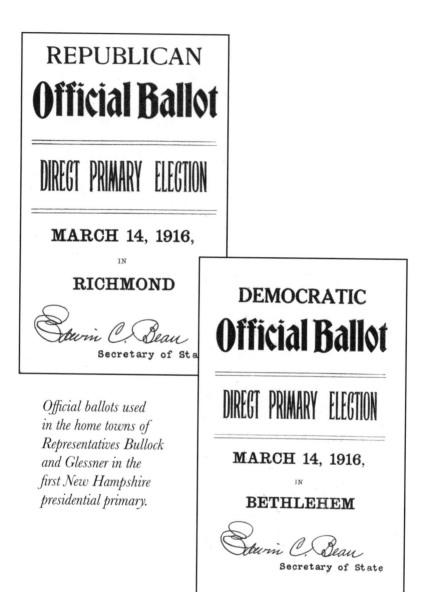

REPUBLICAN

Official Ballot

DIRECT PRIMARY ELECTION

MARCH 14, 1916,

IN

RICHMOND

Edwin C. Bean

Secretary of Sta

DEMOCRATIC

Official Ballot

DIRECT PRIMARY ELECTION

MARCH 14, 1916,

IN

BETHLEHEM

Edwin C. Bean

Secretary of State

Official ballots used in the home towns of Representatives Bullock and Glessner in the first New Hampshire presidential primary.

during the last week of June, 1971, at the very end of the legislative session. The House quickly suspended its rules and passed
the bill to the Senate. On July 1, the final day of the legislative
session, after considerable debate, the Senate suspended its rules
and passed the bill with only one vote to spare. This last-minute
House and Senate action was a deliberate attempt—before they
adjourned due to the constitutional requirement—to make sure
New Hampshire's primary would remain first, and Florida could
not change its date again.

During the time Florida was trying to upstage the New Hampshire primary, the traditional Iowa caucus date was changed by the
Democrats to January rather than late March. Although some in
New Hampshire felt the state should move ahead, the prevailing
opinion was to leave Iowa alone, since it was a caucus. We should
not demand to have the first event but only the first primary. The
state would be in a stronger position later if it protected what
it had—nothing less but nothing more. Thus in January 1972,
Iowa Democrats fot the first time had a caucus ahead of the New
Hampshire primary. The Iowa Republicans kept their caucus in
the early spring but moved up, like the Democrats, in 1976.

This was the first demonstration of New Hampshire's determination not to forsake its long-time tradition of not only being
first, but, equally important, first by a week. Florida's venture was
one of several attempts which have been made to upstage New
Hampshire's first-in-the-nation position. It gave birth to what
later became known as "front-loading."

After the attempt by Florida failed, it was the southern neighbor of Massachusetts, with an assist from its western neighbor
of Vermont, that worked up a regional New England primary
scheme to outfox New Hampshire, by holding it on the first
Tuesday of March. Its eastern neighbor, Maine, also gave passing thought to the idea as did Connecticut. This attempt at a
New England regional primary on the same day as New Hampshire was vigorously opposed by Portsmouth Representative Jim
Splaine, a stalwart supporter of the state's first-in-the-nation

position who then sponsored a bill to move the primary to the last Tuesday of February.

There was opposition to this move by some legislators and local officials. Some thought the primary was not worth protecting while others did not want the town meeting moved up in the calendar again. Due to a lack of consensus, Splaine's idea (in the form of a house bill) had been temporarily laid on the table by the House. Near the end of the 1975 legislative session, Splaine's perseverance paid off and the language was changed to separate the presidential primary from town meeting if necessary and give the secretary of state the authority to set the date in addition to the administrative supervisory responsibility.

Town officials were pleased that town meetings could return to the traditional day and defenders of the first-in-the-nation primary added yet another protection for it. The final part—having the secretary of state set the date—was not without its opponents. Some legislators thought a group of them should set the date, while others thought it should be the governor. Splaine and Governor Meldrim Thomson made the case against both and were successful in placing the decision in the lap of the secretary of state. Governor Thomson was adamant that, in order to keep politics out of the process, neither the governor nor a legislative committee should have the authority to set the date.

The House and Senate let the impostors know the Granite State was not misnamed by enacting an amended version of Splaine's bill, which provided that the presidential primary would be held on "the first Tuesday in March or on the Tuesday immediately preceding the date on which any other New England state shall hold a similar election, whichever is earlier." Splaine had been the only speaker for the bill at public hearings in both the House and Senate and virtually single-handedly saved the first-primary tradition.

Two years later in 1977, the House and Senate further revised the law by removing the words "New England" so that the primary would be held before any other state holding a similar election, not just a New England state.

As the 1980 presidential nomination campaign began, New Hampshire was again the target. This time it came from an unusual source, Puerto Rico, where the Democrats and Republicans had decided to have presidential primaries for the first time. The impetus was a referendum planned for 1981 to vote on statehood. A primary could attract presidential candidates to the island. The two political parties chose not to have primaries on the same day because the Democrats followed national party rules allowing primaries no earlier than March while the Republicans wanted to go ahead of New Hampshire. On February 17,1980 there was a Republican primary in Puerto Rico nine days ahead of New Hampshire. The fact that Puerto Rico was not a state kept the Granite State from moving ahead.

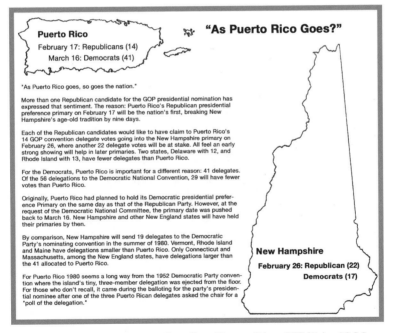

This graphic appeared in "Dateline, Puerto Rico, USA" in 1980, published by the Puerto Rico Federal Affairs Administration.

A critical turning point between New Hampshire and the national political party committees came in 1983. The Democratic National Committee had passed a rule that no state could have a primary earlier than the second Tuesday in March of 1984 with the exception of New Hampshire, which had to have its primary one week earlier, on the first Tuesday of that month. A problem quickly arose because Vermont law still required a primary in that state on the same day. The Democrats said it would only be a beauty contest having no basis for delegate selection. The Republicans however could use it for a partial selection of delegates. This triggered the New Hampshire law to move one week ahead, amid strong opposition from the Democratic National Committee. When the date was officially set for the last Tuesday in February, during the fall of 1983, the DNC chairman said the state would lose its delegates if it had a primary before the first Tuesday of March.

Chairman Charles Manatt dispatched the chairman of the DNC Compliance Review Committee, Nancy Pelosi, to visit New Hampshire, and in no uncertain terms tell the state to back off the February primary or lose its delegates at the national convention. Pelosi, accompanied by State Democratic Chairman George Bruno and two DNC lawyers, met with Secretary of State Gardner and Deputy Secretary of State Robert Ambrose at their Statehouse office in an attempt to convince them to change the date. It was a pleasant meeting, although both sides held to their positions. Just before the meeting ended, Pelosi told Gardner "You have a future ahead of you—you are a young man and you are doing a very foolish thing by this," and then left to meet with Governor Sununu, to see if he would intervene—but he declined. Pelosi returned to Washington, saying New Hampshire, if it continued to hold to its position, would not have delegates seated at the national convention.

Some prominent New Hampshire Democratic Party officials opposed the decision of the secretary of state to move the primary ahead of Vermont. Several predicted that doing so would result not only in the loss of delegates this time, but retaliation by the Democratic National Committee and the loss of the next primary in 1988. Some went so far as to send a letter to attempt to get the Attorney General to interpret the Splaine law regarding a similar election differently than the secretary of state. All during this dispute, Gardner held firm on his decision and believed the first-in the-nation primary would actually be in a stronger position to be retained in the future by keeping the date one week ahead of Vermont.

The state had its primary on February 28th, 1984, amidst a continued threat of having delegates not recognized. On the day before the primary a letter was received from the Democratic National Committee, stating that no delegates selected in the New Hampshire primary would be seated at the San Francisco convention. A month later, in late March, New Hampshire let the Democratic National Committee chairman know that if it's delegation were not seated, it would protest outside the convention hall. As late as May, DNC officials were still saying publicly that the New Hampshire delegates would not be seated at the upcoming national convention. All during this period there was much speculation that this would be the end of the first-in-the-nation primary. But when the convention was held in July in San Francisco, the New Hampshire delegates were seated and the first-in-the-nation primary lived on. (For a detailed review of these events, refer to the *Journal of Law & Politics*, Vol. IV, No. 2. "First-in-the Nation: Disputes over the Timing of Early Democratic Presidential Primaries and Caucuses in 1984 and 1988," by Emmett H. Buell, Jr.)

South Dakota became the next state to challenge the first-in-the-nation primary in 1988. It scheduled a primary for the last Tuesday in February. This was the same day New Hampshire had held its primary since 1976. Splaine's law was used again and the primary was moved ahead a week to the third Tuesday

N.H. primary,
relic or relevant?

California makes play to gain candidates' attention early on

By SCOTT McPHERSON
Sentinel Staff

"California, here I come."
That's one refrain N.H. political junkies don't expect will be echoed

Democrats have an o'
fashioned politica'
Walpole. See '

NH Vs. Delaware In Primary Battle

With a preliminary victory over letter from the DNC has Dela-
Arizona under their belt, New ware's Democrats reconsidering

_e Union Leader, Manchester, N.H.

Iowa: It's war!

Gov. Vilsack wants NH to back down on primary date

From Staff and Wire Reports

Iowa's governor went on the warpath yesterday, hurling combative charges against New Hampshire for unilaterally changing the date of its Presidential primary.

S. Dakota primary gains in stature

■ SOUTH DAKOTA
Continued from Page 1

farms were in trouble."
Still, Erpenbach said, many people are underemployed, and the state' income is only $17,000, below average of $18,685.
Twenty delegates to the Der nal convention will be up fo day. But more impo cided in 1987 to n may play i

THE UNION LEADER, MANCHESTER

Democrats Nix Early P

BY RICHARD L. VERNACI

Dakota must rewrite its delegate-selection pla

ing American Tissue owes it
per mills in million in property taxes that
through its umulated since it filed bank
ruptcy in September.

S.C. Democrats

By ANABELE GARAY
Associated Press Writer

COLUMBIA, S.C. — The state Democratic Party's executive

early as Feb. 3, 2
This facil
Carolina cray

War on primary poaching is declared

High-profile Republicans drawn into skirmish

By M.L. ELRICK
and JORDAN RAU
Monitor staff

In the Lone Star state they say "Don't Mess

The interstate wa-
Senate Majority r
also endorse
said the
Har

words escalated as
b Dole of Kansas
ire's primary and
hould follow New
e it like it is, with

Hampshire on Tuesday and some other state
on Wednesday, nobody's going to notice" the
second state, he said. "They might have a footnote."
Another Republican presidential contender,
former Tennessee Gov. Lamar Alexander, also
supports New Hampshire for the first primary.
But Sen. Phil Gramm of Texas, whose presi-

LIVE FREE OR CRY
The Truth about New Hampshire

By Andrew Ferguson

he's dead.) Because when it comes t
the New Hampshire

Manchester,
nths before the 1964 Ne
ntial primary, the politi
t Alsop took to the pages

The gauntlet is thrown
Arizona challenges N.H.'s primary election spot

By WILLIAM F. RAWSON
Associated Press

PHOENIX — Betting that presidential contenders would rather spend February in the desert sun than the New England

main first," he said.
In 1992, Arizona lawmakers —envious of the attention lavished every four years on the traditional first-in-the-nation primary — set Arizona's first-ever

ELECTION '96

Republican state Sen. B
mon, chief sponsor of Ar
primary law, said her inte
to give the people an oppo
to hear from candidates
their platforms have been

Primary schedule challenged

Golden State wants first-in-nation status

By WILLIAM RAWSON
Associated Press

PHOENIX — Betting that presidential contenders would rather spend February in the desert sun than the New England snow, Arizona plans to hold its primary in 1996 on the same day as New Hampshire's first-in-the-nation contest. Chances are, it won't happen without a fight from New Hampshire.

New Hampshire has a law re...

"I do know New Hampshire is dogged and determined to remain first."

— David Moore o Gallup Organiza

"date," said Margaret

Delaware Republicans bow to New Hampshire

WIMPS

Delaware's Republican Party leadership didn't ha the courage to stand up to New Hampshire. They own and kissed the ring of Granite State poli ly planning a caucus instead of participe presidential primary, Delaware Rep ely what New Hampshire demand Republican Party Chairman happy face on his weak-k

NH's Presidential primary dodges yet another bullet

cord, N.H., said on the convention

Saturday, June 20, 1987

mary in South Dakota

tional party to impose its will on the state.

emocratic party rules prohibit states from

er's Daily Democrat – March 5, 2003

D.C Moves to Upstage N.H. President rimary

Bill Calls for Balloting To Be on Same Day

Maine Threatens NH Primary

By DONN TIBBETTS
State House Bureau Chief

CONCORD — The state of Maine could attempt to hold its Presidential primary on the same day as New Hampshire next year.

A bill that has won preliminary approval of both the House and Senate contains the

"Our law says we have to be a week ahead of anyb y else. If the M bec

should know in a week be funded or not," b New Hampshire Gardner said he received notifi preliminary funding.
"If the the fir

Arizona governor angling to take 1st primary from N.H.

doesn't do well here. He's got a lot a stake but he doesn't seem to much going on."
Arizona could lose most ironic reaso In 1991, initially q

ARIZONA
Continued from Page 1

"People would much rather be here this time of the year, unless you really like that snow and ice ..."
New Hampshire Gov. Stephen Merrill, a Republican who does not want to be known as the governor who lost one of the state's biggest claims to fame, is not amused.
"If I were you, I'd put your money on the 'ice and snow'," Merrill ing that the first-primary by New Hamp

Midwest Dems Want N.H. Primary Fight

By NEDRA PICKLER
Associated Press Writer

HINGTON — Some leading an Democrats want to break pshire's control over the presidential primary nominating caucus

"States other than New Hampshire will ... reward us for challenging New Hampshire's perpetual, preferential, privileged status."

U.S. Rep. John Dingell and U.S. Sen. Carl Levin

has not taken a

has been urging his state to ers, said the union gether:
said yesterday she re "Politics at every level were put sent on diversifying the aside and numerous people

crowd NH prima

Mich.

The Democratic National Com mittee's rules committee approv ed a change this month Cur uld allow early primaries

vin in South of the Demo committee "This i nal Committee

na
national paigns for dates.
"It's bette

ARIZONA BLINKS
Gramm Crafts a Cease-Fire In Primary Battle With NH

of February. The primary remained first by a week and the tradition continued through 1992, when the primary was again held on the third Tuesday of February to keep a week ahead of South Dakota.

During the spring of 1992, the political landscape was changing and party activists and political reporters were handicapping the upcoming contest between Governor Bill Clinton and President George Bush. Under the radar, however, were the actions of two states that would challenge the New Hampshire primary four years later. Without any notice to the rest of the country, Arizona and Delaware lawmakers decided that four years later in 1996 their respective states would, for the first time ever, have presidential primaries.

Both states challenged the New Hampshire tradition. Arizona actually took the existing New Hampshire law and made it their own, as follows, "A presidential primary election shall be held on the second Tuesday in March or on the first date on which any other state shall hold a similar election, whichever is earlier, of each year in which the president of the United States is elected." Delaware law said the state would have a presidential primary on the Saturday after New Hampshire whenever that would be.

Arizona lawmakers had the same idea as counterparts in Florida two decades earlier. They were betting that presidential candidates would rather spend the winter months in the warm Arizona desert sun than the cold New Hampshire snow. Their law was more creative however, as the Granite State could not just change its date like it did with Florida in 1971.

When the mid-term elections concluded and the Republicans took a majority in the United States House of Representative for the first time in over 40 years, all eyes began to look at the next presidential election and who would take on President Bill Clinton. There was a growing field of Republican candidates and the primary calendar was becoming the focus of attention. How would New Hampshire stave off two states—and perhaps others—this time? Was it the end of the road?

New Hampshire Governor Steve Merrill and Republican Party Chairman Steve Duprey asked the candidates for president to help New Hampshire. Merrill was relentless with Arizona Governor Fife Symington, trying to convince him to back off. Two of the top contenders for the Republican nomination, Senator Bob Dole of Kansas and Senator Phil Gramm of Texas, were asked by their New Hampshire supporters to help.

In addition to the political pressure, Arizona was facing other problems as well. The date was outside the window of the Democratic National Committee rules, and because of violations of the federal voting rights act, any election-law changes had to be approved by the U.S. Justice Department. The Justice Department had okayed the switch from a caucus to a primary but were reluctant to okay a February date, because of the difficulty of voting on the Navajo reservation during the bad weather at that time of year, in the remote northeastern corner of the state.

As the pressure continued, Governor Symington said he had been convinced by Senator Gramm that New Hampshire should retain its first position, and offered to support a change in the law to have the primary a day after New Hampshire. That was unacceptable to Governor Merrill and other Granite State officials and, after explaining the significance of the seven days and the conflict with New Hampshire law, he agreed to a week later.

Legislation was introduced to end the conflict by Arizona Representative Jeff Groscost, a Republican from Mesa. He said this would end the game of chicken between the two states and "I don't mind playing chicken . . . but I have a certain aversion to playing chicken when there is no responsible expectation that we could win." The legislature agreed, and changed the law to set the date for a week after the New Hampshire primary and preserve its historic tradition. When the legislation went to Governor Symington for his signature he called the vote to change the date "heroic." He also joked to *Manchester Union Leader* reporter John DiStaso "I hope I can come back to your state now. I have a lot of friends there." He added that his sister lives in Center Harbor

and was on New Hampshire's side. The change of heart pleased
Granite-Staters by ending one more squabble and another effort
to upstage the first-in-the-nation primary.

With one down, there was still one to go. Delaware was set to
have its first ever presidential primary in 1996. Prior to that year
it had been a caucus state. A new law had taken effect which required the primary to be held on the first Saturday after the New
Hampshire primary. As well stated by Gary E. Hindes, a former
Delaware Democratic state chairman, "after 220 years of statehood the people of Delaware were given their first opportunity
to have a direct voice in the selection of the major nominees for
president by voting in Delaware's first presidential primary election." New Hampshire, even older than the First State, had again
led the way.

Delaware had scheduled a filing period for presidential candidates during the middle of December. Before that, New Hampshire's Republican Governor Steve Merrill requested all major

This cartoon appeared in Deleware's Wilmington News Journal,
February 4, 1995. (Courtesy of political cartoonist Jack Jurden)

Republican candidates not to file in Delaware to help protect the Granite State tradition. Kansas Senator Bob Dole, the leading Republican candidate, took a strong stand in support of New Hampshire and most of the Republican candidates followed. As it developed, only Steve Forbes of the major Republican candidates went to Delaware.

On the Democratic side, President Bill Clinton, who had made a special point of visiting New Hampshire every year of his presidency, did not have a serious challenger. While he had repeatedly spoken out in the press in favor of our state having the first primary and of his affection for the Granite State, after his comeback here in 1992 was well-known, some of his national political advisors were concerned about offending Delaware, a swing state in the general election.

In the late fall of 1995, New Hampshire Democratic National Committeeman Terry Shumaker, Clinton's friend and co-chair of his '92 and '96 campaigns in this state, traveled to Washington to meet with the hard-nosed head of the re-election effort, Harold Ickes, Jr., son of one of President Franklin Roosevelt's closest advisors. During a heated discussion, Shumaker reminded the president's campaign team that Clinton would not be president if it weren't for New Hampshire and that he carried the state by a slim margin in '92 and could again in '96, but might not if he didn't keep his word on the primary. Since the filing period had not yet closed, it was also not too late for a primary challenger to file, Shumaker cautioned.

In mid-December First Lady Hillary Clinton came to New Hampshire to personally file her husband's candidacy papers, as she had done in 1991. Shortly thereafter, Ann Lewis, on behalf of President Clinton, formally notified Secretary of State Gardner by telephone that President Clinton was not going to file the paperwork necessary to get his name placed on the Delaware presidential primary ballot.

When the filing period ended in December, Delaware was faced with a ballot without the names of the leading candidates.

Its legislature returned during the first week of January and rushed through the House and Senate a resolution declaring the filing period null and void and requiring the names of presidential candidates who had refused to file to be put on the ballot anyway. It was a hollow victory because the candidates refused to participate.

Even though Delaware's primary was held within seven days of New Hampshire's primary, Secretary Gardner ruled it was not "similar" under the meaning of New Hampshire law because the political parties, not the state, administered Delaware's primaries. They set the number and location of the polling places and did not permit absentee voting. For the Democrats, it was only a beauty contest, as a later caucus would determine the delegates.

Not long after the 1996 election, Governor Shaheen became concerned when she realized Delaware had again scheduled a primary for 2000 to be held on the Saturday following the New Hampshire primary. She was further disturbed that candidate Lamar Alexander, who had refused to campaign and file candidacy papers in Delaware in 1996, took a different position and said he would campaign in Delaware in 2000. If he filed there, then there was the possibility others might follow.

Throughout the winter of 1998, concern about potential competition from Delaware continued to frustrate our political activists. Secretary Gardner and Hugh Gregg secretly set up a meeting with Basil Battaglia, longtime Delaware Republican Party state chairman, and Edward J. Freel, the Delaware Democratic secretary of state who was closely associated with both Delaware Democratic Governor Thomas Carper and Delaware Democratic State Chairman Richard Bayard. Our objective was to seek a compromise which would preserve New Hampshire's seven days without any public notice of the negotiating session.

On March 3, 1998, the meeting was held at the Yale Club in New York City. Battaglia said that his state had no ambition to be "first" or in any way interfere with New Hampshire's first place position. Delaware only wanted to be "up front." Both of the Delaware men seemed to understand that if New Hampshire gave up its seven days, then California or some other big state might move in directly after New Hampshire. In such an event, national attention would no longer concentrate on either New Hampshire or Delaware.

Freel said that nothing could be done to change the Delaware law with the legislature unless both the Republican and Democratic chairmen appeared together before it to plead for a change in the wording "the Saturday after New Hampshire." Battaglia agreed to discuss the matter with the Republican Executive Committee. In turn Freel agreed to approach the Democratic state chairman for his opinion and support.

Unfortunately, by coincidence, on March 7 an editorial in the *Wilmington News Journal* advocated that "Delaware's primary is much better suited as a national bellwether than Iowa or New Hampshire." It quoted a John Morgan, Sr., an important Delaware Republican strategist, who said, the First State "is much more a microcosm of the nation than New Hampshire."

Several New Hampshire dailies, including the *Manchester Union Leader,* the *Concord Monitor* and the *Nashua Telegraph* among others, took exception and the *Boston Globe* ran an editorial very favorable to New Hampshire on March 22 as counterpoint to the Delaware claim. It read: "Every election cycle a few envious states and a few candidates who lack the energy or self-confidence to run a retail campaign try to make trouble. This time it is Delaware. New Hampshire considers a week's grace after its primary . . . an integral part of its status, and it is right. If New Hampshire lost its unique voice, a big state like California would surely move to an early primary date, assuring that only those with huge bankrolls could run."

Although there was communication between the Delaware representatives and Gardner and Gregg after the New York meeting, the New Hampshire representatives never received any encouragement that either of the Delaware duo were making any headway getting their state to change its date.

HOUSE BILL No. *1012* JUN 29 1971   **1971 Session**

INTRODUCED BY: Rep. Cobleigh of Hillsborough Dist. 15; Rep. O'Neil of Cheshire Dist. 12
Rep. Roberts of Belknap Dist. 6; Rep. Raiche of Hillsborough Dist. 34; Rep. Robinson of
Hillsborough Dist. 35; Rep. Vachon of Hillsborough Dist. 40; Rep. Lawton of Belknap Dist.
Read 1 & 2, Ref. Print. Rep. Bednar of Hillsborough Dist. 23

In the year of Our Lord one thousand
nine hundred and seventy-one

AN ACT

relative to the date of annual town meetings and presidential preference
primary and relative to the dates of cooperative school district meetings.

HOUSE BILL No. *73*   **1975 Session**

INTRODUCED BY: Rep. Splaine of Rockingham Dist. 19

REFERRED TO: Statutory Revision

AN ACT   relative to shifting the date of the presidential
primary as circumstances may dictate.

ANALYSIS

This bill changes the date for the election of delegates to national conventions from the first Tuesday in March to the last Tuesday in February. This
election is held in conjunction with the presidential preference primary.

The bill further provides for a special election of delegates to national
conventions to be held in towns one week prior to the regular town meeting which
is held on the first Tuesday in March.

HB 399 – AS INTRODUCED   **1999 Session**

		99-0347
HOUSE BILL	**399**	03/02

AN ACT	allowing the secretary of state to have flexibility in moving the date of New Hampshire's presidential primary.
SPONSORS:	Rep. Splaine, Rock 34; Rep. Flanagan, Rock 14
COMMITTEE:	Election Law

ANALYSIS

This bill permits the secretary of state to select a date for the presidential primary which is on a
Tuesday 7 days or more prior to a similar election in any other state.

These three House bills had a significant impact on setting the primary
date and kept New Hampshire first-in-the-nation.

As more of the major candidates began signing a New Hampshire pledge that they would not go to Delaware, Gardner—from a position of increasing strength—suggested three alternatives to Battaglia: change the proposed Delaware primary to a caucus and hold it on the Saturday after New Hampshire, move its primary to the second Saturday after New Hampshire's Tuesday or go back to a primary on the second Tuesday of February.

Delaware also had a unique provision in its law that all candidates who qualify to receive federal matching funds are placed on the Delaware ballot whether or not they campaign in the state and without their consent. This was as a result of the non-filing of most candidates in 1996, before the law was changed forcing them on the ballot. Texas Governor George W. Bush, one of the major candidates, announced in May, 1999 that he would honor New Hampshire's tradition and not campaign in Delaware if the state violated that tradition. He also decided not to accept federal matching funds for his campaign and thus his name would not be on the ballot. Battaglia said without him it would make "Delaware's primary relatively insignificant."

Meanwhile, Jim Splaine had again seized the reins to keep New Hampshire in control of the primary process. Along with Representative Nat Flanagan he sponsored the second bill in the House which gave the secretary of state the authority to move the primary date seven days "or more" before any other state, including the right to move it into the year "previous" to the one in which a president would be elected. It also provided for moving the New Hampshire filing period dates back from December to November of the previous year.

Speaking to the press, Splaine said, "I see a real potential with New Hampshire becoming irrelevant by 2004 if New Hampshire doesn't do something like this to assert our position."

Feelings were running so high about "front-loading" by Delaware and other states that the bill cleared the Elections Committee of the House with a 19–0 vote and the full House by an almost unprecedented 329–5 vote, for a bill which might easily have been controversial. The Senate was unanimous in its endorsement of the Splaine objective.

Senator Pat Krueger's reaction, "This lets the nation and the leadership in both the Republican and Democratic parties know how strongly we feel New Hampshire should be first in the nation. It's important to let the other states know we are quite serious about preserving and protecting our primary."

Under the provisions of this amended law, theoretically the Granite State's 2000 primary could have occurred on the Tuesday of Christmas week in 1999, and Delaware's primary under its existing law would have taken place on Christmas Day. Splaine said, "This provides us additional flexibility. We don't want to do it, but if push comes to shove, New Hampshire needs to act." This was not a Christmas present Delaware sought.

The law now reads in part:

> The presidential primary election shall be held on the second Tuesday of March or on a Tuesday selected by the secretary of state which is 7 days or more immediately preceding the date on which any other state shall hold a similar election, whichever is earlier, of each year when a president of the United States is to be elected or the year previous.

In early June, when Battaglia realized that Governor Bush could not be forced onto the ballot because he was not taking federal matching funds, and Senator John McCain had made it clear from the start of his campaign that he would not go to Delaware unless it gave New Hampshire a week, Battaglia called Gardner for help to work out a solution. At that time Battaglia did not indicate what action the Republicans might eventually take with regard to holding their previously scheduled primary for the Saturday after New Hampshire. He wanted to have the Delaware House and Senate change the date to Tuesday, one week after New Hampshire. At this point, the Democrats hedged, even though they had been promising to find a solution if only the Republicans would agree. Now that the Republicans were willing, the Democrats changed their minds and the legislation to change the law failed. Just before August first, the Republicans opted out of the state primary as state law allowed, and decided to have it on a Tuesday rather than Saturday, with the party, not the state, paying the expenses. This would allow them to set their own date and end the conflict with New Hampshire. Despite Steve Forbes and Lamar Alexander, both of whom had gone to Delaware this time, the New Hampshire pledge had worked and the first-in-the-nation tradition would continue.

If New Hampshire had not stood up for the primary tradition, it would have been lost. During the several years of dispute with Delaware, never were there harsh words exchanged by those officially representing the two states. It was also true that Republican Chairman Basil Battaglia and Secretary of State Ed Freel never misled Gardner or Gregg nor broke their word, and they can say the same of us.

New Hampshire town meeting day in 2000 fell on March 14, but South Carolina had moved its primary date up to Saturday, February 19 which would have required New Hampshire to hold its primary no later than Tuesday, February 8th. Gardner, who was solely responsible for setting the date pursuant to the New Hampshire statute, still had made no decision by early September 1999 when the 2000 primary would be held. He was waiting for a final word from Delaware.

By late September there was tremendous pressure on the secretary of state to determine the day of the primary. It was becom-

---

Fun along the Campaign Trail

Some contestants have quick solutions to the country's ills or to getting elected, as did Congressmen Morris K. Udall: "The way to slow down inflation is to turn it over to the Post Office."

Or, Senator Phil W. Gramm who had a unique formula for seeking votes: "Courting people in New Hampshire is like getting kissed by Elizabeth Taylor. It's been done before."

ing increasingly difficult for hotels to book reservations around an unknown date, when every room and exhibit area in central New Hampshire would be occupied by journalists, candidates, aides and the press. Yet for over a year and a half, room reservations had necessarily been committed for the primary season without being able to set exact dates.

Sean O'Kane, general manager of the Center of New Hampshire, commented "How do we book these other conventions unrelated to the primary if the primary date is a moving target?" There was also a serious dilemma for the media and TV networks in determining their national schedules for everything from satellite trucks to installation of telephone lines.

Still, with his long-serving experience, Gardner was steadfast in holding out until he knew for sure what the other states would select as their definite dates. For example, two Michigan legislators were talking about moving their state's Republican primary to February 8 after Michigan Senator Carl Levin and fellow Democrats had adopted a caucus plan for February 12. The governor had said, "For too long a time, two states (New Hampshire and Iowa) who are not particularly representative of the nation have had a stranglehold on the selection of the president."

Meanwhile Delaware Democrats also wanted out from their previously planned primary on February 5th. They were in a tough spot, as both Vice President Gore and Senator Bradley, the Democratic contestants, had signed a New Hampshire pledge not to campaign in Delaware. Thus, the proposed Delaware Democratic primary was no problem for Gardner because it did not qualify as "similar" under New Hampshire law. When it eventually was held, only 11,141 voters actually participated.

Battaglia still hadn't made up his mind what date the Delaware Republicans would select and told Gardner in mid-September there was a good possibility their primary might be scheduled as early as Tuesday, February 8, because, among other reasons, it would be easier to get polling locations on that day. This was the day on which, in fact, it was subsequently conducted.

Based on this information, the secretary felt bound to make his decision. On September 28, 1999, Gardner announced that the primary date would be February 1, 2000. Though previously he had been frequently pressed to set the date, at no time prior to the September 28 public announcement had he ever given any firm projection as to what date would be selected. To the contrary, he had studiously refrained from making any final decision.

It would be the earliest date New Hampshire had ever held its primary. The decision was not without its share of critics, some of whom were outraged that Gardner had not consulted with the governor or party leaders. But Gardner recalled that in 1983, to keep ahead of Vermont, he did not forewarn Governor Sununu. The governor had recognized the secretary was just doing his job in moving the primary up.

Gardner commented to the press, "this is the sixth time I have set the primary date. I did it the same way I've always done it. I did not do it any differently this time. We wouldn't have the primary today if we hadn't stood up for it all those years. Over time they will understand."

Delaware did get some revenge. Back in 1819, New Hampshire had commissioned a Concord craftsman to produce a birds-eye maple desk as a furnishing for the new Statehouse. It cost the state's treasury sixteen dollars. In the 1970s, Gardner was made aware by John Page of the New Hampshire Historical Society that the desk was in a Delaware museum and could be bought for five thousand dollars, a pretty good capital gain for the First State! Since repatriation, the antique piece has been used by the secretary of state's office as the candidates' sign-in desk for every presidential primary.

After all of the foregoing, it should have been clear to the country that New Hampshire was not going to give up its claim to the first presidential primary. Or was it?

※

Chapter 14

New Hampshire Holds Its Own

B ACK IN 1983 THE DEMOCRATIC NATIONAL Committee threatened a calendar whereby Iowa's caucus would be scheduled one day before New Hampshire's primary. Nonetheless, David Nagle, Iowa Democratic State Chairman, set the 1984 Iowa caucus date eight days ahead of New Hampshire's primary.

As reported by AP writer, Mike Glover, Nagle argued that "piling Iowa and New Hampshire on top of each other would rob Iowa of any role." He fought his party in federal court and won, which resulted in an agreement with George Bruno, New Hampshire Democratic state chairman, whereby there would be an eight-day separation between the two state events. Such has been the relationship between the two states since that time.

In late summer of 1996, Hugh Gregg suggested to Bill Gardner that it might be a good idea to join hands with Iowa to strengthen the relative positions of the two states for protection of the first caucus in Iowa and the first primary in New Hampshire versus other states which were flirting with the idea of displacing either or both of them. A commission would be appointed to gain favorable public understanding of the service the two states had contributed to the nation's election process. Iowa's caucus had been held eight days before the primary and, because of the dissimilar formats, there had never been any conflict between the two states.

Gardner agreed and immediately received the backing of his

> *Fun along the Campaign Trail*
>
> **At the 1856 Republican Convention, General John Charles Fremont was nominated for president but lost to Democrat James Buchanan in the general election. Nonetheless, New Hampshire named a town after Fremont, which is more than it did for Buchanan, and there have been two of *them*!**

counterpart in Iowa, Secretary of State Paul D. Pate. The commission was to have been composed of both governors, the two secretaries of state, and the chairmen of the two major political parties of each state. The original concept was to have the commission established by joint action of the two legislatures to give it maximum credibility and media attention. As luck would have it the Iowa legislature adjourned before there was time to get the concept up and running.

The alternative was to have the commission established by executive order of the two governors. Unfortunately, because Governor Branstad of Iowa was not going to run for re-election and New Hampshire's Governor Jeanne Shaheen was newly in office with other matters occupying her attention, both concepts lingered until mid-year of 1997.

On June 20th, Secretary Pate thanked Gardner for his leadership in building "a stronger bond between Iowa and New Hampshire in the presidential nominating process, as our states continue to provide an 'open and fair playing field' for all who seek the presidency, the cooperation between us grows essential."

Thereafter a reconstituted commission was established to consist of eight members and entitled: Iowa–New Hampshire First Caucus and Primary Commission. It consisted of both governors and secretaries of state, or their designees, and one person from each of the two major political parties chosen by their respective governors. Democrat Joseph Keefe and Republican Hugh Gregg were appointed by Governor Shaheen to represent New Hamp-

shire. Democrat Michael Peterson and Republican Steve Grubbs
were appointed by Governor Branstad to represent Iowa.

On November 17, 1997, following an earlier telephone conference call between the members, a press conference was held by
telephone between the members of the commission and open to
the media, with the two delegations assembled in their respective
governor's offices. A mission statement was read, general objec-
tives discussed and questions taken from media in both states.
Both governors stated they would support the New Hampshire
law which provided that the New Hampshire primary be held one
week before any similar event.

Thereafter the commission developed a pledge entitled: Iowa-
New Hampshire First-in-the-Nation Pledge. It read: "I, (name of
candidate), pledge that I will support the first-in-the-nation status of the Iowa Caucuses and the New Hampshire primary, and
that I will not campaign in or allow declarations of candidacy to
be filed in any state or territory that holds its presidential caucus
prior to Iowa or its presidential primary earlier than 7 days following the New Hampshire primary." (The "7 days following the
New Hampshire primary" was aimed at Delaware.)

It was proposed that all announced candidates running in the
New Hampshire primary be requested to sign the pledge and that
it was also to be used at the annual Presidential Preference Straw
Poll media event planned for August in Iowa.

The New Hampshire commission members developed an
op-ed piece for the media which stated in part: "What makes
New Hampshire so important to presidential contenders is not
our delegates, but the momentum we deliver to those who distin-
guish themselves in the first, grueling, grassroots campaign. For
the New Hampshire primary to work, candidates must start early
and spend a lot of time here. They need to know that a strong
showing will give them a one-week bump, and crucial publicity
and momentum heading into the rest of the campaign. Without
the seven-day window, therefore, there may be no longer a New
Hampshire primary."

Fun along the Campaign Trail

The New York Institute for Law and Society said it was confident George W. Bush would be the Republican candidate for president and warned him against the selection of New York's Governor George Pataki as his vice president. They felt Pataki liked gambling too much.

Iowa Challenges New Hampshire in 2000

Meanwhile, as the Delaware dispute had been fermenting, without ever having discussed the matter with Gardner beforehand, Iowa had scheduled its caucus date for January 31, 2000, a day which would occur only one day before the February 1 date eventually set by Gardner. Since 1984, there had always been eight days separating the events in the two states.

Even though never blessed by Gardner, the media and the political activists in both New Hampshire and Iowa assumed the Granite State primary would be held on February 8. Their assumption was based on the fallacy that Delaware was no longer in the mix.

There was also the expectation that retiring Iowa Republican Governor Branstad was going to be Lamar Alexander's national chairman. If Alexander were to campaign in Delaware as he indicated he would do, it would mean he could not sign the joint commission's pledge. After Governor Branstad did accept as Alexander's national chairman, it effectively ended the joint Iowa/New Hampshire pledge because the Iowan endorsed his candidate's Delaware itinerary.

Strong efforts were made to convince Tom Rath, Alexander's New Hampshire Chairman, to thwart Alexander's plans to change his position on Delaware. Entreaties were fruitless. Rath did not agree on the importance of the pledge because he thought the other candidates would not agree this time, and he acquiesced to Alexander's campaigning in Delaware. It was also Rath's position that the week-long wait after New Hampshire's primary was not necessary to protect the state's first-in-the-nation position.

Even Steve Duprey, the New Hampshire Republican State Chairman, suggested that "instead of asking them (the candidates) to pledge not to go to Delaware, we can ask them to pledge to support a suspension of the rules at the Republican National Convention, if it becomes necessary to do that, to seat our delegates. This would let them go to Delaware but also lets us have our primary before the first day allowed by the rule, if necessary."

It would have been difficult, if not impossible, to get such a rule-change passed to make special exception for New Hampshire by the delegates of the other states in the national convention of the Republican Party. This was not a practical solution. Apparently Duprey subsequently recognized it would not work, as he actively supported the commission's pledge, saying to the presidential candidates, "Let me make no bones about it. My clear interest is that Delaware not be on your calendar."

The joint Iowa/NH Commission received its final coup de grâce from member Steve Grubbs, the Iowa State Republican chairman, who said he could no longer support a seven day separation between New Hampshire and Delaware when he learned that Steve Forbes also planned to run in Delaware's Saturday primary.

On December 8, 1998, Governor Shaheen held a press conference to announce the issuance of a new pledge similar to the

---

Fun along the Campaign Trail

It's depressing that some presidential office seekers tag the government as nearly beyond hope. So spoke Steve Forbes, "The tax code is a cesspool of special interest and corruption. Nobody knows what's in it any more."

Or, Senator Robert Kerrey, "Citizens are becoming jaded about the power of special interest groups."

Iowa/NH joint pledge. It would be a New Hampshire Commission's pledge relating solely to New Hampshire and its relationship to Delaware. She stressed that all potential presidential candidates would be asked to ratify it and reported the original pledge had already been signed by Representative John Kasich and Vice President Al Gore.

Kasich had previously been the first to sign the original Iowa/NH pledge (which also covered Delaware). He said, "Iowa and New Hampshire are the keys for anyone not born a millionaire. They don't care who you are. They want to know what you are all about." Senator McCain quipped, "I won't even take Amtrak through Delaware."

On the day of the press conference, Senator Wellstone and Congressman Gephardt signed and the media reported Senator Ashcroft had done likewise. Shortly thereafter it was executed by Senators Bradley and Smith. Eventually all of the 13 major candidates agreed to the pledge, except Steve Forbes and Lamar Alexander, both of whom planned to campaign actively in Delaware.

On September 28, 1999, when the actual date was finally set, Governor Shaheen, Joe Keefe, Steve Duprey, Kathleen Sullivan, legislative leaders, the media, hotel managers and the Iowa political community were caught by surprise with Gardner's announcement. Immediately there was widespread criticism of Gardner from all directions exhorting him to find a legal pretext for setting the date back to February 8, the day it had been universally assumed the primary would be, not February 1. Many plans and commitments had been made on that assumption, including the scheduling of presidential debates in both states.

Within a few days of announcing the date of the 2000 New Hampshire presidential primary, Governor Shaheen called a meeting of both state party chairs and national committee members in her Statehouse office. Those at the meeting explained why they thought the date should be changed. Governor Shaheen asked Gardner to accept the decision of those in attendance and defer to their judgment.

She expressed the opinion that Iowa was being placed in a difficult position, having changed its caucus date already and the national parties would react negatively to New Hampshire moving up a week. Gardner responded that Iowa created its own problem by setting the date of the caucus prematurely without waiting to see if any other state would interfere. He also pointed out that Delaware Republicans were planning a primary for February 8, 2000 and New Hampshire had to be on February 1st or earlier to comply with state law. He said he believed his decision was well thought out and was the right one for the state. If on the other hand, he said, his decision turned out to be wrong, he would have to live with it. But better to live with a wrong decision, that was your own, than living with making a wrong decision when you deferred to others contrary to your own beliefs. With that the governor said there was no reason to continue the meeting.

Meanwhile, Iowa Governor Tom Vilsack was raging against New Hampshire, telling the press, "We didn't create this problem, we're not moving." Tell Granite State officials, "you created this problem, you solve it." He called Governor Shaheen to complain and reported "she indicated, I believe, a certain level of frustration that a single individual in her state, without consultation with

---

Fun along the Campaign Trail

George Romney, reputed to be an excellent duckpin bowler, turned up at a New Hampshire alley where candlepins are used. He'd never seen the slender pins before. In demonstration of his prowess, the first roll knocked down all except the head pin, generating great applause from the crowd. But the enthusiasm quickly dwindled when they had to give him an extra ten balls to hit the one pin still standing.

political leaders of either party, unilaterally decided to create chaos."

Vilsack's press secretary, Joe Shannahan, was quoted, "This is just terrible, given the fact that New Hampshire and Iowa worked so closely for two decades, that one lone maverick is causing all these problems that are jeopardizing the first-in-the-nation status in both states." Even many New Hampshire political activists believed Gardner's action would cost the loss of convention delegates, would undermine the state's claim to the first presidential primary and generally give the state a nasty name with both national parties.

Tom Rath, the Republican National Committeeman, was one of the few who took a favorable public position on Gardner's behalf, saying, "Anyone that tries to analyze what Bill Gardner does is making a mistake. He's very up front, and very honest, and does what he needs to do. He's just very vigilant to protect the primary."

Representative Richard "Stretch" Kennedy also took up the cudgels with a statement "for anybody to attack him (Gardner) for doing what he was ordered to do by the legislature in a law signed by the governor is not only wrong but stupid."

The *National Journal's* Political Hotline reported "Every other state in the Union is jealous of their (NH and Iowa) first-in-the-nation status, and now those two states have the gall to feud over how close their dates can be to each other."

Steve Duprey, New Hampshire Republican Chairman, picked up the same theme, "this gives the states that have been looking for an excuse to whack us a piece of evidence that (their relationship) doesn't work as well as they say it does." Kathy Sullivan, New Hampshire Democratic chairman said, "we turned our back on a sister state for no reason that makes sense. My position is New Hampshire doesn't lose anything and has everything to gain by giving a helping hand to Iowa."

It was precedent-setting for both the Republican and Democratic New Hampshire state chairmen to consolidate an attack on the secretary of state for his conduct in allegedly not respecting the sanctity of the presidential primary.

A conference call was held between leaders of both parties in the two states to resolve the issue. "Both party chairs for New Hampshire were on the call and they agree with us. They are in complete agreement that the date should be changed" said Dee Stewart, Executive Director of the Iowa Republican Party. Unable to work any solution over the phone, the Iowa officials decided to hop a plane to Manchester where they could support the locals in attempting to get Gardner to change his mind.

On October 1st, the Iowa delegation arrived in Manchester prepared to join with their New Hampshire sympathizers to take on the secretary face-to-face. A private meeting was held at the home of Joe Keefe, which included Dee Stewart, Rob Tully, Iowa Democratic Chairman, and Chet Culver, Iowa secretary of state (a Democrat). In addition to Joe Keefe, New Hampshire attendees were Steve Duprey, Republican Party chairman, Kathleen Sullivan, Democratic Party chairman, Rich Sigel, Governor Shaheen's chief of staff, Bill Gardner and Hugh Gregg.

The Iowans presented their case that "unequivocally" it would be totally impossible to change the date of their longtime planned caucus commitment to prevent back-to-back election days between the two states. It was asserted that statewide 2,500 caucus sites had already been reserved, hotels in Des Moines were filled to capacity during the earlier week and there would be no accommodations for media if the date were moved back. There was a lot of talk specifically about a great Pork Producers Convention, but no further details on what kind of pork, and the New Hampshirites were too intimidated to ask.

The meeting lasted over two and a half hours, with a friendly exchange of views, except at one point the tension in the room became so great Joe Keefe nearly had to restrain one of the visiting out-of-state house guests. The local residents were just as adamant in their criticism of Gardner's action as were the Iowans. Everybody in the room, except Gregg, took their turn at exhorting Gardner to change his mind. He held his ground saying, "I've set it. I know once you change it, when does it stop?"

After the meeting Gardner told Gregg that he thought the intensity of the visitors was so great that maybe Iowa would not bend and would not move from January 31, in which case he would be under further assault even though Iowa would be the loser in that event, as New Hampshire would get the media attention if the states were only a day apart.

Following the meeting, Culver reinforced Gardner's view by telling the press, "we are leaving here still intent on holding our caucus on January 31. If the Republican National Committee and the Democratic National Committee decide not to seat delegates from New Hampshire, then we would not be in violation of the Iowa law. We could have it on the 31st."

Tully told the media he could not understand why Gardner would be accommodating Delaware as opposed to Iowa, because the public is more concerned with Iowa. Stewart commented, "I wouldn't be surprised if we had back-to-back events."

That night, at the invitation of Representative Kennedy, Gardner and his Iowa counterpart Culver attempted to release the tension between them by attending an evening of boxing events in Salem. During an intermission, the chairman of the New Hampshire Boxing and Wrestling Commission, Bobby Stephens, announced to the capacity crowd that New Hampshire had never lost a bout in its fight to have the first-in-the-nation primary—and never will. The crowd chanted its approval. The

---

Fun along the Campaign Trail

Then there are the modest candidates such as Vice President Al Gore. "I do benefit from the low expectations people have for me."

Or, Senator Richard G. Lugar, "I know people say I'm far too low key, even that I'm dull."

last boxing match featured the popular New England professional boxer Micky Ward who was getting the worst of it, until the very last round when he knocked his opponent out. Culver later told Gardner that he would never forget that night.

The next day, Saturday, Gardner met again with Kathy Sullivan (at her request), a family friend and fellow Democrat, in a vain attempt to ask for his reconsideration. During a walk around the neighborhood he explained his position and predicted that Delaware would have a Republican primary on February 8th and New Hampshire had to stick with February 1st. He would not change the date.

Early the next week following the visit of the Iowa officials, Shaheen paid a rare visit to Gardner's office, just steps down the hall from her own, to plead for his change of mind. Not having been able to storm the fort, she called a meeting of legislative and party leaders to seek a way around the secretary and to appease Iowa. They agreed that New Hampshire should move its date. Representative Raymond Buckley of Manchester, the Democratic whip, said he would sponsor a bill to make this happen. "I don't see what other options we have." The *Concord Monitor* agreed in an editorial, saying "Switch, don't fight. The state should move its primary to accommodate Iowa."

The group planned to consider a special session of the legislature to rescind Gardner's authority. Calls were made to legislative

---

Fun along the Campaign Trail

Lamar Alexander tells the story in his *Little Plaid Book*: "Remember that sometimes it's best to smile and say nothing. One Saturday morning in Dover, New Hampshire, I was sitting on the curb having a bagel for breakfast. A man recognized me. 'You're Lamar Alexander, aren't you?' 'Yes, I am.' He looked again. 'No, you're not,' he said, and walked away."

leaders who had not attended the meeting to assess the chances of success for such a course of action.

Senate President Beverly Hollingsworth reported the next day. "After polling the members of both legislative bodies, it is clear there is no desire to pursue changing the primary date through legislative action at this time." Shaheen had quickly learned that any such bill would never pass.

This was not good news for Iowa which was complaining that moving its caucus back seven days would require rescheduling 2,100 voting precinct sites and shifting various conventions such as the Iowa-Illinois Turf Grass Association. Nor was there any mention from Iowa that by not moving back they would be in violation of their own law which called for their caucus to be held eight days before any primary.

Several days thereafter, Governor Shaheen, along with some legislative leaders and the two New Hampshire party chairmen, saw the light, or maybe just felt the heat from the office down the hall. She issued a prepared statement: "We should be working together with Iowa, as we have in the past. Secretary Gardner's decision will stand, and we must now focus our efforts on protecting our primary."

The governor also promised to seek approval of the Democratic National Committee for the February 1st date and later was successful in accomplishing that mission.

Raymond Buckley, New Hampshire Democratic National Committeeman, still expressed reservations in telling the press he had "grave concerns over the future of our primary. We may be able to slip through this cycle, but the secretary of state's action has made it difficult for us to articulate a rational position to save the primary."

Joe Keefe, accusing Gardner of "colossal misjudgment," authored an op-ed piece in the *Concord Monitor* which read in part: "Last week legislative leaders abandoned the idea of reversing Gardner. I urge them to reconsider and convene a special session to move New Hampshire's primary back to February 8. Although Gardner made a serious mistake, he has always had New Hampshire's interests at heart. He is a decent man, and deservedly popular. His refusal to reverse his decision, however, is pure stubbornness; it threatens the future of the primary. We should be working with Iowa and not fighting it."

Meanwhile, in Iowa, the *Des Moines Register's* respected political writer, David Yepsen wrote a column encouraging Iowa officials to move its caucus to January 24th, adding "Iowa and New Hampshire are dangerously close to messing up a good thing. They are playing political chicken with each other and both could be the losers."

Obviously a strong supporter of Bill Gardner, Yepsen also wrote, "Anyone who knows anything about New Hampshire politics knows Bill Gardner is a respected public servant. Calling him a 'maverick' is inaccurate, gets his Yankee back up and prompts his friends to come to his defense."

David Nagle, original sponsor of the eight-day Iowa window, warned, "When we said we were not going to move, in essence we disarmed ourselves. Eight days was not an arbitrary number. Any candidate that's confronting Iowa right now has to decide if they really want to spend the resources they've committed. We're wrong on this. Once you give it up, you'll never get it back." As reported by AP reporter, Mike Glover, Nagle said the candidates would have nothing to gain by campaigning in either state if it meant back-to-back events.

When Iowans eventually did get the message that Granite Staters were a stubborn lot led by a steadfast secretary of state, they caved. They moved their date to January 24, eight days before the New Hampshire primary on February 1st, which was one week ahead of the Delaware primary on February 8th. Iowa election officials suddenly found accommodations for caucuses and the media, nor was anything further learned about Iowa pork.

It was later learned that the Iowa Pork Congress, so officially identified, was only a two-day affair in one place and was finished four days before the caucus. Iowa Democratic State Chairman Rob Tully said, "We made do."

The election officials had deliberately misled the New Hampshire secretary of state by alleging "unequivocally" Iowa could not change its caucus date of January 31. Further, they had successfully suckered Governor Shaheen, Joe Keefe and other New Hampshire political leaders to agree with them.

Governor Vilsack repented, conceding his tough stance was merely a "bargaining ploy" to frighten the competitor. He said, "The governor of New Hampshire essentially wanted me to take that line in terms of her ability to talk to a legislature. I'm a team player." Pamela Walsh, speaking for Governor Shaheen, immediately denied the charge.

In view of the earlier effort by Governor Shaheen to appease Iowa, publisher Joe McQuaid noted editorially in the *Manchester Union Leader,* "Apparently Gov. Shaheen is also a 'team player.' Only she seems to be playing for the Hawkeye State's team rather than New Hampshire."

Eventually both the Republican and Democratic National Committees blessed the transgressions of their rambunctious offspring and seated all the Iowa and New Hampshire delegates at both national conventions in 2000. Even the Iowa officials later confided to Gardner their apologies. New Hampshire had prevailed once more.

※

Chapter 15

Clouding the Crystal Ball
Perplexing the Pollsters

POLLING HAS RAPIDLY BECOME THE LIFE BLOOD of American politics. According to John H. Fund of the *Wall Street Journal* there were only two media outlets which commissioned polls in 1972. Today it would be difficult to fix an accurate count. Unquestionably our state has become the paramount early test market of candidate and media polls on matters pertaining to presidential campaigns. During the 2000 New Hampshire primary more than twenty different polling firms attempted to measure voter sentiment.

Polling has become so widespread that candidates tend to rely on them to identify popular issues for inclusion in their campaign platforms. These surveys are normally based on small group samples of 200 to 1,000 prospective voters. Very small focus groups sometimes serve the same purpose. New Hampshire, however, with its urban and rural population, offers a far more objective and diversified base to gauge public opinion.

Well before primary day, the candidates working here get a real sense of what's important and what will resonate, along with their personal chance of victory. After the only poll that really counts, the one on primary day, the candidate has learned from the voters what adjustments must be made in order to proceed in the big national race. From a relatively easy experience, the candidate discovers whether he or she has the substance to survive subsequent primaries.

The political poll which really excites the public is the one which predicts who will lead the ticket. It's one marketing strategy to ask a voter which of two toothpastes he prefers, but quite another to ask for whom is he going to cast his ballot. Offhand the voter probably knows from daily experience how he likes to brush his teeth, but the quick choice of a candidate at any given point of time is more transitory.

It raises the question: are political polls reliable? Before the general election in 2000 the *Los Angeles Times* had Bush at 48 percent with Gore at 42 percent while International Communications Research reversed the same percentages, with Gore as the leader. Both polls had the same margin of error. Which one should you have believed?

It has always amazed us that so many people seem to get their political kicks from polls. Worse yet is the addiction to them which many reporters have. Further, to most aficionados it doesn't make any difference whether the polls are conducted two years before a particular election or only two days before. The gambling begins as soon as there is at least one candidate announced for a race or sometimes even as soon as it's indicated someone might run for a particular office.

When campaigns begin early, the press is happy. It offers journalists the opportunity to track presumed shifts of sentiment as the campaigns progress. The candidates are almost as bad. When not satisfied with newspaper poll results, some competitors spend big bucks to hire expensive professionals to do the same thing.

Fun along the Campaign Trail

Referring to the short-lived administration of President Gerald Ford and Vice President Nelson Rockefeller, William Loeb, publisher of the *Manchester Union Leader*, wrote, "Never in the history of the Republican Party have we had two such lemons in the White House."

Everett Carll Ladd of the Roper Center for Public Opinion Research told the *Wall Street Journal:* "Early poll numbers exercise some strange form of tyranny over people that they shouldn't, given how soft they are."

Capping our distrust is the statistical fact that the polls are frequently wrong in picking winners of the New Hampshire primary. Elsewhere in this book we've indicated the specifics of media-misses in predicting end results. One might presume that after the thirteen primaries since 1952, poll fanatics would recognize the fickleness of polling. But we guess its the same kind of allurement which leads many local residents to take repeat trips to the Foxwoods Resort Casino in Connecticut. Others experience a similar thrill merely staying home and auditing the political polls on TV— with the assurance of not losing any money.

The question remains, why aren't these soothsayers better statisticians? When, where and how their questions are chosen make

---

Fun along the Campaign Trail

In the closing days of Clinton's 1992 campaign, after charges of his sexual enterprising, he said he'd keep campaigning "until the last dog dies." On the day before his re-election in 1996, he returned and assured his dedicated supporters there was "still plenty of life left in this old dog." Subsequently, after the impeachment sessions in 2000, he promised again to continue serving in the Oval Office "until the last hour of the last day of my term."

Good to his word, just nine days before leaving office in 2001, he returned to Dover for the "second coming" of the Comeback Kid. He played a student's saxophone at the High School and thanked a gathering of 2,000 excited fans for their loyal support, saying, "The last dog is still barking." This enthusiastic reception said something about the solemnity of the state's politics, or perhaps it was only a tribute to the evangelism of its Democrats.

a big difference. "Push polling" has become a popular trick of the trade. It's the art of framing questions leading to the desired answers of the pollster in an attempt to convince respondents to support or oppose a particular candidate. There's also the technique of how questions are phrased or the order in which they are arranged. Were the interviews conducted in person or over the phone? Were those questioned properly qualified to make a reasoned answer? Are those chosen to respond a representative sample?

Janet Wilson writing in the *Los Angeles Times* reported that, "If properly polled, statisticians say, as few as 1,000 people can accurately reflect opinions of 185 million Americans." If this can be demonstrated maybe we could do away with elections.

We think E.B. White was closer to the truth with his analysis: "We are proud of America for clouding up the crystal ball, for telling one thing to a poll-taker, another thing to a voting machine."

Professional pollsters often defend themselves by saying public opinion can change overnight. Polls are only a snapshot of opinion in time. So, what's the use of polls? If they don't predict the future, why rely on them? Maybe that's why the pros always allow for a "margin of error" and because it can be either up or down, you have to double it. At Foxwoods you don't get that chance!

The worst thing about polls is that, more often than not, they are treated by the media as critical news. Results get front page headlines in leading newspapers, prime-time TV coverage and priority with columnists. Such emphasis adds to the pollsters' presumed authority in predetermining election results. Polling predictions often have a self-fulfilling effect, thereby skewing what otherwise would have led to an impartial judgment.

Many pollsters argue that polls do not influence elections. They claim their profession is only concerned with recording statistical facts. This is rubbish. Certainly they are familiar with the human-nature factor, that everyone wants to be with a winner. Not only does a candidate who is way ahead in the polls capture additional converts, more importantly, many others will feel their vote is unessential. Besides, if polls did not manipulate elections, why are contestants always anxious to release favorable predictions?

Sure, there's always the polling company which get the right result, but that is no more than a tribute to the law of averages. At least once in every four years one or more of them will get it right and occasionally, when it's self-evident, they all get it right.

But there's no one on record who has consistently been correct with so-called "scientific projections" over the course of the primary's history. For example, in 1996 most of them had Dole over Buchanan. In 2000 none of the majors "guessed" anything close to the McCain nineteen point margin over Bush. Some even thought Bush would squeak out a win!

Credit however should be given to the then new Franklin Pierce College Polling Institute at Rindge, which in 2000 came closer than any of the time-tested national polls with its McCain ten point prediction—which is solid proof that even the best of the best cannot be relied upon to predict the future. Credit can also be shared by the University of New Hampshire Survey Center headed by pollster Andy Smith, which predicted the Gore/Bradley race to within one percent.

On June 24–25, 2003, a group identified as "Moveon.org" conducted a national e-mail poll on the presidential candidates, which produced 317,617 votes. Allowing that the poll sponsor may be "left leaning," it was still interesting that former Governor Dean won with 44 percent of the total votes, followed by Congressman Kucinich at 24 percent and all other candidates in low percentages. If the actual results next January are the same for

---

Fun along the Campaign Trail

In 1964, Senator Goldwater didn't add many new friends in the seacoast area when he made this statement: "This country would be better off if we saw off the eastern seaboard and let it float out to sea."

each of these two candidates, we'll refund the cost of whatever you paid for this book!

Presidential speech writer Peggy Noonan spoke the truth in her book, *What I Saw at the Revolution: A Political Life in the Reagan Era:* "I felt that polls are now driving more than politics, they are driving history." It's a shame the public has become so mesmerized that it sometimes is led to vote with the wind even when it's blowing improbable results. Polls are not elections, nor should they be.

After the Republicans surprised and captured the nation in the 2002 general election, it was the Democratic pollster Mark Mellman who said it best, "We're pretty good at predicting the present, but pollsters are not very good at predicting the future—even if the future is only one day away."

❋

Chapter 16

A New Generation Votes

ECAUSE THE CANDIDATES SPEND MORE time here than elsewhere, they frequently visit educational institutions at all
levels, from grade schools to high schools and colleges.
Teachers devote classroom hours to the primary process. Mock
elections are held where the candidates appear. Questions asked
by students differ markedly from those of the standard press conference. It's also a way to guarantee a crowd.

Such opportunities not only serve to introduce fresh perspec-
tives, but provide the candidate with support from first-time voters; many would otherwise have no interest in casting a primary
ballot. For the student, it brings the excitement of democracy directly into the classroom.

In 2000, efforts were undertaken in New Hampshire to address the serious decline in youth voting. Sanford Horwitt of the
Close Up Foundation, a national leader in the effort to get more
of America's youth voting, has pointed out that in the thirty years
since the ratification of the 26th Amendment to the Constitution
which lowered the voting age to 18, there has been a decline of
more than 30 percent in the turnout of 18 to 24 year-olds. This
decreasing trend is of utmost worry to those of us concerned with
the vitality of our democracy.

As stressed by Richard Morin in the *Washington Post* it is even
more alarming that youth interest in the political system has been
declining when it should have been increasing. He wrote, "Yale
political scientist Don Green notes that over the past 35 years,
education levels have soared among young Americans. Participa-

Candidates Bush (upper right) and McCain (lower left) joined other candidates who fielded questions from several hundred young voters at the New Hampshire Youth Forum held on January 9, 2000 at the Dana Center at St. Anselm College. The lively questioning and spontaneous answers were covered by C-Span.

269

tion dropped even in particularly competitive election years, such as 2000. And across the country it's never been easier to register to vote or to cast a ballot."

Because of its national interest and excitement, the state's presidential primary was a logical place to tackle the problem. Students themselves self-started a "get out and vote" campaign a year before the 2000 primary election by forming an alliance, Democracy in Practice, at Conval High School in Peterborough. The purpose was to enlist high school students from all over the state with the same objective. They helped organize a New Hampshire Youth Summit which was attended by several hundred students from schools throughout the state and was addressed by the state's two youngest legislators.

The Close Up Foundation, the New Hampshire Political Library, the National Association of Secretaries of State, the Republican and Democratic Parties also jointly sponsored a Presidential Candidates Youth Forum to promote active political participation by young voters. Pew Charitable Trusts funded the event and it was covered by C-Span as the first of its kind on national television. The high school students assisted in design of the program, which was attended by George W. Bush, Orrin Hatch, Steve Forbes and John McCain.

Though some of the 500 young people in attendance were too young to vote, they had opinions. The *Concord Monitor,* reported, "free-wheeling debates also broke out in the auditorium's lobby as individuals argued over who was the better candidate." A principle mission was to register all students of voting age. Chris Weeks, one of the founding student motivators, said, "they just can't ignore us any more, because we're going to step up to the polls and take part in the process."

Mark Z. Barabak wrote in the *Los Angeles Times,* "Presidential hopefuls yesterday yielded one of the most wide-ranging and free-flowing discussions yet seen in this presidential campaign . . . Each candidate stated his views on issues ranging from sex education to the Northern Ireland peace process and genome research."

"While none of the candidates appeared to sweep the GOP youth vote, the first-of-its-kind event marked a significant step in bridging the well documented disconnect between politicians and young voters," reported Lia Macko of MSNBC.

In the same week a private group of New Hampshire political notables convened the nonpartisan 'College Convention 2000.' It too, sponsored a primary symposium, but was specifically directed at those already of voting age and solicited attendance from across the country. It was a three-day meeting which included presentations by the candidates on specific issues, student leader debates, dinners, exhibits and entertainment for the participants. The program was planned to bring together "dignitaries of every major political party and leaders of issue groups to debate and vote public policy decisions for America."

Pat Buchanan was quoted as telling the new voters, "Let this convention serve as a rallying cry for young people to bring their energy and idealism and march with us on this crusade for political reform."

Efforts such as these, along with national programs such as Close-Up's First Vote, Kid's Voting, Student Mock Election, and other programs of the National Secretaries of State are critical to enlisting young people and convincing them of the importance of their citenzenship responsibility for maintaining the electoral process. In 2000, only 32 percent of the 18 to 24 year olds voted.

Fun along the Campaign Trail

Jacob Pfaff, a thirteen-year old Hookset boy, has seen his share of presidential candidates. His father, Terry, asked him to have breakfast at the Capitol Center for the Arts in Concord at a table with Governor George W. Bush when Bush was campaigning in New Hampshire in 1999. Jacob said, "I can't, Dad, because I have a test, and you know how hard it is to make up a test. I've already met him twice anyway."

We are fortunate to have the world's longest continuous democracy, yet we rank 143 out of 160 countries when it comes to voter participation. Again, it's the uniqueness of our primary which we believe should be the model for a youth training camp. The *Los Angeles Times* in 2000 did exit polling at both the New Hampshire and California primaries about five weeks apart. It found that the percentage of the total primary vote by voters under the age of 30 was more than twice as high in New Hampshire. Perhaps the special youth events in New Hampshire did motivate young voters to turn out in higher numbers.

As campaigns were getting underway for the 2004 primary it was apparent that young voters were going to receive special attention. Senator Kerry, for example, paid an early visit to Dartmouth to seek support, particularly for "hands-on" participation. Competitors Gephardt, Dean and Lieberman used the same tactic at the University of New Hampshire. Students have become a huge resource for volunteer work at all levels of strategy. There are 63,000 of them attending colleges in the state, many of whom get caught up in the excitement of the presidential primary with it's opportunity of promoting their favored candidate and bantering with the media.

Kurt Ehrenberg, a spokesman for Governor Dean, believes student support "gives the candidate people who have energy and believe in the candidate. That's what primary politics are really all about, people who really believe in the candidate themselves." In return, the students have a good chance for intimacy with national figures whom otherwise they'd never have met. Such an opportunity can also lead to valuable contacts later in their lives.

Josh Stern, a leader of Dartmouth's Young Democrats, was asked by a reporter which candidate he would endorse. The student, as reported by Rachel Osterman of the *Boston Globe,* replied, "Only in New Hampshire would I be asked to endorse someone."

※

Chapter 17

It Gets Earlier and Earlier

A S WE LOOK AHEAD TO 2004 it appears that New Hampshire will have its presidential primary for the first time in January. It is likely to be January 27ᵗʰ. Delaware finally changed its law in the Spring of 2003, removing the language that sets the primary for the Saturday following New Hampshire. The law now reads the primary will be on the first Tuesday of February. Gardner again worked with former Secretary of State Ed Freel, Republican Party Chairman Basil Battaglia and the bill sponsor, Senator Robert Marshall, to once and for all bring harmony to the two states and end the conflict. Delaware will have a primary on February 3ʳᵈ, 2004, most likely one week after the Granite State.

Our primary is safe through the year 2004 because the Republicans cannot change their current rules for pre-qualifying delegates until the 2004 convention. Further, President Bush has said, as have all his presidential predecessors since 1952, that New Hampshire should remain first.

Also, the Democrats have updated the permitted starting dates for their candidates. They found themselves at a disadvantage in 2000 because of the month between the Republican starting date in early February and theirs in early March. The gap gave the Republicans a month's advantage in the media. To correct the deficiency, beginning in 2004 states can hold their Democratic primaries as early as February 3 with New Hampshire still being granted a week's grace to go a week earlier.

Although Wyoming was the first to set its GOP county elections for the selection of delegates to the 2004 National Convention on February 3, 2004, the earliest permitted under Republican Party rules, other jurisdictions weren't far behind. The Democrats had far greater reason to pick their frontrunner before spring as it was assumed President Bush would be unopposed and would have a much longer uncontested time to make his case for re-election.

In January of 2003 the District of Columbia announced its intention of holding a non-binding presidential primary on January 13, 2004. This surprising action was initiated by the DC Democracy Fund, Washington's political action committee, which said the plan was designed solely "to bring national media and policy-maker attention to our lack of voting rights." They emphasized that our country is the only democracy in the world that denies residents of its capital city a voice in national government. Delegates from DC can vote in House committees but not on the floor. Since this primary will be a beauty contest without delegate selection, and for other reasons as well, it will not trigger the Splaine law, just as the so-called CityVote did not. (About a dozen of the countries largest cities in 1995 tried to organize a presidential preference primary for November 7, before any state, to force presidential candidates to discuss urban issues. Only two cities eventually took part and no delegates were chosen.)

Because the District of Columbia is not a state, among other reasons, its proposed primary would not conflict with New Hamp-

---

Fun along the Campaign Trail

Though normally self-effacing, Congressman John R. Kasich had a better reason to run as he "got into politics because I wanted to change the world." And he began his changes in the right place when he said, "I never heard of Delaware."

shire's law requiring the primary to be at least seven days ahead of any other state. If the Granite State did move back, the event could occur between Christmas and New Years of 2003. Guam and Puerto Rico held primaries in the 1980s in advance of New Hampshire. DC's planned early event would violate rules of both the Republican and Democratic parties.

Democratic Senator Carl Levin of Michigan has been a long-time foe of New Hampshire's first place on the presidential calendar. He has viewed it as a "perpetual privilege which no state should have" and strenuously objected to his party's rule giving New Hampshire the one week exemption. He said his challenge to compete with New Hampshire would cause other states to view Michigan as "conquering heroes." By March of 2003 he had lined up the Democratic Michigan governor and its state party chairman to sponsor a Democratic caucus on the same day as New Hampshire's primary in 2004, probably to be January 27. They claimed to have the support of most of the presumed major candidates who would be in that race.

While Levin was alleging that Michigan was "more diverse than New Hampshire," its labor unions joined the fight with a threat to New Hampshire that if it passed a "Right to Work" law Michigan would destroy the Granite State's privilege of holding the first national primary, using the argument that Michigan was extremely influential with labor unions everywhere. Fortunately, after the 2003 New Hampshire legislature killed the bill, that possibility did not materialize.

Granite State Democrats reacted vigorously, emphasizing that such action by Michigan would conflict with National Democratic Party rules and they could lose 50 percent of the delegates so elected. It was even suggested that New Hampshire Democrats might ask for pledges from the candidates not to campaign in Michigan prior to New Hampshire's primary. Governor Dean, however, said, "if there's a caucus in Michigan, I want to be there."

Because the threat was designed for a caucus, not a primary, it would not technically be disturbing to New Hampshire's presidential primary law. However, it was unclear whether the event Michigan was planning was called a caucus, but in reality was a "firehouse primary." Its 2000 Democratic caucus was administered by the Democratic Party, not the state, with balloting allowed in union halls and polling places, only open for two hours, and by mail. In 2003, Michigan was prepared to permit first-time voting on the Internet.

Democratic National Chairman, Terry McAuliffe, commented that if Michigan goes ahead with its caucus outside the window permitted by party rules, he would enforce the rules and Michigan would lose half of its 197 Democratic delegation. Michigan also had an "open" state-run primary scheduled for February 24 where Republicans could participate in selecting delegates, which date was not satisfactory to the Michigan Democratic Party for the selection of its delegates. When the state Democratic Party made its final decision in May 2003, it chose February 7, 2004 for its presidential caucus.

It was also reported in the press that Detroit officials had been told the city might be deprived of the possibility of holding the 2008 Democratic National Convention in the city if the party held its 2004 caucus at an earlier date than permitted under Democratic Party rules.

Eventually, perhaps due to the overwhelming influence of the AFL-CIO representation in the Michigan Democratic Party, Senator Levin's plans were thwarted and the party voted to hold its caucus on February 7. At the same time there was talk of setting

---

Fun along the Campaign Trail

Perennial write-in candidate "Love 22" gave away money. But even after handing out thousands of $22 dollar bills with his Uncle Sam likeness centered on the currency in place of Thomas Jefferson's image, he didn't get 22 votes.

up a commission to study the whole process of selecting delegates prior to the 2008 presidential primary.

As a result of the new rule allowing Democratic presidential primaries or caucuses as early as February 3 in 2004, the Democrats in many other states began to take advantage of the opportunity. The following states were quick to announce their intention of staying competitive with the Republicans: South Carolina, Arizona, Missouri, and Virginia; California, New York, Illinois, Washington and Ohio were considering the idea.

The politicians of New Hampshire's sometime nemesis, Delaware, were also giving thought to once again competing for "first" position. But we find salvage in the *Wilmington News Journal* editorial of March 11, 2003 which read, "For eight years, Delaware political leaders have battled with their counterparts in New Hampshire... Delaware has come up a loser . . . We argued that it was wrong to give in because Delaware was the best state for an early primary because it is a true microcosm of the nation. That's still true. But wisdom says that when the forces aligned against you are overwhelming, retreat."

Meanwhile New Hampshire Republicans were encouraged by a visit from its then National Party Chairman, Marc Racicot, who said his party needed more specific rules to protect our first-in-the-nation status. Comparing the Democratic exemption for New Hampshire, he suggested, "We probably need to make ours more definite and certain" which was interpreted to mean that at least the Republicans should do as well for the state as the Democrats in view of our long tradition of being first. Mike Dennehy, then New Hampshire's Republican National Committeeman, said he would attempt to get New Hampshire as the GOP's official first primary.

The *Boston Globe*, which has backed its neighbor's early election, commented editorially, "No one wants Congress setting the primary calendar, so it is up to national party leaders. If they keep shrugging, presidential election years will start the previous year."

✻

Chapter 18

Will New Hampshire Stay First-in-the-Nation?

T HE ISLAND OF GUAM IS ON THE OTHER side of the International Date Line, where America's day begins. If Guam were to schedule its presidential primary on the same day as New Hampshire, it would then take place a day ahead of the Granite State. Even if New Hampshire were to move its date back to Christmas week of the year ahead of a scheduled primary, as it threatened to do in 2000 to upstage Delaware, it still wouldn't make any difference. The voters of Guam would be at the polls one day earlier than whatever date our secretary of state chose.

With global air travel so vastly more convenient than it was in 1920, or even in 1952, the media would perhaps gladly substitute pawpaws and passion fruit for snowballs and ice. They'd already have their tan before returning to cover "frontloading" in California and would have more time to spend in the sun there. But Guam is not yet a state.

There's also another potential. As a crony of oil-rich Alaska, New Hampshire has always been a natural lectern for the candidate who wants to curtail taxes. These are the only two states without a sales or income tax. Up to now, no candidate favoring a tax-free society has preferred to pontificate before eskimos in an igloo as opposed to sympathetic Yankees in a more cordial, warm, general-store environment.

Unfortunately, if immigrants continue to seek sanctuary in this rapidly growing tax-free state with their free-spending habits formed in other heavily taxed states, it may soon become the place where the "Live Free" beginning of its slogan may get swallowed up by its "Or Die" ending. No longer would the state be the only logical citadel to launch a campaign demonstrating how to reduce taxes at the federal level. Alaska might then be the most deserving beneficiary for the first-in-the-nation honor. It, too, has a small population and polar bears make great photo-ops.

There's always the potential that New Hampshire will some day have to yield its judgment completely to the media. A few decades ago there were instances when the media picked the presidents, not the voters. As Theodore H. White wrote in his *Making of the President* books, "The reporting of 40 or 50 senior political correspondents can determine the outcome of an American presidential election. They've become as important as the 100 senators of the U.S. Senate."

The national media can make or break a candidate. If there is a consensus in the press as to what percentage of the vote a candidate has to receive in the New Hampshire primary to be the

---

Fun along the Campaign Trail

Senator John F. Kennedy gained votes here in the minds of those who wouldn't read the statewide daily *Manchester Union Leader,* when Kennedy attacked its owner: "I believe there is a publisher who has less regard for the truth than William Loeb, but I can't think of his name."

Others take an opposite view, as did Jack Kemp, "New Hampshire is unique in the whole primary process. You are the wine tasters for the whole system."

Senator Gary Hart echoed the same theme, "The people of New Hampshire can literally have the power to change the course of history."

Probably Bill Clinton said it best, "I feel your pain. I will not take the Granite State for granted."

He was matched by another Democratic President, Jimmy Carter, "This state has a special place in the political life of this country, shaping the politics of America."

winner, it makes no difference what all the political professional pundits predicted. The final determination will be in the hands of the press. The primary would be irrelevant except as an exercise to take the measurement.

The McGovern/Muskie contest in 1972 was a perfect example of this power of the press. Even though McGovern got only 37 percent of the vote, he was considered the winner over favorite Muskie who had garnered 46 percent, but not the minimum 50 percent his campaign staff had predicted. The same thing happened in 1976 in the Reagan/Ford contest when, before the primary, the media touted that a 45 percent vote for Reagan versus the sitting president would be considered a victory. Yet when Reagan got 49 percent, they considered it a solid defeat.

As Steve Royko, columnist for the *Chicago Sun Times,* wrote at that time, "the results of the primary are meaningless because the winner isn't really the winner unless TV and the pundits decide he is. They make the rules by deciding how big a percentage a winner should get in order to be the winner in their eyes."

Repetition of this kind of extraneous umpiring by those who are not even supposed to be players in the game might also denigrate the political series played every four years in New Hampshire. The cheers of the home-team crowd would not have been heard and somebody who never earned it would have been declared the New Hampshire winner. In that circumstance the crowning of a victor might just as well have been made by television or on the tarmac of an airport in Texas.

Not to be overlooked should be the rapid rise in the 2000 primary cycle of "front-loading." This trend has substantially exacerbated the possibility leading to regional primaries. Opponents, envious of our position, see such action as a solution to the problem of equalizing opportunity for all states to participate in the primary process.

Many variations of how different groups of states could band together for a simultaneous primary day have been proposed. Fortunately, New Hampshire has been exempted from the equation

---

Fun along the Campaign Trail

Dressed as Uncle Sam and hurrying from Massachusetts in a Japanese car to meet the filing deadline, presidential candidate Sam Rouseville got nabbed for speeding in Manchester and never made it to Concord.

---

in most of the scenarios, but there's always the recurring danger it might not be so fortunate in the future.

In such a case, the winning candidate would be chosen as the one who'd probably had national name identification, could hire the best media consultants and who'd buy enough TV time with the snappiest commercials. Contrast that with the candidate who otherwise would have deserved the prize by meeting the voters one-on-one. It's a lot more difficult to be fraudulent in a New Hampshire living room.

Senator John Glenn, who ran in the 1984 primary, spoke from experience when he said, "A New England regional primary would prevent the less well-known, less well-financed candidates in our party from having an opportunity to campaign in a primary where person-to-person, grassroots democratic politics is still more effective than the impersonal media campaign."

The worst-case and most disheartening scenario for New Hampshire would be to get shot down by its own troops in not-so-friendly fire. For example: David Irwin is a Peterborough businessman and occasional columnist for the local papers. He writes seditious stuff like, "it's time we dumped the New Hampshire Primary. The balance of power in New Hampshire elections now rests with couch potatoes in Plaistow and Seabrook and Hollis watching ads on Boston TV." We don't believe the good citizens of those towns who conscientiously turn out on primary day would agree. He just doesn't get it.

Though not affecting New Hampshire, some states, like Colorado, Utah and Kansas which have Republican legislatures, have canceled 2004 primaries. They assume President Bush will have no serious opposition and view a primary as an unnecessary expense. It means the GOP there will not enjoy the excitement and political experience we gain here, even when party nominees are preordained. Meanwhile, in those states, the Democrats may resort to caucuses or conventions to nominate their candidates.

There are also those who suggest the best way to cure the individual egos of each state would be to combine them with a national primary. Professor William G. Mayer of Northeastern University has written, "Perhaps we may decide to bite the bullet and adopt a national primary, as the best in a series of bad alternatives." He points out that it would offer a huge advantage to well-known and well-financed candidates. Or, on the other hand, it might elect someone unacceptable to most of the party's members but supported by a small, yet intense minority.

Of course we've always got to be on the lookout for those misinformed detractors who represent well-read publications like the *Washington Post*. Henry Allen, as an example, alleged that Emerson wrote: "The God that made New Hampshire taunted the lofty land with little men."

Thereafter this sagacious staffer drew his own conclusion: "The question is not who they think they are to be holding us hostage every four years with their presidential primary. Instead, who do we think they are, to let them get away with it, this white, tight and right smidgen of a place, this myth-mongering bastion of no-tax/no spend conservatives with no minorities to speak of and a total of .43 percent of the American people?"

If Emerson really said that about the little men, then at least Allen demonstrates that the small guys have been gifted. The danger is that the "big fellers" who read papers like the *Washington Post* believe the tales they tell.

❋

Appendixes

Appendix A

Chronology of Major Candidates Participating from 1952 to 2000

1952

Republicans	% votes received	Democrats	% votes received
Dwight D. Eisenhower	50	Estes Kefauver	55
Robert A. Taft	39	Harry S. Truman	44
Harold E. Stassen	7		
Douglas McArthur	4		

Republicans:

- General Eisenhower, whose previous party affiliation was unknown, was placed on the Republican ballot by New Hampshire friends. Governor Sherman Adams ran Eisenhower's campaign and thereafter served as Chief of Staff for Eisenhower in the White House. Eisenhower, then serving as Supreme Commander of NATO Forces in Europe was prohibited from campaigning and did not come into the state during the primary, yet won all 14 delegates to the Republican National Convention. The primary was held on March 11th, but Adams first met Ike in June of that year. William Loeb, publisher of the *Manchester Union Leader,* had accused Adams of supporting a "phantom candidate."

- The pollsters had picked Senator Taft, the majority leader of the Senate, as the winner. In the last week, he took a three-day tour around the state and visited 28 towns. He was pained by a photo-op when he was holding a live rooster with a nauseous look on his (Taft's) face.

- Debates arranged between Eisenhower and Taft were conducted by surrogates.

Democrats:

- The pollsters had initially picked President Truman as the winner.
- Prior to election day, Truman called the New Hampshire primary

"eyewash" and announced he would not run for re-election. He'd quietly asked Adlai Stevenson to replace him.

- Kefauver won all of the delegates and was the original "grassroots" campaigner, complete with coonskin cap and sometimes riding on a snowmobile.

1956

Republicans	% votes received	Democrats	% votes received
Dwight D. Eisenhower	99	Estes Kefauver	85
		Adlai E. Stevenson -write-ins	15

Republicans:

- Sherman Adams, Eisenhower's Chief of Staff, had not shared a comfortable political relationship with New Hampshire Senator Styles Bridges. It had been widely understood that Eisenhower did not want Richard M. Nixon remaining on the ticket as Ike's vice president during his second term. But Nixon, in a campaign initiated by Bridges, received 22,936 write-in votes for vice president. This large turnout of write-in votes cemented Nixon's position for a second term as vice president. As Governor Lane Dwinell commented, "it was well-organized spontaneity."
- Publisher Bill Loeb of the *Manchester Union Leader* called Eisenhower "Dopey' Dwight."

Democrats:

- Stevenson did not campaign in the state, as he figured Kefauver remained entrenched from his 1952 win. Kefauver had spent so much time both in the state and promoting it in Congress that he was jokingly referred to as New Hampshire's third senator.

1960

Republicans	% votes received	Democrats	% votes received
Richard M. Nixon	89	John F. Kennedy	85
Nelson A. Rockefeller	4		

Republicans:

- Neither the Republican nor the Democratic candidate had serious opposition.
- Publisher Bill Loeb of the *Manchester Union Leader* called Kennedy the "spoiled brat."
- Just before the filing period Rockefeller unexpectedly announced he was not a candidate.

Democrats:

- Kefauver had laid a good foundation for the Democrats, on which Kennedy capitalized.
- Uninvited fringe candidate, Paul C. Fisher, with a twelve minute speech on abolishing taxes had interrupted Kennedy during a University of New Hampshire convocation. Fisher came in second with 6,853 votes versus Kennedy's 43,372.
- Nashua Democrats take pride in the Kennedy statue in front of City Hall with its plaque:

  In Memoriam—President John Fitzgerald Kennedy on January 25, 1960— This City Hall Plaza Was John F. Kennedy's First Campaign Stop in the Nation for the Presidency of the United States of America.

- In the lobby of the former Carpenter Hotel in Manchester is a plaque commemorating the first Kennedy campaign headquarters in the nation.

1964

Republicans	% votes received	Democrats	% votes received
Henry Cabot Lodge	36	Lyndon Baines Johnson	95
Barry M. Goldwater	22	Robert Kennedy	2
Nelson A. Rockefeller	21		
Richard M. Nixon	17		

Republicans:

- The pollsters had picked Senator Goldwater as the winner on the Republican side. But the senator didn't add many new friends in Rockingham County with his statement, "This country would be better off if we saw off the eastern seaboard and let it float out to sea."

- In 1952, former Senator Lodge had served as National Chairman of the Draft Eisenhower Committee. He did not want his name on the ballot, so his supporters designed a most effective instruction card for the voters to write-in his name. Lodge was serving as ambassador to South Vietnam when his son and friends in Massachusetts mounted a very well planned write-in campaign on his behalf. Like Eisenhower, Lodge never came into the state.

- Lodge had previously told Governor Nelson Rockefeller he would not run against him.

- Rockefeller and Senator Goldwater campaigned vigorously throughout the state. Goldwater had a foot injury which made walking difficult. He proposed making social security voluntary. After New Hampshire, Goldwater eventually won the Republican nomination, then lost to President Johnson in the fall election.

- Rockefeller was viciously attacked by Bill Loeb, publisher of the *Manchester Union Leader,* who charged him with being a "wife swapper" (among other things) although Loeb had weathered divorces of his own.

- Nixon's name, like Lodge's, did not appear on the ballot. He was also a write-in.

Democrats:

- John F. Kennedy was assassinated on 11/22/63, thus there were no Democratic filings as the country was in a state of mourning. Since 1952 when the presidential preference procedure was introduced, it was the only time when there were no candidate's names listed on one of the major party's ballots.

- It was significant that President Johnson received 29,317 write-ins. The votes for Robert Kennedy, John's brother, were also write-ins. Additionally, Robert received 25,094 write-ins for vice president.

1968

Republicans	% votes received	Democrats	% votes received
Richard M. Nixon	78	Lyndon Baines Johnson	50
Nelson A. Rockefeller	11	Eugene McCarthy	42
George Romney (1,743 votes)			

Republicans:

- Romney, businessman and founder of Marriott hotels, held a large rally at his Lake Winnipesaukee summer home. Later, in an argument with the owner of a Concord bookstore and before reporters, he said he'd been "brainwashed" into favoring the Vietnam War. This statement received such nationwide coverage that it collapsed his primary campaign and presidential aspirations. He dropped out ten days before the primary.
- Columnists Robert Novak and Ronald Evans wrote that Nixon's advantage over Romney is "so small it approaches meaningless."

Democrats:

- President Johnson's votes were write-ins. He did not file or come into the state, but advertised heavily. The big issue was the Vietnam War which McCarthy opposed. After the primary, President Johnson withdrew from seeking a second term, stating. "I shall not seek, and will not accept, the nomination of my party for another term as your president." Senator Eugene McCarthy was on the ballot, worked the state hard with views opposing the Vietnam War and won more delegates than Johnson. McCarthy ran again in 1992 and received 211 votes.

- Actor Paul Newman was among the many movie stars and celebrities who came to New Hampshire in support of McCarthy.
- Robert Kennedy was urged to support McCarthy, but refused because he didn't think McCarthy was qualified to be president.
- Publisher Bill Loeb of the *Manchester Union Leader* called McCarthy the "skunk's skunk's skunk."

1972

Republicans	% votes received	Democrats	% votes received
Richard M. Nixon	68	Edmund S. Muskie	46
Paul M. McClosky, Jr.	20	George McGovern	37
John M. Ashbrook	10	Sam Yorty	6
		Wilbur D. Mills	4

Republicans:

- Eighteen months later President Nixon resigned during his term as president due to the Watergate scandal and Gerald R. Ford completed the term.
- Spiro T. Agnew, the vice president, was not a popular running-mate on the Nixon ticket, yet he received an all-time high of 45,524 write-in votes for vice president which reaffirmed his position on the ticket. He also resigned in disgrace during Nixon's term as president. Ford chose Nelson Rockefeller as his vice president.
- Bill Loeb, publisher of the *Manchester Union Leader,* commented on the Ford–Rockefeller team, "Never in the history of the Republican Party have we had two such lemons in the White House."
- McClosky opposed United States participation in the Vietnam War.
- Ashbrook ran as a real conservative, believing Nixon had veered too far to the left once he got to the White House.

Democrats:

- Muskie was damaged by a speech given in a snowstorm in front of the *Manchester Union Leader* building. Because of an editorial critical of his wife, Muskie called the publisher of the paper, William Loeb, "a mudslinging, vicious and gutless liar." Muskie was so passionate in his wrath that the question still lingers with the media as to whether there were tears in his eyes, or just melting snow.
- Muskie's state coordinator Maria Carrier had predicted he would gain 50 percent of the votes, or she would shoot herself. Because Muskie came from neighboring Maine, the media thought he should have done better. Thus McGovern was perceived as the winner.
- McGovern's alleged victory carried him to the eventual Democratic presidential nomination.
- McGovern ran again in 1984 and received 5,217 votes.
- Sam Yorty, Mayor of Los Angeles, was backed by Bill Loeb, publisher of the *Manchester Union Leader,* probably as a foil to attack Muskie and McGovern.

1976

Republicans	% votes received	Democrats	% votes received
Gerald R. Ford	50	James E. Carter	29
Ronald W. Reagan	49	Morris K. Udall	23
		Birch Bayh	15
		Fred Harris	11
		R. Sergeant Shriver	8
		Hubert Humphrey	5

Republicans:

- The Ford–Reagan race was the closest in New Hampshire primary history, with Ford winning by only 1,587 votes. Ford had not been elected to the presidency but, as vice president, had become president after Nixon and Agnew had resigned.

- Reagan had served two terms as governor of California.
- Jack Germond and many other political pundits had picked Reagan as the winner. Publisher Bill Loeb of the *Manchester Union Leader* called Ford, "Jerry the Jerk."

Democrats:

- Senator Udall had been considered the favorite.
- Georgia Governor Carter was totally unknown by the natives when he started out in New Hampshire. Lloyd Robie was playing checkers over the cracker barrel of the family general store in Hooksett when interrupted by a stranger, "I'm Jimmy Carter, running for president." "Jimmy who?" asked Lloyd and thereafter Carter was "Jimmy who." Carter had the advantage of having so many in the race it split the vote in his favor. He ran a traditional one-on-one grassroots campaign and stayed overnight at more than 50 New Hampshire homes during the two years leading up to the primary. Thereafter he won the presidency and returned the favor a year later by inviting all of his former hosts for an evening at *his* house, the White House.
- Senator Hubert Humphrey was realistic about his poor showing, "I never thought my speeches were too long. I enjoyed them."
- Publisher Bill Loeb of the *Manchester Union Leader* called Carter the "wimp."

1980

Republicans	% votes received	Democrats	% votes received
Ronald W. Reagan	50	James E. Carter	47
George H. W. Bush	23	Edward M. Kennedy	37
Howard H. Baker	13	Edmund G. Brown, Jr.	10
John B. Anderson	10	Lyndon H. LaRouche	
Philip M. Crane			
John B. Connally			
Robert Dole			

Republicans:

- Unknown to Bush, Reagan had brought five other uninvited major candidates to what was supposed to have been a Bush–Reagan two-man debate at the Nashua High School gym. When the moderator denied the interlopers the right to speak, Reagan won the day with his off-the-cuff one-liner, "I paid for this microphone, Mr. Green."
- After the debate, Walter Cronkite said Reagan's tactic displayed a thin line between a clever political maneuver and a dirty trick.
- Bill Loeb in the *Manchester Union Leader* took an opposite view: "Bush showed himself to be what he really is, a spoiled little rich kid who has been wet-nursed to success and now, packaged by David Rockefeller's Trilateral Commission, thinks he's entitled to the White House as his latest toy."
- Congressman Anderson, on a recount, received only 9.8 percent of the votes, thereby not entitling him to any delegates. He needed 10 percent. Thereafter he ran as an Independent in the general election. Although he described himself as the "thinking man's candidate," David Olinger said he was "the only candidate running in the left lane."

Democrats:

- New Hampshire Democratic Governor Hugh Gallen supported President Carter, but Carter did not make a personal appearance in the state because of the American hostages in Iran. Senator Edward Kennedy received only 10 percent fewer votes than the president. Carter's relatively weak support contributed to Reagan's November victory.
- Brown was referred to as the "flake" from California.
- Democrat Lyndon H. LaRouche, a New Hampshire-born fringe candidate, received only .0157 percent of the votes cast, and he too called for a recount. He ran in a total of five home-state primaries.

1984

Republicans	% votes received	Democrats	% votes received
Ronald W. Reagan	86	Gary Hart	37
		Walter F. Mondale	28
		John Glenn	12
		Jesse L. Jackson	5
		George McGovern	5
		Ernest F. Hollings	4

Republicans:

- President Reagan received 65,033 votes, and Harold Stassen was in second place with 1,543. Democratic write-ins on the Republican ballot: Hart 3,968; Mondale 1,090; Glenn 1,063.

Democrats:

- The media had picked Mondale to be the winner, but Gary Hart's state campaign director and future Governor Jeanne Shaheen commented, "Lots of New Hampshire people don't read the national press."
- Hart had served as McGovern's national chairman in 1972 and his upset victory managed by Jeanne Shaheen was later hurt by Mondale's question to him of "Where's the beef?" It was his subsequent indiscreet involvement with Donna Rice which ended his presidential aspirations.
- McGovern told the press that Nixon had recently congratulated him for McGovern's statement in the 1972 campaign when, after having been beaten by Nixon, McGovern said to Nixon, "Don't throw away your conscience."

1988

Republicans	% votes received	Democrats	% votes received
George H.W. Bush	38	Michael Dukakis	35
Robert B. Dole	28	Richard C. Gephardt	20
Jack Kemp	13	Paul Simon	17
Pierre S. Dupont	10	Jesse L. Jackson	8
Pat Robinson	9	Al Gore	7
		Bruce Babbitt	5
		Gary Hart	4

Republicans:

- The pollsters had picked Senator Dole to be the winner.
- Vice President Bush referred to Dole as "Senator Straddle." Dole replied, "Stop lying about my record."
- New Hampshire Governor John Sununu ran Bush's campaign and thereafter served as chief of staff for Bush in the White House. Some conservatives scoffed at Sununu as not being qualified for the position because his name spelled backwards would put the UN twice before the US.

Democrats:

- New Hampshire was enjoying an economic boom during the primary campaign and Massachusetts Governor Michael Dukakis was touting his home state as the "Massachusetts Miracle," and pledging to do for America what he claimed to have done for Massachusetts.
- Bush beat Dukakis in the general election where Dukakis had been damaged by a photo taken of him in a military tank.
- After coming in last behind the major candidates, Gary Hart, who had won the previous primary, said, "There are other ways to serve one's country than just standing high in the polls or winning primaries."

1992

Republicans	% votes received	Democrats	% votes received
George H.W. Bush	52	Paul E. Tsongas	33
Patrick J. Buchanan	37	Bill Clinton	24
		Bob Kerry	11
		Tom Harkin	10
		Edmund G. Brown, Jr.	2
		Eugene McCarthy	(217 votes)

Republicans:

- After having defaulted on a Republican Convention promise not to raise taxes, President Bush was hurt by Buchanan, who recalled Bush's statement, "Read my lips, no new taxes," a line New Hampshire primary voters were reminded of daily by the Buchanan campaign.

Democrats:

- Massachusetts Senator Tsongas ran in New Hampshire as a vicarious "favorite son." He lived only a few miles from the state line and had attended college in the state.

- Arkansas Governor Clinton was impaired by an alleged affair with Gennifer Flowers, but later redeemed himself as the "Come back kid."

- Previously, no incumbent vice president had ever filed separately for vice president as permitted under New Hampshire statute. They had always relied on the popularity of the presidential candidate and the party ticket to re-elect them. Endicott Peabody of Hollis, former governor of Massachusetts, ran on the ballot as a Democrat for vice president and received 34,533 Democratic votes. With a friend dressed in a yellow "chicken" suit, he challenged Vice President Quayle, who was campaigning on behalf of President Bush, for not filing for vice president or being willing to debate. Quayle, not on the ballot, received 6,613 Republican write-in votes for vice president.

Libertarians:

- The Libertarian Party was also a legally-recognized party in this primary for the first time in New Hampshire, and cast 3,219 votes for Andre Marrou to be president.

1996

Republicans	% votes received	Democrats	% votes received
Patrick J. Buchanan	27	Bill Clinton	83
Robert B. Dole	26		
Lamar Alexander	22		
Steve Forbes	12		
Richard G. Lugar	5		
Alan L. Keyes	2		

Republicans:

- The pollsters had picked Senator Dole to be the winner. Buchanan successfully hammered away at his long Washington career and all the taxes he had voted for. Although Dole became the Republican nominee for the general election, he lost to Clinton.
- Steve Forbes spent his own money on extensive media and direct mail, setting an all-time record for primary financing, probably more than his major competitors combined.
- Colin Powell, who was not a candidate and had no organized campaign effort, received 6,414 Republican write-in votes.

Democrats:

- Among the registered Democrats, Pat Paulsen, the comedian, came in second after President Clinton with 1,007 votes.

Libertarians:

- The Libertarian Party, recognized on the ballot for the second time, cast 653 votes for Harry Browne for president and 336 for Irwin A. Shiff.

2000

Republican	% votes received	Democrats	% votes received
John McCain	48	Al Gore	49
George W. Bush	30	Bill Bradley	45
Steve Forbes	13		
Alan L. Keyes	6		
Gary Bauer	(1,640 votes)		

Republicans:

- Most pollsters had predicted Governor Bush to be the winner, but none of them anticipated the 19 point percentage of the McCain upset victory. Karl Rove, Bush's chief political strategist, dismissed their loss as "a bump in the road." Bush was hurt by not participating in a candidate debate at Dartmouth and running an overly structured campaign.
- McCain with his "Straight Talk Express" and 114 town meetings ran the typical New Hampshire "grassroots" campaign that's hard to beat.
- Gary Bauer explained his loss, "I heard my words even when my lips weren't moving."
- Senator Dole's wife, Elizabeth, campaigned extensively but withdrew before the filing date, as did former Tennessee Governor Lamar Alexander and Ohio Congressman John Kasich.

Democrats:

- Both Vice President Gore and former Senator Bradley spent considerable time knocking on doors. Gore had the double advantage of the vice presidency and the enthusiastic support of Governor Shaheen and her husband Bill, his chairman.
- Bradley traveled with a smaller entourage, though both candidates had substantial media coverage. Bradley made an agreement with McCain that neither would accept "soft money" if they became the nominees of their respective parties.
- Bradlee's skipped heartbeats, which gained considerable news attention, reminded voters of former candidate Paul Tsongas and made the difference for Gore.

Appendix B

2004 Presidential Primary Calendar

Changes may occur to this schedule. The calendar is based on
state determinations as of July 23, 2003.

*State caucus information was due to the DNC on May 1, 2003, but
some states have received extensions. State caucus information
was due to the RNC by October 7, 2003.*

State	Presidential Primary Election	Caucus Dates	Local Primary Elections May be held on same date as presidential primary; some local primaries may be held on separate dates
Alabama	June 1		June 1
Alaska	*No primary*		August 24
Arizona	February 3		September 7
Arkansas	May 18		May 18
California	March 2		March 2 (may be changed)
Colorado	*No primary*		August 10
Connecticut	March 2		September 14 (may change to Aug. 10)
Delaware	February 3		September 11
District of Columbia	January13	February 10 (tentative)	Date is TBA; Will be set for a date between Sept. 10–14
Florida	March 9		August 31
Georgia	March 2		June 20
Hawaii	*No primary*	Dem: March 2	September 18
Idaho	May 25	Dem: February 24	May 25
Illinois	March 16		March 16
Indiana	May 4		May 4

State	Presidential Primary Election	Caucus Dates	Local Primary Elections
Iowa	*No primary*	January 19 *(tentative)*	June 8
Kansas	*No primary*		August 3
Kentucky	May 18		May 18
Louisiana	March 9		September 18
Maine	*No primary*	Dem: February 8	June 8
Maryland	March 2		March 2
Massachusetts	March 2		September 14
Michigan	*No primary*	Dem: February 7	August 3
Minnesota	*No primary*	Dem: March 2	September 14
Mississippi	March 9		March 9
Missouri	February 3		August 3
Montana	June 8		June 8
Nebraska	May 11		May 11
Nevada	*No primary*		September 7
New Hampshire	January 27 *(tentative)*		September 14
New Jersey	June 8		June 8
New Mexico	June 1 *(GOP ballot will be a pres. primary)*	February 3 will be Dem caucus	June 1
New York	March 2		September 15
North Carolina	May 4		May 4
North Dakota	*No primary*	February 3	June 8
Ohio	March 2		March 2
Oklahoma	February 3		July 27
Oregon	May 18		May 18
Pennsylvania	April 27		April 27

State	Presidential Primary Election	Caucus Dates	Local Primary Elections
Rhode Island	March 2		September 14
South Carolina	February 3		June 8
South Dakota	June 1		June 1
Tennessee	February 10		August 5
Texas	March 2		March 2
Utah	February 27* *(legislature has voted not to fund primary)*		June 22
Vermont	March 2		September 14
Virginia	February 10		June 8
Washington	March 2	Dem: February 7	September 14
West Virginia	May 11		May 11
Wisconsin	February 17		September 9
Wyoming	*No primary*		August 17

Appendix C

March 20, 1986

Testimony of the Honorable Judd Gregg before the Subcommittee on Elections Committee on House Administration

Since New Hampshire instituted its first-in-the-nation primary, there have been over 100 bills introduced in the U.S. Congress designed to effect the scheduling of primaries. In 1985, Congressman Morris K. Udall of Arizona re-introduced his bill to prevent New Hampshire from holding its traditional first-in-the-nation primary. In response, Congressman Judd Gregg of New Hampshire gave this testimony in opposition to the legislation.

Mr. Chairman, I appreciate the opportunity to be here today to testify before this subcommittee on an issue that's important not only to the people of New Hampshire, but also to the people of this nation. It's important that the overall ramifications of this legislation be clearly understood.

This is another ill-conceived effort on the part of Congress to wrest control of the election process from the individual states. In this case, that state happens to be my own. Supporters of these bills want to water down the New Hampshire primary for three basic reasons. First: They say it allows New Hampshire voters to exert a disproportionate amount of influence on the election process, because of the attention the primary receives by virtue of being first. Second: These critics charge that New Hampshire should not host the first primary because it is not representative of the nation as a whole, and third: They claim the New Hampshire primary makes the campaign season too long and expensive. Let's take a look at these charges.

When I consider whether New Hampshire voters exert an influence beyond their numbers and whether they should be penalized for that by having their rights stripped away, I conclude: It is not the voters who exert the disproportionate amount of influence. After all, each voter is only casting one vote. Rather, it is the media that makes the primary a media event, which magnifies the election and makes it an event of greater import than it might otherwise be. Furthermore, what about the public opinion polls which use a sampling of perhaps two thousand people to gauge the sentiment of the nation? These polls receive an enormous amount of media attention, and candidates yearn to see their names at the top of these as much as they hope to win the heart of the New Hampshire voter. These two thousand people represented in these polls are the ones who exert an influence that is out of step with their numbers. Even if you insist that New Hampshire does exert a disproportionate amount of influence in the presidential election process, and I question that, I would submit that it is a small price to pay for keeping alive the dream that, only in America, can anyone grow up to be President. An opportunity of that sort is, after all, what the New Hampshire primary really represents and what this nation is all about.

It's a chance for a person who considers himself or herself to be a legitimate presidential contender, but who has not been anointed by the national media corps or the Washington power base to come into a small state, campaign on a one-to-one basis and be competitive. New Hampshire forces the candidate to stand up to the scrutiny of the individual voter. In this era of big government and big media, the smallness of New Hampshire requires personal contact in a presidential campaign, which is a quality that should be cherished, rather than feared. If we decide to group all of the primaries together to make it impossible for a candidate to take part in a single, small state primary early in the process, we are essentially saying that only the wealthy can grow up to be President, because only the wealthy will be able to afford to compete under such a system. If we go to a series of regional primaries, we can say goodbye to one-on-one campaigning and hello to government by the national media and Washington establishment.

We should also do some reading between the lines. What is really being said by the political leadership of this country is, "let's take New Hampshire out of the spotlight, and keep the process of electing a President in the hands of the few and the powerful within the party leadership. Let's make sure the dark horse does not have an opportunity to gather momentum and media attention in a small state like New Hampshire and thereby foul up all of our carefully laid plans." This is really what is being said in proposing that New Hampshire be grouped in with a series of other states in a regional primary. This message, if I may be so bold to say so, is arrogance in its highest form. The party leadership would tell the George Bushes, the Jimmy Carters, The Gary Harts of this land, all of whom entered campaigns underfinanced and without household names, "You will not be given a fair shot at the Presidency because the Golden Hands of the Leadership and the national media have not been placed upon your shoulder."

With regard to the question of representation—New Hampshire is not as unrepresentative as some would have you believe. New Hampshire is the fourth most highly industrialized state in the Union, the fastest growing state east of the Mississippi, after Florida—and has more cars per capita than any other state. Furthermore, the state presents an opportunity for candidates to come face-to-face with a wonderful mix of metropolitan and rural voters. A large part of the state is rural, yet the southern region of the state is part of the great eastern megalopolis.

Another fact is that since 1952, no person has been elected President without first winning the New Hampshire primary. I wouldn't suggest that this means you have to win-the New Hampshire primary to get elected President, but the fact is New Hampshire voters have demonstrated time and again their ability to select individuals who are palatable to the nation as a whole. The indisputable fact is that New Hampshire voters have a track record of which they are justifiably proud. Should they be penalized for this track record, and for their desire to continue to showcase their political acumen, simply because the national news organizations have decided that the media event that has become our presidential campaign shall start in New Hampshire? I think a decision to do so would be an arbitrary one based upon jealousy.

The claim that New Hampshire contributes significantly to the length of the campaign season and the cost of that campaign is, I believe, a false one. The campaign season really begins at the time an individual aspires for the oval Office. From that point forward, the candidate, whether announced or not, is seeking out the television cameras; sometimes as much as two years in advance of the New Hampshire primary. For an example, we need look no further than Senator Kennedy's statement of several months back that he would not seek the presidency in 1988. That disclaimer became necessary because his actions and words were being framed in presidential terms a full three years before the election. The New Hampshire primary had nothing to do with it. Eliminating New Hampshire's key role in the process is not going to shorten the campaign season. Furthermore, New Hampshire is one of the few states where it is relatively inexpensive to campaign, because of its small area and population. A candidate is not forced to rely upon expensive media centers for exposure to the electorate. One can easily run a presidential primary campaign for between $250,000 and $500,000, which is far below the cost it would take to run a similar campaign in larger states.

Earlier this year the House passed a bill that would force states to keep their polls open until a certain hour on presidential election days. I criticized the measure as an infringement upon states' rights. The proposals before the Subcommittee today are no less an infringement upon those rights of individual states to govern their own elections. Congress seems intent upon nibbling away those rights one morsel at a time. Eventually, the states are going to be left without a cookie.

Nowhere is it written that Congress shall play a role in the nominating process if the convention and party nominating process decide that New Hampshire and Iowa are outside the proper process, they can unseat the delegates at the convention. However, it should be up to the parties, and not Congress, to make such a decision.

The arguments I have raised before you today are not based merely on provincialism. New Hampshire serves a legitimate and serious national purpose; we as a nation need a first primary where the average person can compete on equal footing with the rich and powerful. My concern is that, until the electorate has spoken, we need to keep the process by which we choose a President as open as possible, to keep alive the dream that, "only in America . . . "

Mr. Chairman, members of this Subcommittee, I thank you.

Appendix D

History of Legislation Governing the New Hampshire Primary

The first step toward New Hampshire's first-in-the-nation primary came in 1913 when the state legislature established a presidential primary solely to select delegates to the national nominating conventions.[1] The date was set for the third Tuesday in May, 1916. However, before the first primary was held, the 1915 General Court decided to change the date to coincide with town meeting day, which traditionally had been the second Tuesday in March.[2] This would prevent most communities from having to hold an additional election.

The first primary, held on the second Tuesday in March, 1916 was a week later than Indiana's and the same day as Minnesota's. By 1920 it would become the first-in-the-nation primary, as Indiana changed to May and Minnesota decided not to continue its primary.[3] Delegate selection was the sole purpose of the New Hampshire primary for its first 32 years. Delegates were listed on the ballot either pledged to a specific candidate, or uncommitted.

The 1949 legislature passed a bill to permit the inclusion of a presidential and vice-presidential preference poll in addition to delegate selection.[4] This change permitted the name of a candidate for president or vice president to be placed on the ballot if the proper number of signatures of registered voters (50 from each of the two congressional districts) were submitted to the secretary of state. The name would remain on the ballot unless the candidate filed a disclaimer. Two other changes made in 1949 required pledged delegates to get prior approval from the candidate and allowed prospective delegates to compete in the additional category of "favorable" without a candidate's consent.

The presidential primary law has undergone several further revisions. In 1971 the number of signatures necessary to place a candidate's name on the ballot was increased from 50 to 500 in each of the two congressional districts. And, for the first time, a filing fee was established: it would cost $500 in addition to the required signatures to have the name of a candidate placed in the preference poll.[5] The 1976 primary ballot included a total of 391 names competing for delegate and alternate positions. Because of the large number of candidates, the 1977 legislature voted to remove the delegates' names from the ballots.[6] Instead, the candidates were required to submit their delegate slates to the secretary of state prior to the primary. The law provided that a presidential candidate shall receive at least 10 percent of the total vote cast in his political party to be eligible for a percentage of the apportioned delegates. In 1983 the legislature abolished the signature requirement to place a name on the ballot and increased the filing fee to $1,000.[7]

The state has changed technical and legal details of its primary many times since its enactment in 1913. The major source of revisions, however, has been the effort to protect the first-in-the-nation status by changing the primary date. Between 1916 and 1968 the primary was held on the traditional town meeting day, the second Tuesday in March. New Hampshire changed this date in 1971, after Florida decided to shift its primary, held in May since 1944, to the same second Tuesday in March. As a result of this challenge, New Hampshire moved ahead by one week its town meeting day and voted on March 7 in 1972. This change in the date for town meetings broke a long-time tradition, but the state was determined to maintain its first-in-the-nation primary.

The next change occurred in 1975 when Massachusetts advanced its April primary to the first Tuesday in March as part of an unsuccessful effort to establish a New England regional presidential primary. Vermont was the only other state to join in this effort, but its primary was non-binding: a caucus and state convention continued to award convention delegates in Vermont. In response to Massachusetts and Vermont, the New Hampshire Legislature changed the primary date to "the first Tuesday in March or on the Tuesday immediately preceding the date on which any other New England state shall hold a similar election, whichever is earlier."[8] Therefore, the 1976 vote was held on the final Tuesday in February, a week before the Massachusetts and Vermont primaries.

In an effort to avoid having to take legislative action each time another state challenged New Hampshire's primary status, the 1977 legislature approved another revision on the timing of the primary. This law stated that the primary would be held "on the second Tuesday in March or on the Tuesday immediately preceding the date on which any other state shall hold a similar election, whichever is earlier, of each year when a president of the United States is to be elected."[9] This change also restored the date for town meeting to its traditional second Tuesday in March.

In 1987 the legislature decided that in addition to listing each candidate's name, the ballot would also include his city or town and state of domicile.[10]

As a further attempt to protect the first-in-the-nation tradition, the General Court gave authority to the secretary of state to have more flexibility in setting the date of the primary. It required that the primary be held on the second Tuesday in March or on a Tuesday selected by the secretary of state which is seven days or more immediately preceding the date on which any other state shall hold a similar election, whichever is earlier, of each year when a president of the United States is to be elected or the year previous. The filing period for declarations of candidacy for president and vice president was moved from December to November, beginning the first Monday and ending the third Friday thereafter.[11]

Notes

1. Session Laws of the New Hampshire General Court, Chapter 167, Laws of 1913.

2. Session Laws of the New Hampshire General Court, Chapter 124, Laws of

3. Robert A. Diamond, *Presidential Elections Since 1789* (Washington, D.C. Congressional Quarterly Press, 1975), p. 121.

4. Session Laws of the New Hampshire General Court, Chapter 186, Laws of 1949.

5. Session laws of the New Hampshire General Court, Chapters 562, 369 and 502, laws of 1971.

6. Session Laws of the New Hampshire General Court, Chapter 524, Laws of 1977.

7. Session Laws of the New Hampshire General Court, Chapter 298, Laws of 1983.

8. Session laws of the New Hampshire General Court, Chapter 184, Laws of 1975.

9. Session Laws of the New Hampshire General Court, Chapter 524, Laws of 1977.

10. Session Laws of the New Hampshire General Court, Chapter 284, Laws of 1987.

11. Session Laws of the New Hampshire General Court, Chapter 161, Laws of 1999.

Appendix E

As Others See Us

Concord Monitor—October 29, 1979*

So into This Quirky State Come All the Bandwagons of All Americans Who Would be President. *Why?*

by Sid Moody
AP News Features Writer

The flocks and kine are neatest in New Hampshire,
The song birds sing the sweetest in New Hampshire,
The thunder peals the loudest,
The mountains are the grandest,
And the politics are the damnedest in New Hampshire.

If one lived in Amarillo, say, one might be tempted to think of New Hampshire—if one were tempted to think of New Hampshire at all—that as New Hampshire goes, so goes New Hampshire.

But Americans cannot easily overlook a state that names its mountains after presidents and whose kickoff primary has a mountainous influence in choosing who those presidents will be.

So, considering this barometer, what is New Hampshire?

New Hampshire is a place with a history of:

- *Tolerance:* While Salem was burning its witches, Goody Walford of Portsmouth sued those who accused her of witchcraft for slander. And won.
- *Liberty:* the right of the citizenry to revolt is written into the state constitution.
- *Ingenuity:* In 1869 Enos M. Clough of Sunapee invented a horseless carriage that had 5,463 parts.
- *Variety:* There are 132 ways to spell Lake Winnipesaukee.

---

* This article appeared almost a quarter of a century ago in the *Concord Monitor*. It may be interesting for the reader to note how things have changed—and how they haven't!

- Morality: Around 1820, Dartmouth College fined 39 students $2 each for attending dancing school.

- *Freedom:* the license plates, bearing Revolutionary War hero Gen. John Stark's phrase "Live Free or Die," are made by convicts in the state's one prison.

- *Democracy:* New Hampshire's mob scene Legislature has 400 representatives. If the U.S. had the same proportion, there would be 112,000 congressmen.

- *Forgiveness*: The Legislature has repealed a provision for the governor to pursue and slay "anyone who aggravates New Hampshire."

Paradox and Parsimony

It is also a state of paradoxes. There are white-steepled villages, and the state is 86 percent forest. But it's more urban than rural.

Its government is frugal. The state takes in $130 million in gross receipts for liquor taxes, 60 percent paid by out-of-state bargain hunters. Same with cigarettes.

New Hampshire is the only state with no broad-based taxes. But it hits tourists 6 percent for food and lodging. Unearned income—dividends and interest—is taxed. And state parsimony has sent property taxes soaring.

New Hampshire's tax-free climate has attracted 140,000 newcomers—many "Flatlanders" from "Taxachusetts"—since 1970, making the state the fastest growing besides Florida east of the Mississippi. When the Flatlanders settle in, they learn the tax-free air is purchased at the expense of no kindergartens, of having to drive their refuse to the dump on Saturdays, and of having too few cops to control too many skiers.

As the Flatlanders demand increased services, they create pressure for the very taxes they came to New Hampshire to avoid.

But things don't change too much.

Some town meetings still appoint fence viewers (they adjudicate boundary disputes. Hanover has three, one with a degree from Oxford), hog reeves (porcine dog wardens) and cullers of staves (whatever they do). In Bartlett, Stan Davidson still runs his birch peg factory with a century-old, wood-fired steam boiler. The state still has a day off on Fast Day which dates from the 17th century when citizens were asked to pray and fast for an ailing governor.

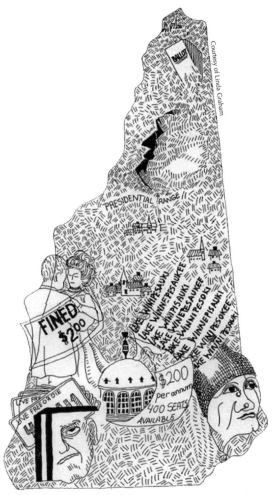

*Illustration by Linda Graham that accompanied
original* Concord Monitor *article.*

There are traditions that New Hampshire has fought for and preserved, and they remain native in the soil even if many of the state's 850,000 people were born elsewhere.

Perhaps the greatest paradox of all is that New Hampshire would perch atop the nation like an old, tarnished rooster weather vane forecasting the political breezes.

Politics and Pomposity

New Hampshire's preoccupation with politics—its town meetings, its opera-chorus Legislature, its staggered terms for state officials, its retention alone in the United States of a colonial-era five-man council to oversee the governor—stems party from a historic distrust of politicians and government.

Take the governor. He has a two-year term. The attorney general is in for five. One reason the Legislature is kept large—third only to Congress and Britain's Parliament in the free world—is that its very size tends to keep things honest.

"By the time you've bought off the last one, you've lost the first," says Andy Anderson, a newsman turned historian. "Besides, there's nothing to steal."

The legislators' 19th century pay scale—$200 a year—keeps the professional pol and the ambitious at bay. The result is not always brilliant legislation, as might be expected in a body that took 45 minutes to call the roll until electronic voting came in recently.

"One-half of the Legislature is incapable of thought, one-quarter never talks, 10 percent are leaders," says Eugene Daniell, Jr. of Franklin. He is an impish 77 year old veteran of political combat that included bringing the New York Stock Exchange to a halt in 1933 with a protest dose of tear gas.

Daniell, in his way, may be a prototype New Hampshire politician. "In Concord, they think I'm a raving radical" for numerous populist proposals dating back to his idol, Huey Long. "In Franklin," where Daniell presides over the school budget with the stinginess of a hired man's breakfast, "they think I'm a raving reactionary."

So into this quirky state, where there is a law against building a fence more than five feet high to spite your neighbor, come all the bandwagons of all Americans who would be president. Why?

Well, a state that can survive Earth's highest recorded wind—231 miles per hour atop Mt. Washington—can withstand a little campaign oratory.

There are no political bosses, no dominant labor unions, no machines. There is only one commercial TV station and only one statewide newspaper, the *Manchester Union Leader,* owned by a choleric uppercase editorialist named William Loeb who is described as a king breaker rather than a king maker.

Loeb's alliterative outbursts—e.g. "Jerry the Jerk"—raise passions if not votes and catch the ears of the Washington press corps when it shows up at primary time. But campaign seeds must be planted years before if they are to flower, as Jimmy Carter proved in 1976. He started in 1974.

Advice and Dissent

The initial step is to locate a sympathetic figure of reputation to head your campaign. An ex-governor would do nicely. But lacking one, the candidate seeks out one of the state's 30 or so political "junkies," people of prominence who enjoy playing the primary game largely for its own sake. The candidate spends a night or two at the junkie's home so his host can eventually boast "the president slept here," meets influentials who are the junkie's allies and hopes the presentation of his creed will enlist enough faithful to labor in the vineyards of the Lord.

"If you can't get the person you want, go to the State House and get the man who's his worst enemy," says Laurence Radway, former Democratic chairman and Dartmouth political science professor who campaigned on foot the length of the state for U.S. Senate. He lost.

"You want to get someone on your side who can activate the activists," says Joanne Symons, also once a state Democratic chairman. "Get the three-by-five card girls to work for you."

Person-to-person contact is the key to winning in New Hampshire. Voters, like shoppers at a vegetable stand, get to handle the merchandise firsthand. There is the trite-but-true joke of the voter who was asked his opinion of a candidate: "I don't know. I've only met him once."

There's a belief that his long exposure to candidates has made the New Hampshire voter politically savvy. Radway dissents.

"The politicians come to New Hampshire like Marie Antoinette going to Versailles to milk cows and get close to nature. For his part, the voter overlooks issues and votes because a candidate looked him in the eye or gave a firm handshake. That's sophistication?"

Radway feels open primaries are squeezing out the professionals from the nominating process. "Instead of reasoned decisions, you get enthusiasts, people who have been temporarily turned on."

Too much significance is attached to New Hampshire, a state with fewer people than Boston, Radway feels. "A candidate gets a 29 to 22 percent plurality with a small vote and bingo! He's on the cover of *Time* and

Newsweek. This adversely affects fundraising for the other candidates in primaries to come."

Hype and Hoopla

Others deplore the national coverage turning the primary into a media event. "Nobody here pays attention to politics until after the Super Bowl," says a local editor, "but we get the Washington pundits up here all winter eating lobster on the expense account while their wives shop for antiques. There's too much hype. Hell, look what they did to Muskie. The media said he lost because he didn't quite get 50 percent of the vote. That's ridiculous."

New Hampshire isn't about to surrender its place at the head of primary line. State law, in fact, decrees its primary will be ahead of any other. The primary gives New Hampshire status and, Andy Anderson estimates, about $25 million spent by candidates and the media. Laurence Radway got a chance to have Walter Cronkite up to his hotel room and send out for grinders.

Besides ego enforcement, publicity and walking-around money, New Hampshire's political return from the primary is modest. Trowbridge warns against putting too many eggs irrevocably in one basket by such a commitment to any one president as accepting a job from him.

"Then you can't play the primary game anymore."

The game started in 1949 when Concord attorney Richard F. Upton introduced legislation for a direct primary.

Upton denies that his motive was to provide Dwight Eisenhower (Loeb called him "Dopey Dwight") a chance to show his popular appeal, although he concedes it had that effect. "I wanted to make the primary more meaningful, to get as many voters as possible involved in the process."

And candidates by the motorcade continue to roll into New Hampshire, even though they must know no loser in the primary has ever moved to the White House. For $500 and 500 signatures, anyone can run.

"I've seen hula girls, wild-eyed ministers and every kind of kook you could imagine," says Floris Lanigan at the secretary of state's office where the line forms. "No, not Chief Burning Wood. He usually runs for vice president."

Index

Index

A

abortion 195
Abrams, Jim 139
AFL-CIO 129
African-Americans 53, 80, 97, 189
Agran, Larry 76
AIDS 75
Alaska 63, 126, 278
Alexander, Senator Lamar 1, 13, 23, 66, 68, 69, 70, 72, 118, 119, 157, 240, 245, 251, 253, 258
Allen, Henry 282
Always First, Always Right 5
Al Qaeda 193
Ambrose, Jay 179
Ambrose, Robert 232
Americans for Democratic Action 218
Americans for Job Security 198
American Federation of Government Employees 218
American Insurance Association 198
American Party 95
American Patriot Foundation 117
American Red Cross 135
American Research Group 121
American Values (PAC) 121
American Women Presidents (PAC) 208
AmeriCorps 193
Ames (Iowa) 115
Anderson, Edward 177
Anderson, Liz 107
Anheuser-Busch Brewery 120
anti-Semitism 86

Apple, R.W. 50
Arctic National Wildlife Refuge 131
Arizona 63, 236, 237, 277
Arkansas 211
Arnesen, Arnie 122
Arsenault, Beth 190
arts 132
Ashbrook, John 142
Ashcroft, Attorney General John 10, 68, 120, 253
Ashooh, Rich 78
Asians 51
Askew, Governor Ruben 199
Asphalt One 154
Associated Press 43
Atkins, Edith 31

B

Baker, Senator Howard 8
ballots xi, 2, 3, 7, 34, 36, 39, 41, 43, 45, 47, 49, 56, 58, 59, 60, 61, 63, 64, 65, 73, 74, 75, 81, 83, 86, 87, 95, 97, 98, 103, 108, 110, 187, 189, 211, 212, 221, 223, 225, 239, 240, 243, 244, 263, 268, 270, 293
Ballot Law Commission 59
Balsams Grand Resort Hotel 43, 44, 45
Baltimore 23
Baltimore Sun 47, 156
Barabak, Mark Z. 270
Barba, Steve 43, 45
Barbour, Haley 218
Barker, Shirley 49
Barnicle, Mike 116
Barrick, Daniel 203
Bartlett, Josiah 20
Bass, Congressman Charles 142
Bass, Governor Robert 31

Battaglia, Basil 180, 217, 240, 241,
    243, 244, 245, 246, 273
Battle of Bennington 21
Bauer, Gary 12, 68, 146, 149, 152,
    153, 154, 155, 156, 161
Bayard, Richard 240
bears 9
Beatty, Warren 73, 184
Bedford 115, 205
Bedford Inn 135
Bennett, Bill 70
Bennett, Bob 218
Bennett, Dick 121
Bennington 7
Benson's Animal Park 182
Ben and Jerry's Ice Cream 90
Berlin 219
Berry, Jr., Samuel H. 1, 88
Bethlehem 32, 35
bible 20
Big Five 98
Big Sky Primary 213
Big Tent 108
Black America's PAC 149
Bosa, Dick 219
Boston 18, 67, 71
Boston College 84
Boston Globe 15, 64, 74, 90, 116, 128,
    169, 177, 182, 183, 241, 272,
    277
Boston Globe Magazine 182
Boston Herald 177
Boston Sunday Globe 78, 219
Bouchard, Steve 128
Bradley, Senator Bill 69, 149, 169,
    172, 174, 246, 253
Branstad, Governor Terry 249, 251
Braun, Senator Carol Moseley 188,
    189, 208
Brereton, Charles 182

Bretton Woods 88
Bretton Woods Monetary
    Conference 159
Bridges, Styles 116
Broder, David 11, 180
Brookhiser, Richard 34, 179
Brown, Governor Jerry 76
Brown, Mary 143
Browne, Harry 95
Bruno, George 232, 248
Bryk, William 83
Bryn Mawr College 64
Buchanan, James 249
Buchanan, Patrick J. v, 7, 23, 66,
    97, 100, 105, 106, 108, 146,
    153, 154, 185, 249, 266, 271,
    295, 296
Buckley, Charles 84
Buckley, Raymond 128, 129, 258,
    259
Buell, Jr., Dr. Emmett 8, 15, 66, 233
Buhr, Tami 65
Building America's Conscience
    (PAC) 128
Bullock, Stephen A. 31, 33, 35, 226,
    228
Bullock Act 33, 35
Bull Moose Party 45
Bunker Hill 19, 21
Burham, Walter Dean 60
Burns, Joe 62
Burton, Austin 19
Bush, Governor Jeb 165
Bush, President George H.W. 9, 15,
    57, 114, 225
Bush, President George W. 6, 20, 50,
    71, 88, 97, 104, 117, 125, 131,
    138, 142, 148, 149, 153, 154,
    161, 163, 164, 169, 175, 185,
    187, 189, 192, 216, 236, 243,

Bush, President George W. *(cont.)*
251, 266, 269, 270, 271, 273,
274, 281
Bush/Quayle Alumni Association
143

C

C-Span 13, 78, 269, 270
C.R. Sparks Convention Center
137, 150, 151, 205
Caddell, Patrick 182
Calhoun, John C. 22
California 2, 8, 21, 97, 121, 145,
180, 214, 216, 218, 225, 241,
272, 277, 278
Calmes, Jackie 138
Campaign America (PAC) 143
Campaign for Working Families
(PAC) 68, 153
campaign spending 70
Canada 21, 51, 175
Capalbo, Kenneth A. 81
Capitol Center for the Arts 271
Captain Climate 90
Carnahan, Governor Mel 121
Carney, Dave 198
Carper, Senator Thomas 240
Carroll, Jim 89
Carroll, Maura 13
Carter, President Jimmy 3, 9, 11, 13,
37, 139, 185, 191, 279
Carter, Willie F. 85
Casey, Carol 218
caucuses 32, 54, 55, 56, 216, 217,
218, 220, 226, 229, 233, 237,
238, 240, 243, 246, 248, 249,
250, 251, 254, 256, 257, 259, 282
cell phones 67
Center for Responsive Politics 62
Center Harbor 237

Center of New Hampshire 246
Chafee, Senator John 115
Chambers, John 63
Chandler, Speaker Gene 45
Charles II, King 18
checklists 41, 42, 60, 65, 103
Cheney, Vice President Dick 70,
193, 206
Chicago Sun 180
Chicago Sun Times 180, 280
Chicago Tribune 38
Chief Burning Wood 19
Children's Educational Opportunity
Foundation (CEO America) 157
China 131, 154
Christian Science Monitor 181
Christmas Day 244
Churchill, Winston (novelist) 49
CIA 126
Cisco Systems 63
Citizens for a Sound Economy
Foundation 157
CityVote 273
civil unions law 190
Civil War 24
Claremont 7
Claremont Eagle Times 176
Clark, General Wesley 211, 212
Clark, Martha Fuller 124, 129
Clear Skies Initiative 198
Clegg, Rev. Billy Joe 93
Cleveland, Grover 50
Clinton, Chelsea 173
Clinton, President William Jefferson
1, 5, 9, 58, 76, 97, 126, 139,
148, 150, 181, 214, 236, 239,
264, 279
Clinton, Senator Hillary 239
Close Up Foundation 268, 271
CNN 14, 78

Cobleigh, Marshall 226
cocaine cartels 135
Coffey, Bob and Howie 141
Cohen, Ben 90
Cohen, Richard 79
Colantuono, Tom 68, 143
Cole, Congressman Tom 225
Colebrook 50
Colebrook Sentinel 118
College Convention 2000 271
Collins, Rachel M. 43
Colorado 281
Colorado College 37
Comeback Kid 264
commercials 56, 141, 158, 281
Committee on Presidential Primaries
    216
Concord 9, 21, 31, 50, 133, 137,
    146, 147, 191, 281
Concord Monitor 5, 38, 59, 78, 109,
    111, 135, 182, 203, 258, 259, 270
Condodemetraky, George 126
congressional caucus 22
Congressional Medal of Honor 127
Congressional Quarterly 213
Conklin, Jr., Edwin A. 90
Connecticut 214, 229, 264
Connecticut River 57, 190
Conservative Political Victory Fund
    120
Constitution, New Hampshire 20, 98
Constitution, U.S. 2, 20, 34
Constitutional Convention, New
    Hampshire 20
Contractor Pig 90
Conval High School 270
conventions, national 7, 30, 31
Conway Carroll County Independent 65
Conway Scenic Railroad 199
Conway Sun 198

Cook, Rhodes 213
Cookie Mom 90
Cornish 49
Costa, Jeff 100, 101
Costantino, Becky 220
Costello, Sam 83
Cotton, Norris 42
Council of State Governments 216
Crane, Congressman Phil 142
Crawford Notch 41
Crow, Randolph "Randy" 86
Crustacean Party 100, 101
Culver, Chet 256, 257

D

D'Allesandro, Lou 123
Daily Telegraph 64
Dallas Morning News 51
Dana Center 269
Daniell, Professor Jere 37
Dartmouth's Young Democrats 272
Dartmouth College 5, 37, 39, 56,
    57, 152, 163, 208, 214, 272
Dass, Michael Eric 94
Davidson, Jean 17
Da Vid 100
DC Democracy Fund 274
Dean, Governor Howard 62, 134,
    188, 189, 191, 212, 266, 272,
    275
debates 23, 47, 83, 84, 89, 143, 172,
    229, 271
Declaration of Independence 19, 20
Delaware 139, 157, 214, 236, 238,
    239, 240, 241, 243, 244, 245,
    247, 250, 251, 252, 254, 257,
    258, 273, 274, 277, 278
Delaware Plan 217
delegates 30, 36, 46, 223, 224, 232,
    273

Democracy in Practice 270

Democratic Congressional
    Campaign Committee 122

Democratic Governors Association
    189

Democratic Leadership Council 99

Democratic National Committee 68,
    223, 232, 233, 237, 248, 257, 259

Democratic National Convention
    214

Democratic Party 5, 14, 22, 24, 25,
    36, 97, 110, 178, 195, 223, 232,
    276, 279

Denison University 8, 15, 66

Dennehy, Mike 167, 277

Densmore, Ned 190

Department of Homeland Security
    199

Department of Peace 203

Derry 196

Des Moines 256

Des Moines Register 111, 260

Detroit 276

Devitte, Jesse 137

Dewey, Thomas E. 47

Dexter, Dean 121

Diamond, David 73

Diaz, Amy 180

Disnard, George 124, 204

DiStaso, John 14, 113, 237

District of Columbia 213, 273, 274

diversity, population 8

Dixville Notch 42, 43, 45, 97

Dole, Senator Elizabeth 8, 53, 69,
    135, 136, 142

Dole, Senator Robert 66, 93, 105,
    109, 135, 137, 154, 237, 239

Dornan, Robert K. 185

dot-com revolution 65

Dover 50, 73, 145, 197, 211

Dowler, Marilyn 42

Do or Die State 6

Dukakis, Governor Michael 7, 122

Duke, David E. 16

dump, campaigning at local 10

Duncan, Dayton 182

Dunleavy, Martin 218

Duprey, Steve 114, 115, 142, 161,
    237, 252, 253, 255, 256

Durham 157

E

Eagle Tribune 107, 116

Earle, Sarah M. 78

Eastman, Robert 14

East Kingston 7

Eaton, John B. 81

Edwards, Senator John 188, 189,
    192, 195, 196, 197, 198

Egan, Ken 146

Ehrenberg, Kurt 272

Eisenhower, Dwight D. 11, 41, 47,
    49, 81

Elections Committee 243

electronic voting 60, 64

electronic voting systems 64

Emerson, Ralph Waldo 282

Environmental Protection Agency
    133

Environment and Public Works
    Committee 115

Epping 7

Executive Council 2, 20, 68, 124,
    143

Exeter 18, 22, 39, 49, 57

F

Fairness in Primaries plan 218

Faith of My Fathers 169

Family Research Council 153, 155
Farmington 49
father of the primary (Upton) 39
FBI 75, 86, 199
Federal Elections Commission (FEC)
       70, 71, 72, 73, 97, 108, 111,
       131, 139, 161, 173
federal matching funds 71, 77, 96,
       98, 108, 111, 158, 185, 243, 244
Federal Tax Code 157
Felker, Samuel D. 31
Fernald, Mark 171, 195
Fifth Provincial Congress 19
filing period 69, 91, 93, 105, 118,
       238, 239, 240, 243
Finnegan, James 39
first-in-the-nation 18, 32, 38, 42, 45,
       104, 216, 218, 229, 230, 238,
       245, 252, 255
First in the Nation 182
First Vote 271
Flanagan, Nat 243
Florida 226, 229, 236
Flowers, Gennifer 6
Flunch, Claude D. 90
Fole, Eileen 126
Forbes, Sabina 159
Forbes, Steve 11, 12, 62, 68, 71, 72,
       138, 149, 152, 153, 154, 156,
       157, 158, 159, 160, 161, 162,
       165, 169, 185, 239, 245, 252,
       253, 270, 296
Ford, Henry 89
Ford, President Gerald 9, 263, 280
Fornwalt, Russell J. 84
Fortune Magazine 178
Fort William and Mary 19
Foster's Daily Democrat 62, 77, 93
Foster's Sunday Citizen 97
Foster, Joe 124

Foxwoods Resort Casino 264
Franco-Americans 51
Franconia Notch 11
Franklin Pierce College Polling
       Institute 266
Freel, Edward J. 240, 241, 245, 273
Fremont, John C. 249
French Canadians 50, 51
fringe candidates 2, 9, 62, 70, 74,
       75, 77, 78, 91, 212, 293
Fringe Candidates Debate 78
front-loading 214, 219, 220, 229,
       243, 280
frontrunners 11, 129, 146, 274
Fulani, Lenora B. 97
Fund For a Healthy America 190

G

Gallup poll 113
Galvin, Secretary of State William
       F. 216
Gardner, Secretary of State Bill iii,
       xi, 2, 78, 82, 93, 215, 232, 233,
       239, 240, 241, 243, 244, 245,
       246, 247, 248, 249, 251, 253,
       254, 255, 256, 257, 258, 259,
       260, 261, 273
geography, New Hampshire 9
Gephardt, Congressman Richard
       69, 122, 123, 128, 142, 175,
       188, 189, 253, 272
Gephardt, Matt 125
Gittell, Ross 5
Glaser, Gerard 64
Glasser, Susan B. 71
Glenn, Senator John 281
Glessner, John W. 32, 35, 226, 228
Glover, Mike 248, 260
godfather of the primary (Tillotson)
       45

Godzick, Dan 150
Goelz, Peter 182
Goffstown 122
Goldwater, Barry 57, 266
Gore, Tipper 52
Gore, Vice President Al 6, 7, 52,
    58, 69, 81, 85, 88, 99, 129, 134,
    143, 148, 149, 170, 171, 172,
    173, 174, 175, 178, 204, 246,
    253, 257, 263, 266
Gore/Bradley contest 58, 171, 175
Gorton, Senator Slade 213
Gospel 78
Gould, Bryan 146
Grace Commission 220
Graham, Senator Bob 188, 189,
    199, 200, 201
Gramm, Senator Phil W. 8, 93, 109,
    237, 245
grandfather of the primary (Stassen)
    45
Granny D 82
Grant, Ulysses 50
grassroots 2, 10, 39, 56, 65, 72, 105,
    109, 141, 150, 154, 168, 221,
    250, 281
Great Betrayal, The 105
Great Stone Face 11, 21, 182
Green, Don 268
Greenstein, Mark 80
Green Party 99, 102
Gregg, Governor Hugh iii, xi, 41,
    47, 48, 95, 220, 240, 241, 245,
    248, 249, 256
Gregg, Senator Judd 126, 165, 190
Griz, The (Morry Taylor) 9
Groscost, Jeff 237
Grubbs, Steve 250, 252
Gruley, Bryan 62
grunt workers 186

Guam 275, 278
Gulf War 206
gun control 194
Gun Owners of New Hampshire
    150

H

Hagelin, Dr. John 97
Halliburton 193, 206
Hamilton, Mark 135
Hamm, Vincent S. 86
handshake ix, 5, 17
Hanover 47, 57, 131
Harder, Anne Heather 80
Harkin, Senator Tom 76
Harnes, Mark 89
Harrigan, John 118
Harris, Katherine 59
Harris, Todd 141
Hart's Location 41, 42, 43
Hart, Senator Gary 7, 72, 129, 175,
    185, 279
Hartford Courant 177
Harvard 37, 56, 65, 76, 80, 99, 188,
    335
Harvard Kennedy School 37
Harwood, John 154, 213
Hassan, Maggie Wood 124
Hatch, Senator Orrin 146, 147, 270
Haverhill 57
Hawkeye State 261
Hawthorne, Nathaniel 21
Hay Fever Association 32
health care 132, 193, 195
Healy, Daniel J. 40
Hemp Lady, The 94
Heritage Foundation 157
Hertzberg, Hendrik 176
Hesky Park 113
Hewitt, Earl S. 47

Hickey, Karen 115
High Tech 61
Hindes, Gary E. 238
Hispanics 51
HMO 174
Hoffa, Jimmy 125
Holiday Inn/Center of New
    Hampshire 14, 78
Hollingsworth, Beverly 259
Hollywood 64
homeland security 193, 195, 197,
    201, 204
Hooksett Kawasaki Polaris
    dealership 164
Hope, Growth and Opportunity
    (AHGO) 156
Hopkinton Dam 42
Hopkinton Fair 107, 145
Horwitt, Sanford 268
House Bill 1012 226
House Bill 210 39
House Bill 430 31
House of Representatives, New
    Hampshire 3, 21, 65, 224
Hudson 6, 7
Human Ecology Party 100
Humphrey, Patricia G. 156
Humphrey, Vice President Hubert
    102
Hunt, Albert R. 48
Husker 100
Hussein, Saddam 132, 206
Hynes, Patrick 146

I

Ickes, Jr., Harold 239
Idaho 214
Illinois 277
Independence Hall 113
Independents v, 3, 95, 100, 102,

Independents *(cont.)* 103, 104, 166
Indiana 32, 226
Indian Stream Republic 21
Inn Unique 41
International Date Line 278
International Harvester Company
    32
International Institute for
    Democracy and Electoral
    Assistance 58
International Monetary Fund 159
Internet 18, 62, 63, 99, 134, 158,
    195, 276
Internet Policy Institute 64
Internet voting 62
Iowa 55, 139, 146, 216, 217, 219,
    229, 248, 249, 250, 251, 253,
    257, 258, 259, 260, 261, 273
Iowa-Illinois Turf Grass Association
    259
Iowa-New Hampshire First-in-the-
    Nation Pledge 139, 250
Iowa-New Hampshire First Caucus
    and Primary Commission 249
Iowa caucus 54, 55, 56, 72, 148, 152,
    156, 161, 171, 217, 229, 248
Iowa Pork Congress 260
Iowa Republican Party 256
Iowa straw polls 145, 159
Iraq war 124, 125, 132, 134, 193,
    199, 203, 204, 206
Irvine 76
Irwin, David 281

J

Jackson, Andrew 22, 23
Jackson, Jesse 53
Japan 131
Jarding, Steve 68
Jefferson-Jackson Dinner 175, 195

Jobs Tour 207
John F. Kennedy School of
    Government 55
Jones, Captain John Paul 22
Jones, Secreatary of State Bill 216
Journal of Law & Politics 233
Justice Department 237

K

Kacavas, John 124
Kaiser, Linda 141
Kalb, Marvin 55
Kalob, Dennis 129, 190
Kansas 215, 281
Kansas City Star 85
Kasich, John R. 68, 139, 140, 141,
    142, 253, 274
Kaye, Peter 9
Keating, Governor Frank 176
Keefe, Joseph 122, 224, 249, 253,
    256, 259, 261
Keene 189, 215
Keene Sentinel 137
Keene State 208
Kefauver, Estes 7, 42, 185
Kemp, Congressman Jack 70, 142,
    161
Kennebunkport 163
Kennedy, President John F. 279
Kennedy, Richard "Stretch" 255,
    257
Kennedy, Senator Edward 166, 190
Kerrey, Senator Robert 10, 69, 76,
    126, 127, 252
Kerry, Senator John 69, 128, 130,
    134, 175, 188, 189, 272
Kerry, Teresa Heinz 128, 131
Keyes, Alan 12, 142, 149, 150, 151,
    152, 154, 156, 161, 296
Kid's Voting 271

Kiernan, Laura A. 78, 90
Killeen, Caroline P. 91, 94, 225
Kimball-Jenkins estate 191
King, aggression against the 18
King, Martin Luther 53
Kingston 7
Kingswood Regional High School 111
King Caucus 22
King of England 18
Kittredge, Clare 64
Klemm, Arthur 45
Knicks 170
Koenig, Sarah 135
Koos, Thomas 87
Kornblut, Anne E. 169
Krueger, Pat 244
Krumholz, Sheila 62
Ku Klux Klan 16
Kubiak, Wladislav D. 82
Kucinich, Representative Dennis
    188, 189, 202, 203, 266
Kyoto treaty on global warming 126

L

Laconia 7, 54
Ladd, Everett Carll 264
LaFollette, Robert 30
Lamb, Brian 13
Lamontagne, Ovide 143
Lancaster 7
Landrigan, Kevin 120, 139, 174
Langdon, John 20, 49
LaRouche, Jr., Lyndon H. 87
Larry King Show 77
Latin American Center 51
Lawrence Eagle Tribune 107, 116
Leavitt, Mike 213
Lebanon 57, 215
Legislature, New Hampshire 3, 65,
    224

lesser-knowns x, 74, 75, 76, 78, 93, 95, 102, 184, 186, 221
Lessner, Richard 154
Levin, Senator Carl 246, 275, 276
Levinson, Michael 93, 221
Lewinsky, Monica 120
Lewis, Ann 239
Libertarian Party 85, 89, 95, 96, 97, 102, 113, 187
Library and Archives of New Hampshire's Political Tradition 45, 54, 78, 270
Lieberman, Hadassah 204
Lieberman, Marcia 206
Lieberman, Senator Joseph 188, 189, 203, 205, 213, 272
Light Party 100
Lilac Luncheon 156, 167
Lincoln, Abraham 24, 50
Lincoln Day Dinner 139
Lippman, Theo 47
Littleton Hospital 32
Little Plaid Book 258
Live Free or Die (slogan) 21, 109, 218, 278
Live Free or Die PAC 109
Lobsterman, The 100, 101
Lockheed Martin Company 78
Lodge, Henry Cabot 7, 57, 185
Loeb, William 263, 279
Loevy, Robert D. 37
Los Angeles Times 17, 263, 265, 270, 272
Lott, Senator Trent 116
Loudon 54
Louisiana 63
Love 22 (candidate) 276
Lowy, Joan 153
Lucas, Jay 143, 153
Lugar, Senator Richard G. 257

lumberjacks 41
Lyford, James O. 30, 100
Lyon, G. Parker 57

M

Macko, Lia 271
MacNeil-Lehrer News Hour 77
Magic (dog) 141
Maine 229
Maine Central Railroad 41
Maiola, Joel 166
Making of the President 279
Manatt, Charles 232
Manchester 9, 14, 48, 50, 51, 107, 123, 137, 143, 150, 153, 157, 209, 226, 256, 281
Manchester airport 198
Manchester Central High School 202
Manchester Union Leader, see *Union Leader*
Mann, Halton Adler 179
Manual for the General Court 31, 32
manufacturing 207
maple desk 247
Margolis, Jon 38
Marland, Mike 59
Marrou, Andre 97
Mars, colonization of 79
Marshall, Robert 273
Martin, Andy 88
Martin, Lynn 114
Maryland 214
Mason, Horace B. 90
Massachusetts 70, 129, 215, 216, 229
matching funds 70, 71, 77, 96, 98, 108, 111, 158, 185, 243, 244
Mayer, William G. 37, 225, 282
McAuliffe, Terry 276
McCain, Senator John 6, 7, 62, 71,

McCain, Senator John *(cont.)* 72, 104, 149, 153, 161, 163, 167, 171, 187, 244, 253, 266, 269, 270

McCain/Bush race 58

McCarthy, Senator Eugene 13, 193

McCloskey, Congressman Paul 142

McFeatters, Dale 178

McGinley, Shannon 154

McGough, Tim 143

McGovern, Senator George 76, 280

McLellan, General 24

McQuaid, Joseph 161, 261

media ix, 1, 14, 15, 16, 18, 34, 37, 42, 50, 54, 75, 78, 94, 95, 149, 250, 253, 262, 265, 274, 278, 279, 281

Media Power Politics 14

Media Research Center 157

Medicaid 175, 201

Medicare 133, 174, 175, 201

Mellman, Mark 267

Mercuri, Rebecca 64

Meredith 113

Merrill, Governor Steve 237, 238

Merrimack 7, 120

Merrimack River 51

Mesa 237

Meyrowitz, Professor Joshua 77

Michigan 246, 275, 276

Microsoft 154

midnight voting 42

Mike's Party 100

Milford 3, 139, 140, 144

Milford Cabinet 181

Milkovits, Amanda 97

Millimet, Joe 207

millionaire 253

mills 51

Mills, Congressman Wilbur 142

minimum wage 125, 193

Minnesota 32, 45, 226

minorities 51

Mississippi 215

Missouri 24, 277

Mondale, Vice President Walter 13, 72

money 10, 11, 67, 71, 73, 118

Mongan, John 48

Morey, Florence 41

Morgan Sr., John 241

Morin, Richard 268

Mormon vote 146

Mosby, Timothy Lee 78

Mount Washington, The 216

Mr. T 45

MSNBC 271

Mt. Washington Hotel 159

MTV 78

Mudd, Roger 77

Mullins, Nathaniel Thomas 89

Muskie, Edmund 7, 280

N

Nader, Ralph 98

NAFTA 107, 125, 203

Nagle, David 248, 260

Nagourney, Adam 145

Nardini, Bob 182

NASCAR 54

Nashua 51, 157, 199

Nashua River 51

Nashua Telegraph 120, 139, 148, 174, 241

NAT0 211

National Association of Secretaries of State (NASS) 60, 215, 217, 270, 271

National Governors' Association 189

National Journal 255
National Review 178
National Right to Work Legal
    Defense Foundation 143
NATO 134
Natural Law Party 97, 102
Nebraska 128
New Castle 49
newcomers 53
Newmarket 7, 141
Newsweek 15, 16
Newton 7, 10
New Alliance Party 97
New Birth of Freedom 159
New England regional primary 229
New Hampshire Auto Dealers
    Association 120
New Hampshire Boxing and
    Wrestling Commission 257
New Hampshire Christian Coalition
    107
New Hampshire Federation of
    Republican Women 156, 167
New Hampshire General Court 223
New Hampshire High Technology
    Council 61
New Hampshire Historical Society
    247
New Hampshire International
    Speedway 136
New Hampshire Patriot and State Gazette
    25
New Hampshire Political Library
    45, 54, 78, 270
New Hampshire Profiles 49
New Hampshire Software
    Association 137
New Hampshire Sunday News 87
New Hampshire Supreme Court 145
New Hampshire Youth Summit 270

New Millennium Project 60
New World Order 108
New York 214, 277
New Yorker 15, 176
New York City 240
New York Institute for Law and
    Society 251
New York Times 14, 15, 50, 95, 145,
    177, 217
Nicholson, Jim 114
Nixon, President Richard 42
Nofziger, Lyn 146
Noonan, Peggy 267
Northeastern University 37, 225,
    282
Northeast Home Heating Reserve
    132
North Carolina 195
North Conway 133
North Country 45
North Korea 135, 193
Notchland Inn 43
No Child Left Behind Act 125, 166,
    190, 198, 201
No Way to Pick a President 179
Nyhan, David 15, 74, 116

O

O'Beirne, Kate 178
O'Donnell, Edward T. 79
O'Kane, Sean 78, 246
O'Neill, Tip 179
Ohio 214, 277
Ohio Plan 218
oil drilling 126, 131
Old Man of the Mountain 11, 21,
    182
Omaha 128
optical scanner 60

Oregon 31, 61
Osterman, Rachel 272
Oyler, Tom 85
Oyster River High School 199
Ozone Action 91

P

PACs 68, 109, 195
Page, John 247
Paletz, David 14
Palmer, Dr. Niall 38
Panama Canal 74, 154
Parliament of England 21
Pataki, Governor George 251
Pate, Secretary of State Paul 249
Patterson, Professor Thomas 37, 56
Paulsen, Pat 5
Payne, Doug 90
Peace Conference 49
Peace Corps 133
Peet, Richard C. 86
Pelham 208
Pelosi, Congresswoman Nancy 232
Pembroke 7
Pennsylvania 31
Pentagon Pork Pig 90
Perot, Ross 107
Perry, James 14
Peterborough 270, 281
Peterborough Public Library 130
Peters, Jeffrey B. 82
Peterson, Michael 250
Pew Charitable Trusts 220, 270
Pfaff, Jacob 271
Pfaff, Terry 271
Phillips, Howard 113
Phillips Exeter Academy 39, 50
Phoenix 145
photo-ops 15
Pianin, Eric 139

Pierce, Franklin 22, 23, 49, 100, 102
Pioneer (PAC) 68, 139
Plymouth State College 152
pods 218
Politics and Eggs 115, 205
polls and polling, political 17, 30,
    34, 262
Pork Producers Convention 256
Portsmouth 18, 49, 137, 160, 193,
    206, 229
Portsmouth Navy Yard 22
Port of Portsmouth 193
Powell, Michael 113
Powell, Secretary of State Colin 70
Prairie Primary 213
Presidential Beauty Contest 41, 47
Presidential Candidates Youth Forum
    270
Presidential Preference Ballot 39
Presidential Preference Straw Poll
    250
Presidential Primary Act of 1996
    213
Pride, Mike 109
Progressive Movement 30
Project Vote Smart 97
Providence Journal 177
Province of Massachusetts, 18
Pro Tem Committee for Decency in
    Government 69
Puerto Rico 231, 275
Putney, Susan 211

Q

Quayle, Vice President James
    Danforth 68, 79, 143, 144, 146,
    154, 165, 215, 280
Quebec 50

R

Racicot, Marc 37, 277
radio 11, 14, 30, 47, 71, 89, 106,
     114, 153, 157, 158, 161, 195
Raiche, Robert 226
Rapsis, Jeff 181
Rath, Tom 118, 120, 251, 255
Rauh, Mary 169
Reagan, President Ronald 11, 57,
     165
Real Democracy Project 73
recall 2
Reform Party 97, 102, 107, 187
regional elections 217
registration, same-day 61
Republican Leadership Council 161
Republican National Committee
     173, 223, 257
Republican National Convention
     214, 252
Republican Party 6, 12, 22, 24, 31,
     36, 37, 47, 57, 105, 108, 113,
     114, 116, 117, 142, 145, 176,
     220, 223, 237, 240, 251, 252,
     256, 263, 273, 274
Revere, Paul 18
Revolution, Right of 98
Revolutionary Assembly 18
Revolutionary War 21, 38, 49
Rhodes Cook Letter 189
Richmond 7, 31
Rigazio, John Donald 92, 93
Right to Work law 275
Rindge 266
Rivier College 157
Robie's Store 200
Robinson, Melissa 131
Rochester 7
Rockefeller, Governor Nelson 56, 263

Rockefeller Center 56
Rocks, The 32
Rogak, Lisa 181
Roko, Mike 180
Rollinsford 7
Romney, George 254
Roosevelt, Franklin D. 13, 239
Roosevelt, Teddy 45, 49, 165
Roper Center for Public Opinion
     Research 264
Rosenthal, Phil 180
ROTC 133, 204
Rouseville, Sam 281
Rove, Karl 197
Royko, Steve 280
Run Some Idiot, One Schmuck's Odyssey
     79
Russo-Japanese War 49

S

Sacramento 21
Safire, William 14, 177
Sanbornton 7
Sanders 78
San Antonio Express-News 54
San Francisco 233
San Francisco Examiner 179
Scanlan, David 212
Schoof, Les 42
Scripps Howard News Service 153,
     178, 179
Seacoast Board of Realtors in 137
Secret Service 20, 174
Seib, Gerald F. 72, 128, 171
Shaheen, Bill 173
Shaheen, Governor Jeanne 166,
     173, 175, 192, 195, 240, 249,
     252, 253, 254, 259, 261
Shannahan, Joe 255

Sharpton, Reverend Al 188, 189, 208, 210

Shaw, Bernard 14

Shea, Jim 177

Shumaker, Terry 239

Siegel, Mark A. 30, 225

Sigel, Rich 256

Simon, Roger 124

Simon, Senator Paul 221

Simpson, Glenn R. 62

Sixty Minutes 116

Skok, Michael 82

Smith, Andy 266

Smith, Bradley 72

Smith, Mary Jo 115

Smith, Senator Bob 68, 105, 110, 112, 150, 185, 218, 253

Social Security 11, 80, 85, 124, 131, 133, 156, 159, 174, 192

Sorlucco, Jerry 190

Souter, Justice David 154

South Carolina 195, 245, 277

South China Morning Post 64

South Dakota 31, 233, 236

South Korea 131

special education 132

Spiliotes, Dean 56, 152

Spirit of America (PAC) 120

Spirou, Chris 181

Splaine, Jim 229, 230, 233, 243, 244, 273

St. Anselm College 122, 208, 269

St. Louis 114

St. Paul's School 133

Stanford University 87

Stark, General John 21

Stars and Stripes 22

Stassen, Harold E. 42, 45, 46, 47, 48, 87

Statue of Liberty 181

Stearns, Matt 85

Stengal, Richard 93

Stephens, Bobby 257

Stern, Josh 272

Stewart, Dee 256, 257

Stickney, Wallace E. 156

Sitnick, Fred (the "Messiah") 91

Stirton, Ian 97

Straight Talk Express 6, 167

Strauss, Mike 100

Stremsky, Kenneth 93

Student Mock Election 271

student participation 268, 272

Sullivan, John 49

Sullivan, Kathleen 253, 255, 256, 258

Sumner, Frederic Augustus 24

Sununu, Governor John H. 143, 165, 247

Sununu, Senator John E. 117, 166

Super Tuesday 213

Supreme Court, U.S. 132, 225

Supreme Executive Magistrate 21

Swarthmore College 64

Swett, Katrina 124, 129, 195, 204

Swiezynski, Joe 3

Symington, Fife 237

T

Taft, Robert 8

tax, income 10, 53, 82, 96, 150, 171, 278

tax, sales 10, 53, 190, 278

tax-cuts 195

Taxpayer's Party 115

tax code 88, 107, 158, 160, 197, 252

Tax Code Termination Day 158

tax cuts 125, 133, 174, 192, 197, 201, 204, 206, 208

Taylor, Elizabeth 245
Taylor, Jim 79
Taylor, Morry 9
television   ix, 11, 14, 15, 18, 66, 71,
    79, 88, 106, 108, 109, 121, 137,
    141, 148, 153, 157, 158, 159,
    161, 175, 181, 214, 246, 264,
    265, 280, 281
Tennessee 97, 174
Teschner, Douglass 168
Texas 51
Thayer, Judy 111
Third Parties v, 95
Thomson, Governor Meldrim 230
Thornburgh, Secretary of State Ron
    215
Three Fathers 39
Tiffany, Gordon R. 81
Tillotson, Neil 43, 44, 45
Time 15, 93
Touhy, Dan 62
town meeting 3, 24, 32, 38, 226, 230
Trump, Donald 64, 73, 184
Tsongas, Senator Paul 6, 7, 58, 76,
    77, 126
Tuck, Amos 22
Tully, Rob 256, 257, 261
two-party system 103

U

U.N. 124, 134
U.S.S. Ranger 22
U.S. News & World Report 77, 124
U.S. Supreme Court 184
U.S. Taxpayer's Party 113
Udall, Congressman Morris K. 3,
    142, 245
Uncle Sam 276, 281
Unfree Speech 72
Union, Teamsters 125

union halls 276
Union Leader, The 1, 14, 39, 68, 79,
    88, 90, 93, 94, 109, 113, 120,
    139, 154, 161, 173, 180, 237,
    241, 261, 263
University of New Hampshire 5, 62,
    77, 157, 163, 166, 193, 266, 272
University of New Hampshire
    Survey Center 266
UPI 67
Upton's Law 39
Upton, Speaker Richard F. 34, 39, 40
urban issues 273
Uribe, George 150
Uscinski, Shelly 107, 108
Utah 213, 281

V

Valelly, Rick 64
Valley News 215
Van Buren, Martin 22, 24
Vermont 2, 8, 45, 190, 192, 229,
    232, 233, 247
viagra 137
vice president, running for 16
Vietnam War 128, 169, 193
Vilsack, Governor Tom 254, 261
Virginia 277
volunteers xi, 2, 3, 5, 7, 34, 36, 39,
    41, 43, 45, 47, 49, 56, 57, 59,
    60, 63, 64, 65, 73, 74, 75, 81,
    83, 86, 87, 95, 97, 98, 103, 108,
    110, 187, 189, 211, 212, 221,
    223, 225, 239, 240, 243, 244,
volunteers 263, 268, 270, 293
voter turnout 5, 34

W

Wall Street Journal 14, 34, 48, 62, 63,
    69, 71, 128, 138, 154, 159, 171,

Wall Street Journal (cont.) 179, 213, 264

Walsh, Pamela 261

Ward, Micky 258

Washington 7, 174, 215, 216, 277

Washington, George 20, 49

Washington, Mount 13

Washington Post 11, 71, 79, 113, 139, 180, 268, 282

Washington Times 113

Watts, J. C. 149

Wayfarer, The 14

weather, New Hampshire 13

Weber, Thomas E. 63

Webster, Daniel 21, 116

Webster-Ashburton treaty 21

Weeks, Chris 270

Weirs 49

Weld, Governor William F. 128

Wellstone, Governor Paul 69, 134, 253

Wenck, Rick 13

Wentworth, John 19

Wentworth by the Sea Hotel 49

West, Paul 156

We The People Party 99

Whalley, Mike 164

Whalley, Purr 164

What I Saw at the Revolution: A Political Life in the Reagan Era 267

Wheeler, David 143

White, E.B. 58, 265

White, Theodore H. 182, 279

White House 9

White Mountains 41

Wilder, Governor Douglas 76

Willey House 41

Williams, Ken 78

Williams, Ted 163

Willis, Gerald 16

Wilmington News Journal 241, 277

Wilson, Governor Pete 180

Wilson, Henry 49

Wilson, Janet 265

Wilson, Woodrow 50

Windham 156

windows 224, 260

winner take all 214, 218

Winnipesaukee 216

Winnipesaukee Scenic Railroad 107

Wisconsin 30

Witcover, Jules 179

WMUR-TV 88, 107, 109, 121, 181

Wolfeboro 48

Wolfeboro High School 112

women's suffrage 34

Woodburn, Jeff 56, 126, 134, 173

Wyoming 220, 274

Y

Yale 268

Yale Club 240

Yankees 8, 50, 51

Yankee Day Primary 214

Yeager, Dorian 89

Yepsen, David 111, 260

York, Michael 78

Young, Paul 159

Youth Forum 270

youth voting 268

IN APPRECIATION OF OUR READERS

Publication restraints required data in this book to have been collected before August 15, 2003.

We regret not knowing what will occur hereafter, before or at our tentative January 27, 2004 *primary.*

Who will be the frontrunners in January? What new issues will direct campaign strategies? Will all current candidates stay in the race? Will retired General Wesley Clark join the race? What new fun will occur on the campaign trails? How will polls and money influence the results?

These and a myriad of other questions will be of major concern to all of us. Please know we share with you the anticipation of what is going to happen four months down the road and wish we could continue with you as things develop.

But, most important of all, we are grateful you have come this far with us and sincerely express our thanks for your interest in having read this book.

At the same time, we recognize those many individuals who have dedicated their talent and resources to supporting and preserving the New Hampshire primary.

August 15, 2003

ABOUT THE AUTHORS

Born in New Hampshire, co-author HUGH GREGG has had politics as a life-long avocation. He served as Alderman-at-Large and Mayor of his home city of Nashua, and as a Republican governor of the state. A graduate of Yale and the Harvard law School, Gregg was a Special Agent of the Counter Intelligence Corps in World War II and the Korean crisis.

He was New Hampshire's chairman for Nelson Rockefeller, George H.W. Bush and Ronald Reagan in the presidential primary campaigns.

Lest anyone think that a former Republican governor cannot be bipartisan in co-authoring this book, the author possesses a scroll signed by former Democratic Vice President Al Gore expressing "Great Appreciation" for his service as an honorary member of the Gore 2000 National Steering Committee. Hugh never took any money for his services from Al—not that any of his services or Al's money were ever offered.

Gregg writes from a broad background, with a unique perspective on the Granite State ethos and its political temperament. He is a freelance writer, and author of *The Candidates: See How They Run; A Tall State Revisited,* and other publications relating to the first-in-the-nation presidential primary.

～

Born in New Hampshire, co-author BILL GARDNER has followed his grandfather's example and was elected three times to the House of Representatives from his home city of Manchester.

Elected secretary of state in 1976, at the age of twenty-eight—as a Democrat by a Republican legislature—he is now serving a fourteenth consecutive two-year term. He is the youngest ever to hold the office, the longest to serve in it and the first from the minority party to be elected by the majority.

He has an undergraduate degree from UNH and graduate degrees from UNC-G and Harvard.

As secretary of state, he is responsible for administering and overseeing all state primaries and elections. He has set the date for each presidential primary for over a quarter of a century. His position, and his Statehouse presence spanning four decades have offered him a privileged window to witness the colorful and storied history of presidential primaries. He has a unique perspective on why—and how—New Hampshire has remained the first-in-the-nation primary state.